The Case for Buddhism

An exploration of Buddhist values in the modern world

by

William Woollard

Grosvenor House
Publishing Limited

This book is published by
Grosvenor House Publishing Ltd
28-30 High Street, Guildford, Surrey, GU1 3EL.
www.grosvenorhousepublishing.co.uk

A CIP record for this book
is available from the British Library

ISBN 978-1-78148-615-3

Dedicated to Daisaku Ikeda for his constant inspiration throughout all the years of my practice, and to my beloved wife Sarah for her constant love and support

Acknowledgements

Inevitably, many people have played a part in the writing of this book. It's impossible to go to discussion meetings and seminars with interesting and passionate people without the seeds of ideas being planted that later emerge in the writing. So my sincere thanks to all my Buddhist colleagues particularly in West London. But I am particularly grateful to the dozens, indeed hundreds of people who have written to me over the past couple of years suggesting that there was a need for a book that could be given to the *most* sceptical, the *most* disinterested, hopefully to spark their interest in what a Nichiren Buddhist practice has to offer to anyone trying to make the very most of their lives in today's busy, crowded, time-slicing, media-addicted society.

And finally my gratitude to Mr Makiguchi, the great visionary who founded the now global, lay Buddhist organisation the Soka Gakkai, back in 1930, for sowing the seed of the idea in my mind when he wrote, '*I could find no contradiction between science, philosophy, which is the basis of modern society, and the teaching of the Lotus Sutra.*'[1]

A Note on the Author

Producer, director, writer, presenter, William's career has covered the entire spectrum of television production, but he has experienced several other careers in an eventful life. Oxford Graduate. A fighter pilot with the RAF, although he was never called upon to fire a shot in anger! A trouble shooter for an oil company in the jungles of Borneo and the deserts of Oman. A social scientist working on corporate social responsibilities with major international organisations in Europe and the USA. Finally an award-winning television producer, working on documentary programmes for several of the world's foremost networks in Europe and the USA.

Much travelled. Twice married. Four wonderful children. A life time interest in comparative religion among many other things. He writes, *'I came to Buddhism with the deepest scepticism about it's appropriateness or relevance in a modern western environment. I am now wholly convinced of its profound value to any life, anywhere, in any circumstances. I see that initial scepticism as perhaps my primary qualification for writing this book.'*

Contents

CONTENTS

CHAPTER ONE

Setting out on a Journey

Every book is a journey, and at the start of every journey you need a certain minimum amount of baggage, a certain minimum amount of information to enable you to set off confidently in the right direction. In this case that minimum information consists I think of two items in particular. One is that I have been a science journalist for well over 30 years, enjoying myself immensely in taking difficult and often obscure and intractable bits of science, and working hard not just to explain them, but to make them interesting and accessible and entertaining even, to a wider general audience. The second is that for over 20 years I have been a Buddhist, a Nichiren Buddhist as it happens, seeking to put into practice a set of values and principles that have greatly enriched and enhanced every aspect of my life, and I believe the lives of those around me.

Everything that follows in this book really flows from those two bits of baggage.

But if I'm totally honest that's not quite enough information is it, to allow us to move on comfortably? Why do I say that? Because the fact is that the mention of Buddhism immediately raises in the minds of most people more questions than it answers. Indeed, partly perhaps because of the apparent mismatch with my quite tough and rigorous journalistic background, people frequently approach me and actually pose the question, 'A practising Buddhist? What's all that really about?

What's all that really about…is basically what this book is about. Because of course the practice of Buddhism is still so rare, so relatively unusual in the western world that it inevitably stimulates that sense of surprise and inquiry. When we get to talking casually many people want to know more than can possibly be conveyed in a brief conversation, and yet at the same time, there is often a reluctance to get closer to something as seemingly alien and other-worldly as Buddhism. I can wholly empathise with that view. No one wants to seem weird to his friends. I didn't. And for all the claims about our living in a multi-cultural society, the underlying cultural fabric of Europe is still very much Western Christianity. Indeed that is true of the entire ex-European empire spread around the globe from the Americas to Australia. One manifestation of that deep cultural tradition that we would all immediately recognise is that somebody who might never go into a church from one year to the next, is nonetheless completely at home slipping into a church for a moment of stillness, or even, in a moment of stress, asking for help from a God he or she doesn't really know. Whereas, understandably enough, that same person would find it infinitely more difficult, impossible even, to slip into any place Buddhist in an attempt to deal with this particular bout of anxiety or stress.

For most people in the West, when we hear the word Buddhist, we are forced to take refuge in a bunch of vague and shadowy stereotypes, because we don't have any clear or familiar markers to hang onto. That is I think a key point. With Christianity there are plenty, even complete non-Christians know the basic outlines of the Christian tradition. Whereas the mention of the name Buddhism summons up not much more than a series of vague National Geographic-type images; a vast, interesting perhaps, but nebulous mystical philosophy without any clear boundaries, lines of orange-robed priests weaving amid the traffic in downtown Bangkok, or prayer flags waving against the backdrop of Tibetan peaks. And that's about it. Not much to go on for the typical hustling and bustling time-pressured westerner.

So that is part of the purpose of this particular journey, clearing away those vague and totally unhelpful stereotypes, and replacing them with a much clearer, sharper under-standing of what Buddhism is about. I believe strongly that Buddhist values and principles can enhance any life, lived anywhere, in any circumstances, whether or not that person has the slightest interest in taking up a Buddhist practice. My primary objective is understanding, not recruitment. So this is certainly a serious, committed, personal account of Buddhism, but only in the sense that Buddhism is about *ordinary daily life*. It is not in any way about a remote, inaccessible and other-worldly philosophy. Not at all.

It's about the problems and the challenges and questions that we all encounter every day. What should I do in this difficult situation? How should I best handle this relationship or that problem? And it's about some of the deeper issues we're all concerned with, even if they rarely actually surface in conversation in families or among colleagues at work, because they are too deeply buried in our life. Concerns we all share, such as the fundamental desire for a stronger and more consistent sense of well-being amidst the unexpected and challenging turbulence of our lives; the crucial deeply-felt need we have for a genuine sense of connectedness and engagement with other people, and a concern for their well-being too; and the intimate relationship that we now know exists between a resilient sense of hope and optimism, and a fit and healthy and fulfilling life. How do we maintain that spirit of optimism amidst the hurly burly of life? As one psychologist expressed it to me in conversation, *'Cheerfulness matters. Hope and optimism really matter. They make a huge difference to the quality of our lives. They are not just a sort of optional salad dressing on the surface of life!'*

So put simply, this particular case for Buddhism is basically about learning in a wholly practical way, how to build a stronger and more resilient sense of well-being for oneself, and others, *no matter what* the circumstances we find ourselves in. And that's clearly a hugely important qualification. We tend to persuade ourselves that our *external* circumstances are the determining factor in our overall sense of well-being. Buddhism offers us the astounding truth that building or creating this sense of well- being at the core of our lives is essentially a matter of *choice,* how *we* choose to live. That in itself is a life-changing lesson, and in my experience we don't have to be especially knowledgeable, or dedicated, or indeed religious in any way, to learn it.

But there is a another question

But as important as that clarification and exposition of Buddhist ideas undoubtedly is, as I began to pull together some of the many disparate ideas and propositions that contribute to the themes in this book, I came to realise that they really address an equally important issue. It's one that we may never put to ourselves in any formal sense, but which nevertheless…whether we choose to acknowledge it or not…sits behind all our lives, all our behaviour, all our relationships. Namely… where do we turn these days to establish our values? Where do we turn to re-calibrate what you might call our *moral compass*, in the increasingly secular, powerfully cynical and culturally diverse world that surrounds all our lives? And this is by no means a purely personal issue is it? It's a question that more and more frequently has come to occupy centre stage in a wider public debate. Many sociologists tell us that we seem to be living through a kind of moral vacuum,[1] and as we all know, a vacuum of any kind is an extremely uncomfortable and disorientating place for human beings to live.

But you might say, that may well be true, but what's all that got to do with Buddhism? Good question. And the short answer is I think, just about everything!

Because as I pulled together these different threads from so many different fields of study, they revealed a surprising and unexpected conjunction. Namely that fundamental ideas about the principles and the values that really empower ordinary people like us, and enable us to live fundamentally creative and fulfilling lives, in all kinds of circumstances and environments, ideas that Buddhism has been talking about so constructively for so long, now find echoes and amplification and confirmation, in the kinds of findings that are coming out of the latest work of the social scientists, right across the spectrum of sociologists and psychologists and neuroscientists even, and on into the field of classical economics.

It's crucial not to fall into the trap of using definitive words like *'prove'* or *'validate'* in this context, because that would be wholly inaccurate. The findings of these modern social scientists don't prove or validate Buddhist teachings. As far as I'm aware there has never been a piece of research specifically to validate a Buddhist teaching. And in any case my argument would be that Buddhist insights about the nature of human life don't need anything resembling validation from modern science. They have proved their value many times over in the toughest laboratory there can ever be...namely human life itself.

But what these research findings *do* provide is absolutely invaluable, in the sense that they deliver into our hands a set of new, and quite different, and profoundly illuminating perspectives that illustrate the *astounding modernity...* I really can't think of any better way of expressing it...the astounding modernity of Buddhist insights into the values and behaviours that enable us to live the most productive and satisfying and creative lives of which we are capable, for ourselves and for those around us. That is absolutely the key point that cannot really be overemphasised, their continuing *value and relevance,* if we choose to work towards an answer to that fundamentally important question, where do we turn these days to establish our values?

Replacing inaccurate stereotypes

It's not a question we have to answer of course. Nobody's making us. We can if you want just duck away from it, as we frequently do when we're faced with difficult stuff. But if we *do* make the positive choice to grapple with it, because it helps us to build a vision of a bigger life for ourselves, as we scan across the fields of study where bits of the answer might emerge, it is extraordinary just how readily the elements of classical Buddhist teaching slide into place with modern knowledge, so that you can scarcely see the joins.

It has been said by religious historians that perhaps Buddhism's greatest contribution to mankind's spiritual heritage is that it introduced the concept of *choice*. When Buddhism came into being some 2500 years ago that was truly a revolution. At a time when mankind was hemmed in by powerful controlling and limiting concepts such as destiny and the commandments of divine beings, Buddhism introduced this extraordinary idea that human beings are truly answerable only to themselves.

We have the freedom it teaches, and the inner resource, to make our own choices, to take control of our lives, provided only that we accept *complete responsibility* for the *causes* that we make, and the *effects* that those causes plant in our lives. It was certainly revolutionary then, in many ways it remains revolutionary today. It may seem esoteric, outlandish even to look to Buddhism for a solution to many of society's seemingly intractable problems, but that is largely because our view of Buddhism in the west is limited by so many inaccurate stereotypes.

One of many such stereotypes for example, that obscures the general perception of Buddhism in the West is that it is very much about giving things up, or at the very least about introducing a kind of spare asceticism into our lives. The plain fact is that Buddhism is very much focused on *increasing* the richness of our experience of our lives, and in the *here and now*, rather than in some heavenly hereafter In the process it talks to us a great deal about what we mean by happiness or well-being. In fact it is alone among the major world religions in proposing the extraordinary idea that happiness isn't a matter of chance or accident, as we commonly believe, something that comes to us if we just happen to be particularly lucky or fortunate, but essentially a matter of choice. Indeed Buddhism goes further and argues that we can all, without exception, learn how to make that choice. The learning process it declares, is neither particularly difficult, nor exclusive, nor, most important of all, is it dependent upon our *external* life circumstances. Again that's a truly life-changing idea, and one that is clearly worth discussing at any time, since what we all want, one way or another, is a greater measure of well-being in our lives.

But it is I would suggest, an idea of particular relevance at the time we happen to be living through. Why do I say that? Because for the very first time in its history, science too seems to have become keenly interested in the idea of happiness, and how it might be achieved. So, it could be argued, we are privileged to live in very unusual times, when very considerable and genuinely *scientific* energy is focused on understanding precisely what it is that makes people feel good about their lives and their relationships, *in all kinds of circumstances,* not just in wealthy, or well-heeled or fortunate ones. The kinds of things you might argue, that are of the very greatest interest to all of us, since these are the most important issues we all face in our lives. What values should we embrace, what behaviour should we adopt, to enable not just individuals but *whole societies* to live and work more peacefully and productively? Basically we all want to live in peace and harmony with our neighbours, don't we, both near and far?

Some knowledgeable observers even suggest that we might be looking at the beginning of a whole new science, a science of happiness indeed. Perhaps. But at the very least we are being offered a whole new way of looking at so many things about our motivation and behaviour, that Buddhism has been talking to us about for many many years. We just haven't been listening!

Buddhism is not passive

Another of the most enduring stereotypes about Buddhism that crops up in almost any discussion of it, is that Buddhism is somehow *passive*. Buddhism is most certainly *pacifist*, because it believes strongly…and correctly if we take the judgment of history…that war and violence are wholly destructive, and in all but the very rarest of occasions, serve only to create and perpetuate more violence and destruction. But the word itself, *'pacifism,'* is very often taken to include within it so to speak the idea of *'passivism.'* Hence the commonly held stereotype that Buddhism is essentially a form of *escapism*, and that personally, Buddhists are likely to be quiet, withdrawn and somewhat diffident people, mainly intent upon seeking some sort of refuge from the pace and bustle and chaotic complexity of modern life.

Nothing could be further from the truth. Buddhism is a huge and multi-layered philosophy so it certainly provides plenty to think about and mull over, but above all Buddhism is about *taking action*, it's about the way people *live* their lives, rather than simply the way they *think* about them. So it is constantly challenging people to move out of their comfort zone, to look for new ways of developing and realising their own potential, and new ways of creating value in their lives and the lives of those around them.

Indeed, without wishing to push the analogy too far, Buddhism might be said to provide a significant bridge between a living spiritual philosophy, and the ever increasing lines of books in the *self-help* section of your local bookshop, with their various forms of instant advice on how we might get better at the game of life. Because Buddhism in a sense has a foot in both camps. It has the bed-rock of a profound and all-embracing philosophy that touches upon every area of human life, and which has truly stood the test of time. But it is also just as genuinely about *self-help* and about *self-belief.* The very heart of Buddhism is about our learning how to handle the business of living more confidently and more buoyantly.

As Daisaku Ikeda, one of the greatest living authorities on Buddhism has expressed it, *'Buddhism is a movement emphasising self-education.'*[2]

The basis of individual responsibility

We have become accustomed in the West to seeking our solutions not so much in individual change, but through political manoeuvring, or through the promises of science and technology. But it's quite clear that both have severe limitations when it comes to achieving profound *social change.* Inevitably societies are made up of *individuals,* and in essence, Buddhism is about transforming society in the only way that profound social change can be sustained, from the bottom up, by transforming individual lives. It talks indeed of *human revolution,* individual by individual. We could certainly argue I think, that rarely in human history, has there been a greater need for a philosophy of society, based upon *individual responsibility,* and profound *respect* for the welfare of others. Both describe what Buddhism is really about. And, as I've mentioned above, one of the most remarkable things for me as I went about the research for this book, was the realisation that many of the most persistent and most valuable findings that have come out of today's social research, into what it is that enables people to feel good about their lives, and experience a genuine sense of meaning and purpose, are powerfully *prefigured* in the principles and the practice of Buddhism.

We encounter many example in the chapters that follow, but let me just mention two or three examples here.

We have Daniel Goleman for example, psychologist and best-selling author in his ground-breaking book *Emotional Intelligence*, confirming for us that hope and optimism can indeed be learned;

'Optimism and hope' he writes, *'like helplessness and despair – can be learned. Underlying both is an outlook psychologists call self efficacy, the belief that one has mastery over the events of one's life and can meet challenges as they come up. Developing a competency of any kind strengthens the sense of self efficacy.'*[3]

One could argue I think that a Buddhist practice is entirely about life-competency, and building an altogether more capable individual. It might well be described as the *ultimate* self-help practice.

We have a modern polymath like Professor Owen Flanagan from Duke University, philosopher, psychologist, and neurobiologist, in his book *Varieties of Moral Personality*, describing for us the immensely close connection that has been established between the strength of our values, having a strong ethical or moral compass, and manifesting that in our behaviour, and our overall physical and mental well being.[4] Once again, as we've been discussing, Buddhism is all about folding strong positive values into our lives and demonstrating those values in our actions.

We have an eminent UK economist, Professor Layard from the London School of Economics, arguing that a society simply cannot flourish without a strong sense of shared purpose, a sense of shared values and principles between individuals. Human beings he explains are deeply social beings. We want to trust one another, and equally we want to be trusted and respected. All that is part and parcel of our being committed and integral members of a society. So that breaking that trust, in the sense of seeking our own advantage over others, seeking to get the most we can for *ourselves*, regardless of others, becomes a source of great personal anxiety.[5] That is a sentiment that echoes to the very heartbeat of the Buddhist vision of how society should work.

And we have several of the leading research psychologists in the field in the US, in a paper somewhat ominously entitled, *Zeroing on the dark side of the American Dream*, explaining for us what they believe is the long term downside of living a life driven largely by the values of materialism. What these researchers did was to examine the attitudes and the ambitions of a very large sample of undergraduates studying at US universities. They interviewed over 12000 students when they were 18 years old and so just formalising what it was they were really seeking from life. They then revisited these same people when they were in their late 30's, when they'd had some time to work towards realising those early ambitions. What they found was that those students who had expressed the strongest *materialistic ambitions* in their college days, described themselves as being far less fulfilled and far less satisfied with their lives fully eighteen years later. Pursuing those strongly materialist ambitions it seems, had not delivered anything like the life satisfactions that they had expected of it.[6]

So what might we conclude from this all too brief a sample? It would seem that the great consumerist, materialist, grab-what-you-can-while-you-can ethos of the past 20 years may still have some way to run. But it's no longer anything like so strong or so all-inclusive. Today there would seem to be a strong *counter-current* gathering momentum. There's much more to well-being than financial gain, write the social scientists. To find themselves now being echoed by the politicians declaring that there must be more to their policies than simply a concern for GDP. And many more people saying that there must be *more* to life than just acquiring more *stuff*, yet another outsize flat-screen tv, or another Mercedes outside the front door.

That essentially, is what this book is about, the *something more* that can genuinely transform our lives.

CHAPTER TWO

A Personal Story

So why am I a Buddhist? It's a longish story but since it's an important and a very relevant part of the argument that I wish to make, let me explain in as brief a compass as makes sense, at this early point in the journey.

The story really starts in South East Asia. For a considerable portion of my working life I have lived and worked overseas, initially in South East Asia, and then for several years in the deserts of the Middle East, and throughout that time I worked hard to establish good and close relations with people of all the local religions, Hindus and Muslims, as well as Buddhists. Even making a shot at mastering the languages, Malay and then Arabic, so that I could converse at least on a casual basis, and relate to these people at a deeper level than purely work issues. That effort paid off in that it added immensely to my experiences and the quality of my relationships during those years. I spent many weeks for example up-country, living in long-houses in the jungles of Borneo, and many weeks travelling and encountering villagers in the vast and empty deserts of Oman.

I've also always had a keen interest in religions on a cultural and historical level, so I studied Islam and read the Koran for example, and was well aware of the depth and the beauty of much Buddhist thought, and how well it fitted into the norms and rhythms of the societies in which it had been created and nurtured for so many centuries. But unquestionably it didn't really touch my life during those years abroad. I could see and respect just how profoundly these beliefs drove my colleagues lives, but there it ended. I had been brought up in an actively Christian household and my life and behaviour I believed, largely reflected Christian values, but that was about as far as it went. I have elsewhere described my then Christianity as rather like a comfortable, well worn jacket; a bit crumpled and loose fitting, and a bit worn at the elbows, but it slipped on easily, and once on I scarcely knew it was there. And I didn't feel any need for any more substantial religious scaffolding to support my life.

It's worth adding perhaps that the general view that I acquired of Buddhism during those long years overseas, comes pretty close to the way in which the western world has viewed Buddhism over the past few hundred years. It has been seen, historically speaking, as an interesting and often extraordinary body of *humanist* philosophy, full of insights into the nature of human motivation and behaviour perhaps, but somewhat remote and other-worldly and more than a little obscure. And it has been that viewpoint that has largely driven the Western response to Buddhism over the years. It has been seen very much more as a focus of philosophical and doctrinal studies for the academic, rather than any kind of *practical guide* to ordinary daily life. Particularly daily life today, in the fiercely competitive, time-slicing, achievement-driven, hustle and bustle of our post-industrial western society.

Getting on with the daily stuff

And that I think is by no means an unimportant consideration for so many of us; we are indeed overwhelmingly concerned with *getting on* with the business of our lives, being swept along by the relentless tide of events that swallows up most of our day, and often perhaps not so much *making decisions* about our life, as having them made for us by what might be called our deeply ingrained *habit energy*. We tend not to spend much time, if any, just standing still for a bit. Contemplation isn't a particularly fashionable place to be.'*What is this life if full of care, we have no time to stand and stare…*' the poet asks, and most of us are travelling so fast to the next place we need to be that we don't have the time to even attempt an answer.[1]

And when I think about it, that was pretty much my own personal situation when, many years later, I first encountered Nichiren Buddhism in this country, through Sarah, my partner at that time. My response was to some extent coloured by that earlier overseas experience, but to say that I was profoundly sceptical would be an understatement. It seemed well...*simply irrelevant...* to the kind of life that we were living. I was being swept along by my passion to make the most of my journalistic and writing career, and I certainly didn't feel any need for something that I saw as outlandish and ostensibly *alien* as Buddhism in my life. For starters there was no space. Like most people I was far too busy. But busy or not, there was no way that I could envisage that some remote and mystical philosophy, born out of a wholly different time and place of which I had some experience, could help me deal more *effectively,* more *creatively,* with the kinds of challenging, often exciting, sometimes anxiety-creating problems, that came up every day of the week.

I was prepared to accept that the Buddhist ideas were interesting, and worthy of discussion over the supper table from time to time. I was prepared to concede that most of us put far too little energy into nurturing our spiritual life, but that was about it. It simply didn't make sense to me to suggest that it could help me deal with the issues and the strong ambitions that pressed in upon me at work and at home.

I knew who I was and pretty much what I wanted out of life, which was essentially more of the same, more exciting work and more critical acclaim; both were far more important to me than more financial success. I was pretty much addicted to the stimulation and the pace and the movement of the career I had ended up in, which was writing and producing television programmes. Every programme was both demanding and stressful and yet immensely challenging and rewarding, so that the creative process was very much like a drug, when one programme-fix had ended I wanted another one. And the endless demands on my time and my energies didn't leave any space for something as supremely out of left field as Buddhism.

The best laid plans of mice and men

But as we all know, life is full of ironies that take us completely by surprise. Within a few months, and with considerable reluctance, I decided to take up the study of this Nichiren Buddhism. Why the change of mind? Well it was undoubtedly partly as a result of a relationship that had become very much more important to me; Sarah, who is now my beloved wife, had begun to take Buddhism very seriously, because of the benefits that she was experiencing; the clear set of values for example, and the sense of purpose and structure she felt it brought into her life. But my decision came mainly from the realisation that I simply didn't know what I was talking about. My casual brush with Buddhism overseas had in a sense been more confusing than enlightening. In order to deal with this new dilemma at the heart of my life…I wanted the lady, I didn't want the Buddhism that she was now firmly attached to…and this was the only strategy that presented itself to me. Before I could do anything I had to know much more about what I was dealing with. My initial thoughts I have to admit, were that eventually, with a much deeper knowledge, I would be able to *reason* Buddhism out of our lives so to speak; explain coolly and rationally, just why this practice was wholly inappropriate to the sort of life we were living in twentieth century Europe, so that we could then get married! So much for the best laid plans of mice and men.

The fact is that the study of philosophy, any body of philosophy, is I think, immensely seductive, precisely because it *challenges* us, and our preconceptions. It forces us to stop and think, and face up to the big questions about ourselves and our life that in the general rush and hurry of things, we spend all too little time thinking about. So, inevitably perhaps, I soon got a great deal of pleasure out of the study. In a sense it took on a life of its own. I read everything I could lay my hands on, and just about everywhere, on planes and trains and buses, and in the gaps between filming sessions.

A man made philosophy of life
Buddhist philosophy is wholly about human motivation and behaviour, and how we function and relate to one another. It has been well described somewhere as perhaps the greatest creation of the human mind, because of course, unlike all the other great global religions, Buddhism is entirely man-made if I may put it that way. Created wholly

by men, for men. When Shakyamuni first began to talk to people about his new understanding of the nature of human life, nothing remotely like it had ever been seen before. At no time in the 50 years or so of his travelling and teaching life did Shakyamuni, the first historically recorded Buddha, claim to have anything like a hot line to God, or anything resembling divine inspiration. So it was astoundingly fresh and challenging of conventional ideas. But it is also a philosophy that has evolved immensely over the past 2500 years, with additions and commentaries and interpretations by some of the greatest minds in human history, so it is scarcely surprising that there is much in it that is confusing and even contradictory.

But, as it turned out, it wasn't simply a case of picking up a book and understanding what it said. I had, seemingly inadvertently, come upon something that was changing how I felt about myself and the way I lived my life and, above all, how I handled my relationships with other people.

Interestingly the modern American philosopher Robert Solomon writes about something very similar in his book about his own spiritual journey, *Spirituality for the Skeptic*. Having defined himself as having been a profound sceptic, *'dismissive of both spirituality and religion'* for most of his life, he goes on to describe how an awakening sense of a spiritual depths in our lives can fundamentally transform our sense of who we are;

'Spirituality,' he writes, *'is ultimately social and global, a sense of ourselves identified with others and the world. But ultimately spirituality must also be understood in terms of the transformation of the self. It's not just a conclusion, or a vision, or a philosophy that one can try on like a new pair of pants. How we think and*

feel about ourselves has an impact on who we actually are.'
These kinds of thoughts, he goes on…*'do not just move us and
inform us, or supplement our already busy day-to-day existence.
They change us, make us different kinds of people, different kinds
of beings.'[2]*

So my personal journey of exploration and discussion and
debate and argument went on for perhaps a couple of years.
And alongside the intellectual journey, almost without
my being aware of it, there had clearly been a substantial
spiritual journey as well. We still argued Sarah and I, but
the arguments had subtly changed. They weren't in any
way the progressive dismantling of the practice that
I had envisaged. They were much more part of this process
of exploration and understanding. So there wasn't in any
way a sort of damascene moment of change, or anything
approaching that. It was a relatively slow growth of
understanding and respect, and admiration, for the values
and the principles and the attitude to life embodied in these
Buddhist teachings.

Back to basics
To squeeze it into a nutshell, Buddhism is essentially about
seeking to create the greatest value, *whatever circumstances*
we find ourselves in, good, bad and indifferent. So the
memory of that period in my life is one of great pleasure,
since it was so positive. A time of new ideas and stimulating
discussion and evolving relationships. Above all perhaps,
a time of real spiritual growth, and an awareness of the
importance of that growth.

Professor Richard Layard, economist at the London School
of Economics has also written about the social implications
that such an individual journey can have;

'Through education and practice, it is possible to improve your inner life- to accept yourself better and to feel more for others. In most of us there is a deep positive force, which can be liberated if we can overcome our negative thoughts...A happier society requires us to attend much more to the quality of our inner life and to proven methods for improving it.'[3]

It's immensely significant I think, that here we have an eminent, hard-headed, and undoubtedly forward-looking economist, writing about how we might improve the way we *run* our modern societies, and choosing to mention on several occasions, the contribution that Buddhist teachings might make to that process. Not, it's important to make clear, in any specifically *religious* sense, but on an individual and on a social level, since its values are indeed aimed at creating the sort of compassionate, constructive, value-creating society in which we would all choose to live and bring up our children.

And I could clearly see something of that going on in the people I began to encounter at meetings and seminars. People from a wide range of cultures and backgrounds, but with a common approach, in that they clearly sought to be positive and resourceful and optimistic about their lives, even when they were deeply embroiled in problems, as we all are of course, for a fair bit of the time. Life for these people was clearly about learning how to see these difficulties, not simply as *problems,* a burden to be borne, or worse, to *complain* about, but as a challenge, an *opportunity* even, for change and personal growth. Because when you think about it even momentarily, that is the only way we can grow and develop the confidence and the resilience to challenge and overcome problems isn't it? By tackling and overcoming problems. How else?

Sometimes succeeding and sometimes failing of course, but having the courage and the resilience to pick themselves up and try again. That is easy enough to say of course, and putting it down in a few short sentences like that makes it seem pretty effortless. It's only when we try to do it that we realise just how much effort it takes, and how much courage and resilience. And that in essence, is what the daily-ness of the Buddhist practice is about. It provides the structure and the discipline that stiffens the resolve to meet the challenge.

That is perhaps why, despite their own problems, these people always seemed to have enough energy and vitality left over to support one another, with noticeable warmth and sincerity. There was none of the judgemental comment, or the corrosive cynicism that is perhaps one of the most dysfunctional and destructive qualities of modern society. I'm not saying that these supportive qualities are unique to Buddhist groups. Of course not. Simply that these ordinary everyday Buddhists were clearly teaching *themselves* how to develop an enduring spirit of optimism and compassion.

One of those life-changing moments

So I gradually became aware that I had reached one of those genuine, life-changing moments. It's very difficult to achieve profound change in our lives. Indeed it is perhaps *the* most difficult thing to do. We've spent so many years grooving our beliefs and patterns of behaviour into our life, that they represent nothing less than who we are. So it takes real energy and real commitment, and overcoming not a little apprehension, to set about changing them. We need if you like the *wisdom* to see that we need the change, the confidence that we have enough *commitment* to carry it through, and the *courage* to set the change in motion.

Did I have enough commitment? Here I was with my life seemingly set on a well-defined course, comfortable, moderately successful, with no profound perception of religious need.

But perhaps the most surprising thing for me was that when I finally made the decision to fold a Buddhist practice into the fabric of my life, it didn't seem so profound a change after all. Indeed it seemed to have a certain *natural inevitability* about it, as if I had been on this gradual journey towards a greater understanding of myself and my life.

And again the philosopher Robert Solomon seems to me to express something very similar when he writes, that achieving an active and meaningful spiritual dimension in our lives…

'… is adopting a framework or a positive attitude in which all sorts of possibilities open up that may not have been evident before… The facts of the world remain pretty much as they were before. Nevertheless everything changes. The world is born anew.'[4]

'a positive attitude in which all sorts of possibilities open up'… captures the very essence of what I'm talking about. I cannot say that at the start of my practice, there was any clear vision or sense of direction. There wasn't an overriding idea or an obvious goal towards which I was heading. Why should there be? There was however I now realise a clear resolution. There seemed no point otherwise. If I try to put myself back into that situation, I was determined that once I had set out on this somewhat surprising road, I would continue until I was sure, one way or another, about the value of this practice in my daily life. It was easy enough for people to say to me, *'Buddhism is daily life,'* as they did.

The question was, did it actually work at that level? Did it make a fundamental difference to the way I viewed the ordinary stuff of every day?

Where have I ended up?

I've never spent much time looking backwards. That has never been of much interest to me. I'm much more concerned about the projects I have in hand now, and where they are leading. But if I look back over the past twenty odd years, and ask myself, where have I ended up; what has been the result of these years of regular daily Buddhist practice, what sort of answer emerges? That's a tough question for anyone of course, and not one that can be answered lightly.

But I am prepared to say that my Buddhist practice has had a greater and more profound effect on the way I live my life than any other single experience. That's a big thing to say about a long and eventful life. Moreover I simply can't think of any negatives. I have ended up with the most powerful and enduring sense of well-being and gratitude for all the things that are in my life…and I mean *all* the things. I can honestly say that for much of my life that was not the case. I can well remember for example that I would very rarely allow myself to use the '*happiness*' word, because as soon as you had uttered it, it seemed that whatever it was that you were trying to describe had either passed by or simply evaporated. Better not to pin a label on the experience.

Somehow, I can't claim to be entirely sure how, since causal connections are inevitably so difficult to trace, but undoubtedly I've been able to develop a much greater *awareness* of, and a much greater sense of *gratitude* for, the immense richness of my life. I also seem to have grown a much greater capacity to embrace everything that I encounter in my life. Not just the easy things, the good and the golden things, the stuff we all want, but all things, good, bad and indifferent. And there has been plenty of bad and indifferent stuff, as there is in all lives. Near bankruptcy as a result of fraud in the City for example, and losing most of the material possessions that I thought were so crucial to my happiness. For the past three years I've been engaged in a battle against cancer that has involved me in a fair bit of mental and physical pain. But as I have written elsewhere, as soon as I became aware of the cancer, so too I was aware of my ability to face up to it, to embrace it even, as part of my life. And those responses came as something of a shock to me. The knowledge that my sense of well-being and optimism about life wasn't dependent on only good things happening to me.

So what I'm saying is that this gradual transformation towards a profound and stable sense of well-being has occurred almost sub-consciously, as I have gone about my ordinary daily life…as a Buddhist. And that is a crucial point that cannot really be overstated. Basically I've just got on with living my life. The only major change has been that I have tried hard to do that within the framework of those Buddhist principles and values that I slowly acquired. So I've maintained a strong daily practice, for example, difficult in the early years because I was often questioning its value, but now about as much a part of my life as breathing. I've made a real effort to respond *positively* to all the 'stuff' that confronts all of us on a daily basis. As you would expect I haven't always succeeded, but when I've made a mess of things I've made the effort to re-evaluate so that I can make a better shot at getting it right next time around. Sometimes that's been easy, sometimes difficult, but as Buddhism tells us so often, *trying, actually making the effort, is in itself succeeding*. It's *not* trying, *not* making the effort, that we can count as failure.

And I think I'm being wholly accurate when I say that I've worked hard to create value in the lives of people whom my life has touched. Not in extraordinary ways I might add, just the ordinary everyday ways of courtesy and support and encouragement and active help when it was needed. As both Buddhism and now modern social science tell us repeatedly, *altruism*, concerning ourselves with the needs and welfare of others is without a shadow of doubt, one of the most powerful contributors to our own sense of well-being. Giving to others is an immense source of personal benefit.

So what does that all mean?

But what we need to focus on I suggest, are the *implications* of that brief account, which I have no doubt, could be said to describe the lives of just about all my Buddhist colleagues. And those implications seem to me to be *inescapable*. Put simply it suggests that a Nichiren Buddhist practice, provided it is lived with some degree of care and commitment...nothing extraordinary or even particularly demanding, certainly nothing we would consider to be overtly religious in any formal sense... that simple practice has the *potential* to transform the difficult and unlikely stuff of our ordinary daily lives, into a profound sense of well-being and gratitude for the joy of living.

Because that is describing nothing more than what has actually taken place in my life.
And in writing it, I am fully aware of the scale of that claim.
It's huge

OK so that's the Buddhist side of the story, albeit briefly told. But let's leave it there for the moment and move on to the other key contributor in this journey, the science, and the key question clearly is where does the science fit into the argument? What has science got to do with a Buddhist practice?

Buddhism and Science

The answer to that question is slightly more circuitous. Over recent years there has been something of a movement to link together the words Buddhism and science, as if to imply that in some way, not often explained in detail, they occupy to some extent the same or similar territories. I believe that approach to be profoundly misleading on many counts. Buddhism is not and doesn't claim to be the in the least *scientific* in its approach to resolving the deepest issues of human life. But then it doesn't need to be. On the one hand, Buddhism doesn't in any way need scientific justification or validation for its philosophical insights into the nature of human motivation and behaviour. They have been tested and proven over many centuries, as I've said, in the toughest laboratory of all, the trials and tribulations of daily human life. And on the other, science simply isn't equipped, even if it were interested, to deal with the area of religious belief.

Many scientists as individuals do of course have strong and active religious lives, but that tells us nothing about the relationship between science and religion except that they can clearly co-exist. It is simply testimony if you like to the enduring power and support provided by religious thought. But the basic fact is that science doesn't *do* religion. Issues like faith and belief and fundamental spirituality essentially lie beyond the range of scientific tools. You can't put courage or compassion, or faith and belief into a test tube and weigh and measure them. This issue was most eloquently dealt with by the late Stephen Jay Gould, the brilliant American palaeontologist and writer on science, who famously coined the *definitive acronym* on the subject. That acronym is NOMA. It stands for '*non-overlapping magisteria,*' which is simply a somewhat academic or high-flown way of saying that science and religion occupy quite different *dimensions* in our life.

However academic and inaccessible that particular definition might be, we know instinctively that it's accurate don't we? It makes complete sense to us on a sort of workaday, pavement-level basis. We know full well that we live in a world that is dominated by science and technology, and we know the colossal benefits that we derive from that situation. No one would want in any way to question that. But if we give it a moment's thought we also know that academic science is only a very small and highly specialised part of what we all know. Most of our *knowledge* about ourselves and our relationships comes from our own experience of life. We learn about life you might say, *from life itself.*

We also know that we *don't* turn to science when it comes to some of the biggest and most puzzling questions of all. Questions such as why are we here? Or is there a fundamental purpose to life? Or what is the meaning of suffering? Or what happens to this item called me after death? We may not ask those questions very often, but that's not the point. The fact is that when we do, we don't turn to *science* for the answers, we turn to a completely different dimension of our experience. And we happen to call that dimension religion, which *does* attempt to give us answers.

So clearly we have an absolute need for both sources of illumination or inspiration, if we are to make the very most of our lives, in this remarkable universe that we inhabit.

As the great 18th Century Austrian philosopher Immanuel Kant expressed it so forcefully, science is the organisation of knowledge, but wisdom, in the sense of spirituality, is the organisation of life. Indeed, I would argue that we need to stand up and take serious issue with scientists, when they choose to argue that in some way our lives would be richer, without the religious bit. It wouldn't!

But what about behaviour?

But back to the main thrust of my argument, and to Stephen Jay Gould. His analysis has long been widely accepted as the most authoritative statement, on what obviously remains a complex and somewhat controversial issue. But that having been said, I think we could certainly put up a case *at this time*, that there is...not so much a *flaw* in Gould's analysis, that would be going too far...but a gap perhaps, a lacuna. And it has arisen mainly I think as a result of the sheer volume of research that has been carried out in this area over the past ten to fifteen years. Put at it's simplest, science still cannot tackle issues of fundamental *faith* and *belief* and *spirituality*, and frankly isn't particularly interested in doing so. However, over the past couple of decades science has been immensely interested in observing and analysing what might be called the *consequences* of belief, namely our *behaviour*. What we do. How we live. What values we hold. How we handle relationships. How much compassion or altruism we show towards others. How we respond to problems and challenges. What makes us angry or sad, or happy or despairing? The questions are endless.

And it goes without saying that if we happen to have a strong religious or spiritual belief, then that *will have* a powerful effect on our behaviour. What we deeply hold to be true *reveals* itself in every aspect of our lives, from how we think, and what we say to the actions that we take in almost every circumstance. People as we know are quite commonly prepared to *die for their beliefs*, that is just how far our beliefs can affect our behaviour.

So in this case there is undoubtedly a big *overlap* between science and religion, in the sense that *behaviour,* influenced by profound belief, is of course *infinitely accessible* to observation and analysis by the scientists, in all its infinitely manifold and varied forms.

So why is that so important?

A quiet revolution
Well in a sense I think that we have been living through a kind of revolution over the past 20 years or so, a *quiet revolution* you might say, since this kind of research may take some time to yield up its findings, and is rarely if ever the stuff of headlines. But over this time, social scientists have sought to explore and to understand in ever increasing detail, the motivations and the compulsions that drive human behaviour, and their effects on our sense of self and on how we feel about our lives. The results have been sometimes astounding, sometimes predictable, but always interesting. With immense patience and care, and on a truly objective basis, sometimes with research projects that have run, and continue to run for many years, these social scientists have begun to put together an understanding of the nature of human life and motivation that goes way beyond anything that might have been imagined even a few decades ago.

As the briefest of insights into what I'm talking about, let me just quote a passage about a relatively recent research finding. It comes from the psychologist Daniel Goleman.

'A decade ago,' he writes, *'the dogma in neuroscience was that the brain contained all of its neurons at birth and it was unchanged by life's experiences. The only changes that occurred over the course of life were minor alterations in synaptic contacts... the connections between neurons...and cell death with aging. But the new watchword in brain science is 'neuroplasticity,' the notion that the brain continually changes as a result of our experiences... whether through fresh connections between neurons or through the generation of utterly new neurons. Musical training where a musician practices an instrument every day for years offers an apt model for neuroplasticity. MRI studies find that in a violinist for example, the areas of the brain that control finger movements in the hand that does the fingering grow in size. Those who start their training early in life, and practice longer show bigger changes in the brain.'*[5]

'...the brain continually changes as a result of our experiences.' So that's an interesting and radically new finding in science. But why you might ask is it of interest to us in this particular discussion? The short answer I suggest, is that a Buddhist practice is just such an on-going *daily experience* that Daniel Goleman is talking about, and as this analysis explains, it will undoubtedly have an effect on the way our brain functions. And the musical analogy Goleman uses is also directly relevant. Buddhist practitioners could be said to be very similar to musicians, in the sense that they too *'practice,'* day after day, week after week, year in year out, seeking to nurture hope and optimism and courage and resilience in their daily behaviour. The clear implication of Daniel Goleman's revelation, is that the Buddhist practitioner too, through that continually repeated *experience,* is strengthening the structures in the brain that enable him or her to manifest ever *more readily,* those very qualities of hope and optimism and courage and resilience in their behaviour. Just as the

musician undoubtedly develops the ability to play his instrument, more readily and more fluently, as a result of the sheer regularity of his practice.

A unique opportunity

So here it seems to me, there is a wonderfully rich and meaningful *overlap* to be explored. Because with religion of course...and in this case it's Buddhism that we wish to put under the microscope...it is only meaningful when its values and principles and its teachings become manifest in *human behaviour*, otherwise it's just a matter of words, just airy philosophy. One of the most profound things ever written about Shakyamuni for example, the first historically recorded Buddha, the seed from which this great tree of Buddhism has grown, who lived around 500BCE, is that the real significance, the real purpose of his mission in this world lay precisely in his *behaviour* as a human being. In what he did, at least as much as in what he said.[6]

But the question I asked was, why is this important? And the answer I think is that it gives us this great *opportunity* which has never been around before. It goes without saying that Buddhism doesn't exist in a bubble. Buddhism *is* daily life and its great strength is its claim to continuing relevance despite the vast changes that have gone on in our social circumstances, because fundamentally, *human nature* hasn't changed. So we are immensely privileged. We can, essentially *for the very first time*, look at the complex understanding that Buddhism has evolved of human motivation and behaviour...over several hundred years of contemplation and reflection... *in the context of* the wholly new ways of looking at our motivation and our behaviour, that we are only now learning from the formal studies carried out across the world, by the social scientists.

That, in essence is the something more that this book is about, that journey of *exploration* and *comparison*. Looking in detail not simply at what Buddhism has to tell us about living a full and meaningful and creative life, but looking sideways at what sociology and psychology and neuroscience have to tell us as well, so that we can see where and how they relate to one another. And that, it seems to me, is an immensely beneficial journey, whether or not we happen to be, or have the slightest wish to be, a practising Buddhist. Because these are precisely the areas we might turn to if we are genuinely seeking an answer to that question we asked right at the beginning, where do we turn these days for our values? Where do we turn these days to recalibrate our moral compass?

A dual track

So, for the past couple of years or so, I have been exploring as much as I could handle of the social research that has gone on in this area in recent years, and the result has been surprising. There is no question in my mind but that fundamental ideas about the nature of human motivation and behaviour that Buddhism has been teaching for centuries, find the most interesting and stimulating echoes and parallels and amplifications, in the studies carried out by today's social scientists. So this book pursues what you might call a *dual track.*

It is indeed a serious, committed, admittedly personal account of Buddhism in today's world, as it is manifest and expressed in the daily lives of very ordinary people; people holding down a day job you might say, caring for their kids, watching the ball game on a Saturday afternoon, worrying about the mortgage or the tax bill or the care of an aged relative, or whatever. Activities that we are all involved in. Buddhism that is, very much *in daily life*. And about the qualities that we all seek in our lives, such as a stronger and more consistent sense of well-being at the core of our life, that is not so easily dismantled by challenges and problems.

As we mentioned earlier, Buddhism teaches this extraordinary truth that happiness is not a matter of chance or random good fortune as we commonly believe, but essentially a matter of *choice,* and that with a certain amount of effort and commitment, we can all learn how to make that choice. That in essence is what a Buddhist practice is all about, learning how to make that choice.

But what about this statement, from a fully paid up scientist, a professor of psychology in fact, Sonja Lyubomirski from the University of California,

'To step back and consider your deep-seated assumptions about how to become a happier person and whether it's even possible for you...is to understand that becoming happier is realiseable, that it's in your power, and that it's one of the most vital and momentous things you can do for yourselves and for those around you.'[7]

That statements is from the other side of the tracks so to speak, from the scientific side. And yet it clearly emphasises two things, both of which have always been central to Buddhist teachings. One, that we *can* undoubtedly go into training if you like, to strengthen our own sense of well-being. And two, that in doing so we inevitably enhance the lives of those whom our lives touch... *'one of the most vital and momentous things you can do for yourself and for those around you,'* she says. Indeed one of the most remarkable experiences for me, as I went through some of the best of this modern social research, was the realisation of just how many of the findings about what it is that makes people feel good about themselves and their lives, and experience a sense of wholeness and purpose in their lives, are prefigured in the kinds of ideas that Buddhism has been teaching for so long.

So it's that scientific context, the new viewpoint that it brings to us, that makes up what I have come to call the second main track of this book.

The proposition

What I would like to do therefore is to take a number of issues that are central to the practice of Buddhism, issues such as compassion and altruism and gratitude for example, or creating meaningful relationships, the dilemma of suffering, how we deal with destructive emotions such as anger and greed, the complex matter of ethics and morality, and so on, and look at these issues, from both the classical Buddhist and from the scientific point of view. These issues aren't by any means concerned with the margins of our life are they? Most of them indeed are profoundly life changing. The kinds of things you might say that are of the greatest significance to all of us. Buddhism as you would expect, has a great deal to say about how we might approach them in a way that creates the most value for our lives and for those around us. And now modern science offers us this immensely *supportive* perspective.

Of course, if we ask the direct question, 'Do we need an understanding or an awareness of the science to develop an effective Buddhist practice? There can only be one answer, and it's in the negative. We do not.

But listen to this from the late, great, historian and philosopher, Arnold Toynbee,

'Science and religion need not and ought not to be in conflict. They are two complementary ways of approaching the universe mentally in order to cope with it.'[8]

Or this from philosopher Robert Solomon,

'Spirituality is supported and informed by science. The more we know about the world the more we can appreciate it.'[9]

So they are telling us that in order to make the very most of this rich and complex life that we are living, we benefit from both kinds of illumination, the spiritual and the scientific. That unquestionably rings true doesn't it? And this, from Tsunesaburo Makiguchi, the visionary Japanese educational reformer who founded the lay Buddhist organisation that today is at the forefront of the spread of Buddhist values and beliefs into the western world,

'I could find no contradiction between science, philosophy, which is the basis of our modern society, and the teachings of the Lotus Sutra.'[10]

The fact is that we live and practice in the *real world*, and the real world is changing rapidly, perhaps most rapidly in the *knowledge and the understanding* of human nature that lies so close to our Buddhist teachings. In a sense you could say that this social research takes our *personal* experience of the way Buddhist values and principles shape our daily lives, and places them in a wider, *global context.* And my argument would be that if we genuinely wish, as Buddhists, to reach out to a much wider non-Buddhist audience, then we can only be helped in that endeavour by some understanding, however peripheral that might be, of this new and immensely revealing knowledge.

But more than that, I think we gain genuine *benefit* from stretching our understanding in this way. Why? Because, as I've mentioned, we happen to be living in privileged times. We are witnessing if you like the slow building of a wave that is bringing immense social change. The debate and discussion about what people really want for their lives, the obvious concern for personal growth and self realisation, the understanding of the kinds of values and behaviour that enable people to feel good about their lives and their societies, has long since passed out of the hands of philosophers and religious teachers into mainstream social debate. It has become the stuff of everyday political discussion.

That is I believe a crucial point. Moreover it links in directly with an understanding that has always been at the very heart of a Buddhist approach to life, namely the idea that the pursuit of a sense of well-being at the *individual* level has an infinitely deeper and wider significance at the level of *society*.

As Daisaku Ikeda, one of today's greatest thinkers and writers on Buddhist issues has expressed it;

'In an age when both society and the religious world are wrought by turmoil and confusion, only a teaching that gives each individual the power to draw forth his or her Buddha nature can lead all people to happiness, and transform the tenor of the times. In other words…there can be no lasting solution to the problems facing society that does not involve our individual life state.'[11]

It is unquestionably a powerful vision, and one that is immensely relevant to the communities we all live in.

It proposes that a movement towards a better society, based on the principles of respect for the lives and values of others, and with peace and individual happiness as its objective, cannot just be created as a *top down* process. It has to start from the bottom up, with a profound change taking place in the lives of countless individuals, gradually changing the way the whole of society functions.

That is in essence, the goal to which this book is dedicated. And I ought to add perhaps right from the start, that it is written very much for people who have little or no knowledge of Buddhism, and for those who could well be as deeply sceptical as I was, about it's relevance or appropriateness to a modern western life style.

The plain fact is that we have a *great opportunity* to move on from the commonly held and largely superficial stereotypes of what Buddhism is about, because we now have this unusual and unexpected conjunction of views. They may be using different idioms and different methods, but essentially, both Buddhism, and now the social scientists, are telling us that a greater sense of well-being at the heart of our lives is fundamentally what we are all seeking, and that there are some *clearly defined* ways of achieving that objective, however tough and challenging the modern world may be.

So I'm suggesting that it's clearly worthwhile to invest a certain amount of time and energy, to clearing away those persistent stereotypes that obscure our view of what Buddhism is about, to see more clearly what it has to offer. And we start by unpacking the concept of belief or *faith* in Buddhism. What's that all about?

CHAPTER THREE

Buddhism and Belief

The essential starting point for anyone seeking to understand a little more about Buddhism is that it doesn't have a god at its centre. It is atheistic or humanistic. That is to say it doesn't have at its heart, or anywhere else for that matter, the all-seeing, all-powerful, creator-god figure that sits at the heart of all the other major world religions, particularly those with which we are most familiar in western societies, Christianity and Judaism, Islam and Hinduism.

That is very easy to say, and very easy to comprehend on an intellectual level, but in my experience it is much more difficult to grasp on a sort of daily, practical, down-to-earth level, because the implications are profound and never ending. Thus there is no divine hierarchy in Buddhism. It is this characteristic above all that gives Buddhism its wholly distinctive character. Instead of there being a set of dogma and beliefs, *handed down* to mankind in various ways by a divine presence or divine being, Buddhism is firmly rooted from first to last in ordinary humanity. Moreover, since it is not attached to *any* definition of divinity Buddhism doesn't have any *boundaries.* It doesn't have for example the boundaries that have been the source of so much conflict down the centuries that divide the Islamic definition of divinity from the Judaic, or the Judaic from the Christian, or the Christian from the Hindu. It is wholly inclusive. No one and indeed no thing is excluded. It is wholly inclusive.

So it is a colossal *humanist* vision that reaches out to embrace every man's relationship with himself, man with his fellow human beings, and man with his universal environment. Buddhism in effect draws three concentric circles around our lives. Ourselves at the centre. Then other people or society as a whole, a truly global society. Then the outer ring of the universal environment. So Buddhism is immensely forward looking, immensely modern you might say, in that it has always argued that all three are intimately interconnected in every way. No one of them is complete without the others, and for us to live a truly full and fulfilling life, it argues, we need to learn how to be connected creatively to all three. That is to say we have to know how to fully respect our *own life* with all its qualities and all its *imperfections;* understanding and embracing our faults and imperfections as well as our qualities, is essential to our well-being. We need to support the *lives of others* in every way that we can conceive. And we need to play a consciously constructive part in protecting and preserving the *natural environment* that sustains us all.

There is no clearer way of expressing this idea I feel, than to say that Buddhism is in every way, a *man made religion,* although you won't of course find those words, in that form, in any Buddhist text. So the body of Buddhist teachings essentially represent the wisdom and the insights initially of one man, Shakyamuni himself, immensely extended and developed and amplified down the succeeding centuries by some of the greatest minds in human history. But none of them at any point claimed any sort of divinity, or divine connection. Shakyamuni constantly makes this clear in his teachings, and there are many references in the various commentaries that we might use to buttress the point, but two perhaps will suffice.

One is from a renowned Buddhist teacher and it goes as follows,

'Buddha was not a god. He was a human being like you and me, and he suffered just like we do.'[1]

The other is from an eminent Buddhist Historian,

'The Buddha always stressed that he was a guide, not an authority, and that all religious propositions must be tested, including his own.'[2]

There are of course many profound implications that arise from Buddhism's basic humanism. By no means least is the fact that since it isn't about a God, or gods, we have to be careful about how we use key words like *'faith'* for example, and *'prayer.'* They occur all the time in the writings of all religions, including Buddhism. But if there isn't a God to have faith in, or to pray to, then clearly these words will mean something very different in Buddhism, from the way we commonly understand them on the basis of our Judaeo-Christian heritage. And it goes without saying doesn't it, that it's crucially important we have some understanding of what that difference is?

The fundamental notion of equality

One key implication that is absolutely fundamental to anyone approaching Buddhism for the first time, is that the wisdom and the understanding that has been generated by this process of evolution down the centuries, on the nature of human life and motivation and relationships, is passed on to all men and women on the basis of *equality*. Complete equality. That is such an important point, but it's one that is extraordinarily difficult to grasp, even for those who have been practising for many years. Because we are so accustomed in the West, we might even say conditioned, to believing that there is a vast *unbridgeable* gulf that normally exists between the teacher, the *bearer* of the wisdom, the Jesus or the Mohammed figure, and the rest of humanity, us ordinary human beings. That gulf simply does not exist in Buddhism.

Shakyamuni tells us repeatedly, so that there should be absolutely no doubt, that he is simply one of us.[3] Indeed for him to be deified in any way by his followers would run completely counter to the central thrust of his teaching. It would deny if you like the central idea that the life state he achieved, filled with hope and optimism and courage and resilience, despite the toughness of his life, is available to all of us. We can all learn that is, how to achieve it *in this lifetime*. That learning indeed is what the practice is all about.[4]

So if we strip away all the stories and legends and the mythologies that have inevitably accumulated around so great a life lived so long ago, Shakyamuni, and indeed all the historical Buddhas down the years, have been *ordinary* human beings. They were undoubtedly *extraordinary* in terms of their wisdom, and the clarity of their vision, and their profound grasp of the reality of human life. And no doubt extraordinary too in their charisma, and their ability to convey that understanding to others. But apart from that, they manifested many of the ordinary human frailties. And they too struggled as we all do, to bear the trials and tribulations of ordinary men and women.

And the clear message that we should take from this, is that the fundamental quality at the centre of their lives, which happens to be described as their *Buddhahood or Buddha nature*, was part of their *ordinary humanity*, it was not a thing apart. Conversely Buddhism teaches, that all the rest of us ordinary human beings have within us the *potential* to attain this same life state. The importance of that understanding becomes evident when we get to talking in more detail about what this word Buddhahood means, but the key point is that it has nothing to do with an aspiration towards perfection, or elevation of any kind. Not at all. It's not a *religious* quality in any way, that is perhaps the biggest misconception. It is simply a *human* quality, an inner resource that, Buddhism teaches, we can all learn how to harness and make use of in dealing with all the stuff of our ordinary daily lives.

As one Buddhist text neatly expresses it,

'We ordinary people can see neither our own eyelashes which are so close, nor the heavens in the distance. Likewise we do not see that the Buddha exists in our own hearts.'[5]

Thus a Buddhist practice is essentially about *empowering* people, enabling us to use all the resources we have, spiritual as well as intellectual, to build strong and meaningful lives for ourselves… and for *others*…the two are inextricably interlinked. It's about learning how to think of ourselves in terms of our relations with other people, in terms of compassion and altruism, rather than our acquisitive individualism. Because Buddhism, perhaps more than any other religion… except possibly the 'religion' of science…brings constantly to our attention the profound implications of the fact that we all live in a *totally joined up* world. The world's media may have been talking about the Global Village for only a decade or so, but Buddhism has always taught it. And now we've all caught up. We all now understand so clearly that nowhere in the world is very far away any more; that what happens to ordinary people on a dusty street in Palestine, or in an African township, or on a remote part of the Japanese coastline, can touch and change all our lives.

Buddhism's modern relevance

These distinctive elements of Buddhism, its essential humanism, its *dynamic humanism* as it's sometimes called because its purpose is to change and move our whole lives towards the positive end of the spectrum, and its *unbounded inclusiveness,* are perhaps the key qualities that give Buddhism its universal relevance and its astounding, everlasting modernity. It may have begun in the deer park in the little town of Sarnath in Northern India all those years ago, when Shakyamuni first sat down to talk to a small group of people about his newly-won ideas, but in no sense is it ancient, in no sense is it *stuck in time,* or backwards looking. It continues to be powerfully about the here and now of our daily lives.

Witness to that is the fact that over the past 40 or 50 years, many tens of thousands of people in Europe and the Americas for example, and elsewhere, have chosen to place a Buddhist practice at the very centre of their lives. For the very first time in its history, during what might well be described as the most materialistic, and possibly the least spiritual of all the ages of man, Buddhism is flowing strongly westwards out of Japan and Asia, and into the western-way-of-life parts of the world. Indeed never before in its history has Buddhism spread so rapidly or so widely in terms of geographical area, and never before have so many people in the West turned to Buddhism to find answers to their questions about life, the universe and everything.

Moreover there are no easy answers to explain away this process. It's not an age thing, young or old, nor is it confined to any particular social grouping. Indeed it's noteworthy that the people who have adopted a Buddhist practice in the West come from all walks of life, all kinds of backgrounds, all kinds of careers; from actors and accountants to plumbers and television producers and taxi drivers and traders in the city. Ordinary people, living in the real world, bringing up their families and pursuing their careers, and individually making the choice to put it all together within the overarching framework of a Buddhist set of principles and values. It is a genuine revolution of sorts. Indeed it has been described by some religious historians as a new departure in the religious history of the West. One knowledgeable commentator has gone so far as to describe this modern movement as being of similar significance in the history of Buddhism, as the Protestant Reformation was in the history of Christianity.[6]

What makes it all the more remarkable is that this global movement is taking place not on the backs of missionaries or itinerant teachers as you might expect, or anything resembling them, but slowly, steadily, almost imperceptibly, in a truly modern way; as a result simply of people talking to other people, largely on a one-to-one basis.

This is my experience. *You might find it useful in your life.'* The very basis in a sense on which this book is being written!

Moreover it's taking place in an age, as I've said, that is far more notable for its rampant materialism and its widespread cynicism than for its religious commitment, and despite the fact that a Buddhist practice is genuinely demanding. It calls for application and effort and commitment, because we are learning a new set of life skills, fundamentally new ways of thinking about ourselves and our relationships, and how to tackle the tough and challenging stuff that is inherent in all our lives.

Clearly it is fulfilling some perceived need for a stronger and more meaningful spiritual life for many people, a searching for something *more* to life; a reaction perhaps *against* the powerful influences of cynicism and materialism at work in society. There is just so much available to be done these days, and so much more to hunger after in shopping malls and supermarkets and on the web, that we can find our lives almost entirely taken up with 'stuff,' with the doing and the arranging and the acquiring and the moving on from one event, one party, one club to the next. But is that enough? Is that what we really want? The point is that we are undoubtedly *spiritual* animals, however much we may try to convince ourselves that we're not.

Madonna once told us most persuasively, that this is a *material* world, and that she is very much a material girl. That may indeed be so, but there is a powerful line from Bruce Springsteen that brings us a completely different message, and one that reflects perhaps a growing change in social sentiment..

'It's time to start saving up...he says... *for the things that money can't buy.'*[7]

The things that money can't buy...what can he possibly mean, other than a deeper and more meaningful spiritual life beyond the bounds of mere materialism? What is remarkable I think, is just how close that sentiment comes, to something that a great and influential Buddhist teacher called Nichiren Daishonin wrote to his followers, all those years ago.

'*More valuable than the treasures in any storehouse,*' he wrote... that is to say, more material stuff... '*are treasures of the body,*'... that is to say good health... '*and the treasures of the heart are most valuable of all,*' ...that is to say, an active and meaningful spiritual life.[8]

And in our deepest selves we know that to be true don't we?

The nature of enlightenment

But back to this central question of faith in Buddhism, what can it possibly mean in a religion that has no gods to have faith in? One hurdle we have to leap over before we get to that, is the subject of Shakyamuni's own *enlightenment*, the nature of the reality he came to understand. Enlightenment is in a sense a *technical term* in Buddhism, and I think it really helps to see it in that light. Indeed the word Buddha itself essentially means *the enlightened one,* it comes from a Sanskrit verb that means to be awakened, or to be aware of, or to know deeply. And the key thing to note is that those are quite human-scale activities aren't they? Nothing divine about them. We can all wake up, or be aware, or know deeply.

So how should we deal with the fact of Shakyamuni's enlightenment? In many ways the concept of a state of being, or a state of mind labelled *enlightenment* is strange to us, not to say alien. It's a word we're not likely to use often, if at all. In an essentially intellectual and materialist age we are much more attuned to, and likely to be much more comfortable with, down-to-earth explanations and scientific patterns of proof. But of course, as we all know, there is much more to our humanity, particularly our humanity when it is lived at the highest level, than can be observed and measured in a laboratory. So we have to accept I think that in using an unusual word like enlightenment, we are reaching out in an attempt to describe something that may be very difficult to actually *pin down*, but which nevertheless remains a wholly valid part of human experience. Put simply we might say that enlightenment involves a completely different view of reality. One analogy that comes to mind is the sort of phase change as it's called in physics, that happens when water turns to ice. It is the same stuff so to speak, precisely the same molecular substance, nothing has been added or taken away, but it is also a complete transformation.

The interconnectedness of everything

But in truth, metaphors only take us so far don't they? Many attempts have been made to bring the *implications* of Shakyamuni's experience closer to us. They contain many ideas that have become the central pillars of Buddhist thought, ideas that underpin the entire structure. So let's look at a couple of those ideas to see if they help to clarify things for us. Take the profound *interconnectedness* of everything in the universe for example, from the dust beneath our feet to the great galaxies spiralling out on the edge of space. *Everything*, Shakyamuni tells us, *is* interconnected, way beyond anything we can possibly perceive and understand with our senses.

Perhaps the strangest thing for most of us is the fact that today's most eminent scientists talk to us in a disturbingly similar way. The late, great Nobel prize-winning American physicist Richard Feynman for example tells us,

'First of all there is matter, and, remarkably enough, all matter is the same. The matter of which the stars are made is known to be the same as the matter on earth...The same kinds of atoms appear to be in living creatures as in non-living creatures;

frogs are made of the same 'goup' as rocks, only in different arrangements.'[9]

It's hard to think of any other scientist who could use the word 'goup' in a scientific text and get away with it! The fact that Feynman describes a profound connection between frogs and rocks is surprising enough, but what he is clearly telling us in plain English, is that all matter, animate and inanimate, is deeply interconnected.

And then there's the great philosopher-scientist Daniel Dennett telling us almost exactly the same thing from a slightly different perspective.

'There is just one family tree,' he tells us, 'on which all living things that have ever lived on this planet can be found – not just animals but plants and algae and bacteria as well. You share a common ancestor with every chimpanzee, every worm, every blade of grass, every redwood tree.'[10]

'...*all living things that have ever lived on this planet.'* It's a phrase that takes the breath away. But just think of the implications. It means that the bunch of roses you give to your beloved partner on your anniversary carries DNA that connects them closely to the hand that holds them. The family dog that takes you lovingly for a walk every morning, as mine does, hangs from the same family tree as yourself. There could surely be no clearer confirmation of Shakyamuni's perception of a universal interconnectedness all those years ago?

The profound truth of universal change
Then there is his perception that lies at the very heart of Buddhism, that change or *impermanence,* is the very nature of

all things. However much we cling on to the idea that what we have we hold, however fiercely we may desire things to remain as they are, *nothing* ever stays the same from one moment to next. Everything that is or ever was, every life, every relationship, goes through the same endless cycle of birth, growth, decline and death.

Becoming, growing, subsiding, dying.

Forming, continuing, declining, disintegrating.

Once again this is *absolutely in tune* with the message from modern science. The only thing that varies is the period of the cycle, from a few millionths of a micro-second for the life of a sub-atomic particle say, to the life span of a mayfly, or a man, or a mountain, or the dramatic events that occur in the life cycle of a star like our Sun, spread over many millions of years. Science has steadily discovered, and we have steadily come to understand, that they all become, grow, decline and die.

It's worth adding perhaps that there is an extraordinary paradox in all of this, one of so many in Buddhism, in that *underlying* this universal cycle of flux and change that affects *all* things without exception, there is a single constancy; the unchanging constancy of the *rhythm* itself, that sustains and supports the endless cycling from birth to death.

Life is not a rehearsal, it's the real thing

But in all of this, whatever elements of the enlightenment story we find difficult to grasp or to understand, perhaps... we do well to remember...simply because of the *limitations* of our own experience or imagination, or our unwillingness to believe; whatever the precise nature of the truths that Shakyamuni came to perceive, the key thing to hang onto I would argue, is that what *resulted* from his experience is clear enough. The immense moving power of the experience that he went through changed him forever. He became truly a *different man.* In many ways it seems very similar to the experience that Saul went through on the road to Damascus, that transformed him from a fierce persecutor of Christians, into Paul, the great teacher and primary architect of the Christian Church. It wasn't Jesus who created the Christian church, or indeed Peter, it was Paul. But in the case of both Paul and Shakyamuni, the experience they went through was like walking through fire, and it lit a fire in them that was so strong that it was never extinguished.

Shakyamuni was never able again to separate his existence as a human being, from his desire to teach the truths about the life we all lead, that he had come to understand, and to improve the well-being of all of humankind. He set out if you like to reveal a new *understanding of reality,* which is what enlightenment ultimately means. And central to that new understanding is the seemingly simple, and yet truly revolutionary idea, that life is *not a rehearsal* for some sort of afterlife, it is the *real thing,* and it makes sense therefore to learn how to build a better life for ourselves, *today,* in the here and now.

He taught for a surprisingly long time, over 50 years, and throughout that long period he was tireless in his efforts to convey the essence of his new understanding of reality, in ways that made a *practical* difference to ordinary people's lives. Right at the heart of his teaching was the clear message that the new understanding that he had gained of human life and motivation, although *radical* in its direction and its implications, it was not in any sense *divine,* or alien to ordinary human existence. How could it be since *he* was no more, nor no less than that. What he had come to understand was simply the highest reach of an ordinary human mind.

He was clearly a man of great charisma and an inspirational speaker and he talked of taking people up a sort of *staircase of understanding,* pitching his teaching always at a level that could be received and comprehended by whatever audience he encountered. So it wasn't remote and theoretical and removed from the concerns of ordinary people. But when seen against the centuries-long background of Brahmanism, nothing like it had been taught before. Because his teaching eliminated the received wisdom of a pantheon of gods who basically controlled human destiny, and introduced a wholly new perception of reality, concerned with the growth and liberation of the individual human spirit. The *'true great adventure of self reformation,'* as it has been described.[11]

It was this powerful *human-scale* philosophy focused on daily life, and deliberately expressed in the dialect of ordinary people rather than in the dialect of the priestly class, that touched and drew in people from all backgrounds and all walks of life; the rich and the poor, young and old, the educated and the unschooled. They all wanted to see him and hear him speak in person. The image that most readily comes to mind perhaps is of a Ghandi-like figure, immensely approachable, immensely compassionate, surrounded by a crowd listening intently, as he taught about a new kind of hope and a new kind of possibility for ordinary lives.

The radical teaching of the Lotus Sutra

But what precisely was that new hope and that new possibility? It is expressed most completely and most powerfully in a teaching, or a sutra, called The Lotus Sutra. This was the mainspring of Shakyamuni's mission during the final phase of his long teaching life. It represents if you like the summit of that staircase of learning up which he was steadily taking his followers, and it is properly described as the very core and essence of his life's work. The Lotus Sutra is the central text of Mahayana Buddhism, which embraces Nichiren Buddhism. It is a long involved work full of stories and parables which stands alongside the Bible for example and the Koran as one of *the* great religious texts of human history. As Daisaku Ikeda, one of the world's greatest authorities on the Lotus Sutra, describes it, at the very heart of the philosophy it teaches, is the perception that '...*the inner determination of an individual can transform everything; it gives ultimate expression to the infinite potential and dignity inherent in every human life.*'[12]

The lotus of the title is seen to be a powerful and many-layered metaphor for many things, but undoubtedly one of the most important, the very heart of the message that it seeks to transmit, is that the lotus is a plant that grows in a muddy, swampy environment, and yet produces flowers of extraordinary beauty. Thus it is symbolic of the *immense potential* that can be revealed, created, brought out of, the ordinary muddled, mundane circumstances of our daily lives, no matter how difficult and challenging the initial circumstances of that life may be.

Thus in the Lotus Sutra Shakyamuni essentially turned the religious world on its head. At a time when people saw themselves as being limited and hemmed in by powerful, external controlling concepts such as destiny and the will of the gods, Shakyamuni taught them that was not the case, that was not an *accurate representation* of the reality of human life. Everyone he said, could come to understand that man carried his own destiny *in his own hands*. That our lives are our *own*, to shape and to make. That we have the resources *within us*, and the freedom, to make our own choices, to take control of our lives and move them in the direction we wish to go. Provided only that we accept full responsibility for the choices that we personally make, and their implications for others around us. That concern for others is the very basis of Buddhist morality, which we look at in greater detail later on.

It was unquestionably, a revolutionary teaching then, which is why it spread like a bushfire across South East Asia. But what is also unquestioned I would suggest, if you give it a moments thought, is that it remains pretty revolutionary today. This accumulated wisdom about learning how to create for *oneself* a better and a happier life, no matter what our circumstances, no matter what problems or challenges we all encounter every day of our lives, continues to be about the *present* and not about the past. It continues to demonstrate its direct immediacy and relevance, despite the vast changes mankind has lived through in every area of our lives, immense, immeasurable changes.

But those are of course *external* changes, whereas our *inner humanity* remains unchanged. We still find ourselves for example, *limited* by all kinds of disabling doubts and fears. Fears of so many things, fear of inadequacy, fear of rejection, fear of loss, of failure, and much else. We still find ourselves knocked down and disabled by problems and difficulties that sometimes seem so overwhelming that we don't know where to turn. We still find it difficult to *acknowledge*, let alone to draw on, our inner resources of courage and hope and optimism, to make the very most of our lives.

Indeed some of Buddhism's central teachings about how to recognise and draw upon our inner resources, and so overcome many of the negative impulses and responses that we experience, have been taken up and are used on a regular basis by some of today's leading psychologists, in helping people with severe and persistent depression or unhappiness.[13]

So Buddhism continues to touch and to change people's inner lives, in the West now as well as in the East, in increasing numbers. If we ask the question why that is, there are of course many threads to the answer. But undoubtedly one of them will be that there is something immensely powerful, immensely empowering, about this central idea that comes directly from Shakyamuni and Nichiren Daishonin, of taking hold of our lives in a rational and positive way, and moving them in the direction we wish to travel. We all want to know how to do that. And that really brings us back to this question of faith, which is where we started out in this chapter. So what have we learned about faith in Buddhism?

This key question of faith

You might say that in some ways it is the most important question of all, because faith is a chameleon of a word, and in trying to pin down what it signifies for Buddhists, we are clearly concerned to establish both what it does mean... and what it doesn't. So that we end up with a much stronger, much clearer understanding of the territory. There's really no point in our constantly being advised to '*have faith*,' is there, if we don't fully understand what that means?

So in all the major religions with which we are most familiar, in Christianity and Judaism and Islam for example, we know that the word faith is used to bind together all those elements of the teaching that are *beyond the reach of proof*, or beyond the reach of human experience. And inevitably in religions that deal with the nature of divinity itself, and how it works in the world, and the unknowable after life, those un-provable, unknowable elements are very substantial indeed. So faith of this sort has a truly immense role to play. The believer is asked to make what we have come to call a *leap of faith* to accept those elements of the teaching or doctrine.

And the word *'leap'* in this context describes very accurately what we are being asked to do, namely to leave the *solid ground* of our experience, of what *we absolutely know* to be the case, and put our trust and belief in something that is way outside our normal experience, and what's more, will *always* be outside our normal human experience. That is not of course suggesting in any way that such a leap of faith is immensely difficult. Clearly it isn't, given the sustained and hugely sustaining power of Christianity and Islam for countless millions of people over the past two thousand years. And of course I should make it absolutely clear that in no way should this be interpreted as a value judgement. Not in any way. I am simply trying to explore differences in the way in which we use this key word faith. I have been to many Christian and Islamic funerals for example, and there can be not the slightest doubt about the immense consolation and support provided by the deep faith of the people there.

It is clear therefore that in all these major religions, faith has much to do with the firm *belief* in the powers of God and of Allah, and the *decisive* role that power plays in the daily lives of men. That is to say, this kind of faith, which is so deeply embedded in our western culture, has very much to do with entities, powers, people, that are *outside of oneself.*

I would go so far as to argue that this idea of taking a 'leap of faith' is now *so deeply embedded,* that it has become the *essential* meaning of the word itself; *whenever* we use the word faith in the West we are normally talking about faith in something *'out there,'* something very much *outside ourselves.* And I think it helps to be totally aware of that.

Which brings us back to the central fact that since there is no all-powerful creator god 'out there' in Buddhism, the word *must* carry a very different meaning. And right from the start we learn that the fundamental difference in Nichiren Buddhism is that faith is not in any way to be equated with belief in something external, something *outside of oneself.* The word *only* has meaning in relation to a quality or a strength that we are seeking *within.* As Nichiren Daishonin expresses it on so many occasions,

'...perceive the true nature of your life... If you seek enlightenment outside yourself, then your performing even ten thousand practices and ten thousand good deeds will be in vain. It is like the case of the poor man who spends night and day counting his neighbour's wealth but gains not even half a coin.'[14]

So what must faith mean then in this context...if we are to *perceive the true nature of our lives?*

The somewhat surprising answer is that faith in Buddhism is essentially about belief in oneself, *self-belief.* And it is related directly to the strength of the *desire* or the *determination* that we can summon up, *within our own life,* to act or to live in accord with Buddhist values and principles. It means going into battle if you like against our own inner weakness or lack of self-confidence or self-belief, so that we can create for ourselves a life that is overwhelmingly resilient and positive and optimistic and compassionate, and always concerned with creating value out of whatever circumstances we might encounter.[15]

Faith in Buddhist terms then, is not all that different from the sheer determination or the self-belief we work hard to summon up, to pursue *any* major goal or objective in our life. We do find that we have to *dig deep* within ourselves to achieve success in a chosen career, or to turn a crisis situation around, or to overcome a life-threatening illness, or create a lasting and fulfilling relationship. The fundamental difference, and of course it is fundamental, is that in this case the self-belief is *anchored* firmly in the powerful humanistic philosophy introduced into the world by Shakyamuni, and developed and amplified by a series of remarkable thinkers and teachers over the past two and a half thousand years.

So faith in Buddhism is also very much about *method*, about *how* we can develop such a life, such an enduring self-belief.

To bring this story bang up to date we need now to look briefly at one of the greatest and most controversial of these teachers, who has already been mentioned on several occasions, and who has had a huge role to play in the evolution and transmission of Buddhist teaching into the modern world. His name...Nichiren Daishonin.

Nichiren Daishonin

Nichiren was born in 1222 into an ordinary family living in a fishing village on the south eastern coast of Japan. He went into a monastery at the age of 12, essentially because a monastery was about the only place where a boy could receive an education. He became a priest at the age of 16, and clearly he had very unusual qualities of commitment and perseverance, in that he devoted the next phase of his life, virtually his entire youth, to a personal quest to unravel the confusion in thinking and the conflict between the various Buddhist schools that prevailed in Japan at that time. He spent fifteen long years travelling round the leading monasteries in the country, to study the collections of ancient Buddhist texts that they held. Painstakingly he traced the central thread of Shakyamuni's teachings back through Japanese and Chinese and Indian commentaries, to the heart of the Lotus Sutra itself. So we could say that Nichiren's letters and other writings, which are still extant, and now widely translated into many other languages, put us *directly* in touch with Shakyamuni's original words and his intent.

That personal quest led to Nichiren becoming, very much like Shakyamuni before him, the most authoritative, and the most outspoken and persistent religious and social reformer of his day. And he was utterly fearless. He was living in a rigidly feudal society ruled over by a powerful and ruthless military dictatorship, within which various sectarian priesthoods had immense power and influence over the detail of the lives of ordinary people. Women and those in the bottom layers of society had virtually no rights. Yet here was Nichiren actively preaching a Buddhism that spoke of absolute equality in the rights of man, men and women alike, respect for the individual regardless of his or her status in society, and the potential for all men and women to create a better and more fulfilling life for themselves, no matter where they sat in the social hierarchy. It was genuinely revolutionary stuff, and inevitably he became a marked man. In the event he was pursued and persecuted in various ways by the military authorities and the religious establishment virtually throughout his life.

Despite these severe and constant challenges to this mission that he'd taken on, to communicate these revolutionary truths far and wide, Nichiren spent his entire life living among ordinary people, peasants and farmers and craftsmen, clarifying the essence of Shakyamuni's teachings, encouraging them to see their Buddhism as a wholly practical approach to living, not a thing apart, but part of the detail of their daily experience. He wrote to them constantly, and as I've said, these letters, or *gosho* as they are called in Japanese, still exist to be read today, supporting and encouraging and guiding ordinary people through countless everyday problems. Everyday then and just as everyday now; anxiety over a sick child, grief at the death of a husband, conflict with an employer, uncertainty about how to handle a really challenging circumstance.

Always his message is realistic and down-to-earth, always the positive one of hope and optimism. But always seeking to deepen their grasp of the *paradox* that lies at the very heart of Buddhism; the understanding that although we instinctively reject and shy away from the troubles of life, the plain fact is that it is only by facing up to them, embracing them, challenging them as they occur, that we can build the courage, and the strength of spirit, and the enduring self-confidence that we all seek. We can only learn that we are immensely capable of overcoming problems...by overcoming them. There simply is no other way.

So he taught that when we feel ourselves to be low in spirits, or when we lack the self-belief and the courage we've just been talking about, almost any problem can seem huge and overwhelming. Whereas when we've built up our courage and our confidence by challenging and overcoming problems, even the most difficult situations no longer seem so daunting, or so insuperable. The essential issue on which we should focus our minds therefore, is not how to eliminate problems from our lives, which is a manifest delusion, a sheer impossibility, there is no such life. What we should be seeking he argued, is that inner strength of spirit, that inner confidence that we can overcome them, which is eminently achievable.

That in essence, is the very *faith* that Buddhism asks us to have belief in.

Throughout his life, writ large in all his letters, Nichiren was very much like St. Francis in the Catholic tradition; he demonstrated deep compassion for everyone, and an unshakeable courage in his own life, so that ordinary people were immediately drawn to follow him and support him, whatever challenges they faced. Some of his followers even chose to give their lives for him, when they were threatened with execution if they did not withdraw their support.

If we were to cast around in more recent history to find a similar figure, to give us a stronger feel for the sort of person Nichiren was, someone who also struggled, virtually alone, in the face of entrenched resistance, to galvanise similar profound changes in society, it might well be a Ghandi, or a Mandela or a Martin Luther King.

Nichiren's Legacy

When he died at the age of 60 Nichiren left an extraordinary legacy, in the sense that his personal quest to re-establish the primacy of the message wrapped up in the Lotus Sutra, provided the essential basis for the modern spread of Mahayana Buddhism, out from Asia into the western world. Although it lay locked up inside Japan, until the widespread liberalisation and opening up of Japanese society that occurred immediately after the Second World War.

But it could be argued that Nichiren went further than any other Buddhist teacher, in that from the depths of his own enlightenment, and his profound understanding of human nature, gained from all those years living and working among ordinary working people, he created an immensely simple, down-to-earth *method*, to enable ordinary people to establish an *effective Buddhist practice*, as part of their ordinary daily lives, no matter how busy they might be, no matter what demands were pressing in upon them from other areas of their lives. That was his great, in many ways incomparable contribution, creating a model of Buddhist practice that is *wholly accessible* to ordinary people today for example, living busy, active, time-slicing lives in a modern society. That is why he is sometimes known as The Buddha for the Modern Age.

There is no question, countless people in the western world today will attest to the fact that the combination of self-belief, and the determination to achieve personal change, that can be generated through the daily discipline of Nichiren's practice, can be a very powerful beneficial and life changing force. And once again it is quite surprising, and very affirming, to find similar views expressed in very similar terms, in modern, secular, scientific literature. It is very much a question of self-belief, and of effort and determination. As one psychologist among many has expressed it for example,

'...*enjoying a real increase in your own happiness is in fact attainable, if you are prepared to do the work. If you make a decision to be happier in your life – and you understand that this is a weighty decision that will take effort, commitment, and a certain amount of discipline- know that you can make it happen.'*[16]

Actual proof

So it could be argued that the Buddhism of Nichiren Daishonin is offering you the opportunity to put the claims that it makes to the test in your own life. Make the decision it says, summon up from within this self-belief, this determination, that you are prepared to tackle the things about your life that you wish to change…*'exert yourself in the two ways of practice and study,'*[17] as Nichiren puts it, and observe the results in your own life, to see whether or not it delivers it's promise.

And that 'whether or not' is crucially important of course. Both options are wholly valid. It's not a practice that one could continue on the basis of someone else's belief. But basically, that is the process that I went through some 20 odd years ago, with no small measure of doubt and scepticism as I've mentioned! But there is nothing wrong of course with a dash of healthy scepticism, or even a heavy dose of it. Scepticism is a great asker of difficult questions that demand answers. In the event I've travelled, as I'm sure many others have before me, and since, from a profound scepticism, to an equally profound commitment to a practice that has brought immense value and joy into my life. And, I have not the slightest doubt, to the lives of those around me.

People frequently ask me,*'Where do you get your constantly positive spirit from?'* I have only one answer, from the daily practice of Nichiren Buddhism.

CHAPTER FOUR

Buddhism and Happiness

Do we really need a discussion about the nature of happiness you might ask? It's such a slippery and elusive emotion to define, and so intensely subjective, that we're in grave danger, aren't we, of just going around in pointless circles? And in any case, however difficult it may be to pin it down in a *definition*, does that really make any difference? Isn't it very much like the taste of the strawberry, we may not be able to describe it, but we all know it well enough when we actually experience it?

But those arguments clearly cut both ways don't they? It's precisely because it *is* so slippery and so elusive a term, that we might get a great deal out of even a brief discussion of what we really mean when we talk about happiness in this world. And personally I think there's a great virtue in being a bit *tougher* on ourselves, so that we take the time and the trouble to think our thoughts through more completely, and set them down more precisely. Not least because this particular word is, in my view, in danger of being so immensely *overused* that it's meaning becomes gravely diluted.

And there are other equally compelling reasons. Above all else perhaps, the fact that if you are vaguely interested in, or practice Buddhism, you simply can't escape it. You can't have failed to notice for example the number of times the word happiness has cropped up in the text so far, which mirrors the fact that it occurs a great deal in Buddhist discussions. In fact Buddhists will often say that the *fundamental reason* for their practice is nothing less than greater happiness for themselves and for those around them. And if we give it a moments thought, that too is somewhat surprising, in the sense that if I were to ask you to go away and search for the word 'happiness' in other religious liturgies, you might never come back! Why? Because the simple fact is that we have to search very hard indeed to find the word happiness in those contexts; happiness in the here and now that is, *in this life*, rather than in some heavenly hereafter. That's a very important distinction. The fact is that most religions don't talk about happiness in this life as having anything to do with the *purpose* of their existence, or indeed talk about it at all.

The power of choice

Buddhism unquestionably does, and I hasten to add, that observation is not in any way a value judgement. Not at all. It's simply an observation. It is one of the fundamental qualities that, we might argue, sets Buddhism so clearly apart, because it presents itself right from the start, as being about ordinary people attaining happiness in this life. Not happiness after death. Or in some idealised utopian life space in this world. Or some vision of a pleasant life we might hope to achieve *when* this or that qualification has been achieved. Or when this or that obstacle has been removed.

And that word 'when' is important too. Many of us can find ourselves mentally trapped in the prison of the 'when,' as it has been called by the psychologists; this tendency to persuade ourselves that only *when* this or that change has taken place, only *then* we might perhaps achieve the happiness we seek. It becomes if you like a self-imposed barrier to moving on to a better place.

The way Buddhism responds to that situation is to say that we need to recognise the immense power that resides in our *freedom of choice*. That whether we realise it or not, whether we believe it or not, we have within us all the resources we need to *choose* and to *establish* a stable sense of well-being in our lives. Not when anything has been added, or removed, but *now*. It argues strongly that we can *learn*, that we can *train* ourselves, to achieve that goal now. Not just in the good and the golden times, but any time. No matter how challenging and disturbing the vicissitudes and circumstances of our life may be.

That is of course a huge and potentially life-changing idea, but it is also so unusual, so *counter-intuitive*, that it is extremely difficult for most of us to come anywhere near accepting it when we first encounter it. It just doesn't make sense we say to ourselves. There must be some sort of *catch*. It took me personally a long time to learn that there isn't, that the catch is primarily our lack of self-belief, our lack of conviction in ourselves. And it was only later that I came to learn just how strongly this perception, which is utterly central to Buddhist belief, is echoed in the work of many today's sociologists.

Martin Seligman for example, Professor of Psychology at Pennsylvania State University, and one of the founding fathers of the school of positive psychology, in his illuminating book, *What you can Change and What You Can't*,

'Optimism is a learned skill. Once learned it increases achievement at work and improves physical health.'[1]

That is a crucial point that he is making isn't it? It's not just about having a nice warm feeling within. The happiness associated with optimism he is saying, is *life-giving*, it serves to enhance and improve the entire spectrum of our lives, at work and at play.

And as we've already seen, Daniel Goleman psychologist and science writer, says almost exactly the same thing.

'Optimism and hope -like helplessness and despair-can be learned. Underlying both is an outlook psychologists call self-efficacy, the belief that one has mastery over one's life and can meet challenges as they come up.'[2]

So they are saying, we have a clear choice. If it so happens that we have built the absence of hope into our lives up till now, or even pessimism and despair, once we become fully self-aware of that fact, we can learn how to *replace* those negative life states with optimism and hope. That is a powerful confirmation of the proposition that Buddhism has always presented to us. A Buddhist practice is entirely about building a wholly capable individual who can do precisely what Goleman is talking about, having the courage to meet those *'challenges as they come up,'* rather than being knocked down or disabled by them.

The Buddhist vision…and the scientists

So Buddhism, with its essential humanism and it's focus on the power of the human spirit sets out to define greater happiness, for oneself and others, as *the* fundamental objective of human life, in the here and now. And as I write that, after many years of Buddhist practice, I am intensely aware of just how bold and uncompromising and *value-creating* that is as a vision of life. No if's and but's and maybe's. That it says, is what we are seeking. All the more remarkable in that it was set out all those centuries ago, when life was considerably rougher and tougher and certainly less forgiving than it is now.

And once again the extraordinary thing is just how closely that principle accords with the views of today's evolutionary biologists and positive psychologists, who argue, strictly on the basis of their research, that the quest for happiness is the *ultimate motivational force* in life. What does 'ultimate' mean in this context? It means that it doesn't require any further definition. It speaks for itself. We may initially express it to ourselves in other terms; we want to be healthy for example, or have better relationships, or a better job or achieve a qualification, and many other items of desire that we might list, but all those items are only important in the sense that they *contribute* to our happiness. They are stepping stones that is, on the way to our ultimate goal. Moreover the scientists have clearly demonstrated to their own satisfaction, that it is a truly *universal quality*. It cuts across all the boundaries that you can think of, national and religious and ethnic and status. It is if you like, a fundamental element in the human condition.[3]

So that close alignment of views does give us a very different perspective doesn't it? It means for example that this powerful and life-changing idea that Buddhism offers to us, an idea that many people find unusual, and hard to swallow, because it is so bold and uncompromising, is doing *no more* than recognising the essential character of our universal human nature. Doing no more than pointing out to us that this *is* the most powerful motivator in human life, and that it *can* be harnessed as an instrument of change, to enable us to lead fuller and richer lives.

A common understanding

Given that it plays such a key role in our universal motivation, let alone our Buddhist practice, my key point is that it's just as well that we all share a *common understanding* of what we mean when we use it, this much over-used word, rather than just assuming that we have a common understanding.

And that would seem to be a genuine issue, both within and beyond Buddhism. Someone as supremely eminent in the field as Martin Seligman for example, is driven to exclaim in his latest book *Flourish,* that the word happiness,

'... is so overused that it has become almost meaningless. It is an unworkable term for science, or for any practical goals such as education, therapy, public policy or just changing your personal life.'[4]

'*Almost meaningless'* is bit strong perhaps, but you can see the point can't you, that the word happiness in the modern idiom, or to the modern ear, is unquestionably a bit...well a bit *lightweight!* To many people, and I would include myself, it means primarily such things as merriment and laughter and good cheer and smiley faces, and I don't think we can simply ignore those connotations as if they were unimportant. We would be doing ourselves and our discussion a grave disservice. Particularly since good cheer and smiley faces is certainly *not* what is meant by happiness, in both Buddhist teachings and in the scientific research centred around positive psychology.

What about well-being?

Perhaps the closest we come to an appropriate word, or phrase, in both those contexts, certainly one that I find much more meaningful, and one that has already been used a great deal in this text, is well-being. Why? Because it clearly expresses a much broader and deeper and more solidly based emotion. On one recent occasion for example, when I was talking to an audience of businessmen about Buddhism, the phrase *'happiness in the work place,'* got a noticeably cool and even a somewhat cynical reception. But as soon as I switched to talking about *'well-being in the work place,'* there was an immediate understanding of what we were really talking about, a much more substantial, an altogether more stable and focused state of life, than laughter and good cheer.

And once again, that distinction finds support among the scientists. As Daniel Goleman explains in some detail in his book *Working with Emotional Intelligence,*[5] when comparisons are made between the effectiveness, or the productivity of people at work, the difference is very often found to lie not so much in the know-how or the purely *technical skills* of different people, but much more broadly in their overall sense of *well-being,* and therefore their greater capacity for handling relationships, or dealing in a calm and focused way with difficulties that arise.

But perhaps most important of all, this phrase *well-being* has so much greater depth and breadth and capacity, that it can even embrace the idea of mischance and misfortune. Buddhism for example when it speaks of happiness, has in mind a solid, lasting, resilient sense of well-being at the core of one's life, that can endure and be experienced, even *in the midst of* sadness and loss and crucial challenge. That again finds multiple echoes in the work of modern sociologists. Professor Tal Ben-Shahar for example, who for many years taught in the positive psychology programme at Harvard, talks about the need to *get real*.[6] Optimism and happiness he argues cannot be about being eternally cheerful. That would be hopelessly *unreal*. It has to be about getting up close to, getting to grips with and embracing the pains and problems we encounter, so that we truly understand them, and learn how work through them to a better place. And he talks of the immense value that we can generate in our lives by learning to look for the *seeds of the positive* in things that go wrong in our lives, rather than continually being eaten up by the sense of loss or damage.

And both Buddhism and social science would want to embrace several other dimensions that are difficult to see wrapped up in the simple word happiness, but that we would all freely recognise as central to a durable sense of well-being. Dimensions such as,

- rich and positive relationships with others,
- a sense of accomplishment in our endeavours,
- a sense of meaning and purpose in our activities. And let's not forget,
- a sense of compassion and altruism.

In this same book Martin Seligman recounts for us a brief but telling anecdote which goes as follows;

'My friend Stephen Post, Professor of Medical Humanities at Stony Brook, tells a story about his mother. When he was a young boy, and his mother saw that he was in a bad mood, she would say 'Stephen, why don't you go out and help someone?' Empirically, Ma Post's maxim has been put to rigorous test, and we scientists

have found that doing a kindness produces the single most reliable momentary increase in well-being of any exercise we have tested.'[7]

A powerful life-lesson there in just half a dozen lines. Ma Post's natural wisdom he tells us, has been put to *rigorous* scientific test, and it reveals that showing compassion and altruism towards others produces the single most reliable increase in well-being. Evolutionary biologists have the devil's own job trying to explain for us the evolutionary purpose of altruism, and here we have a psychologist telling us that even the smallest acts of *kindness and compassion* towards others, can have the most powerful effect on our own sense of *well-being.* We will spend more time later in the book examining the importance of altruism in our lives. But this simple human story illustrates two other fundamental qualities that are deeply interwoven into the Buddhist understanding of well-being, both of which seem to be borne out equally by what the scientists tell us they have learned more recently.

Not in someone else's gift

One is that well-being, happiness if you will, doesn't exist just in our own heads, although we commonly believe that to be the case. We evolved very much as members of a group. That basically is why we have been so successful as a species, and we are in our deepest nature very much gregarious animals. We need strong relationships. Our inner sense of well-being is generated essentially through the nature of the *relationships* we establish with the world around us, from the basic pleasure we take in our environment, through to the experience of lasting and fulfilling and harmonious relationships at all levels in our lives. When we experience them they strengthen and reinforce our creative energies, so that we feel *liberated,* and we find that we can achieve so much more in our outward lives. When those relationships break down for whatever reason, the effects can be devastating in all areas of our life, not simply those associated with the relationship. We are not only less happy, we operate as individuals *under stress*, out of *harmony* with ourselves and our environment, and our performance is greatly reduced.

The second understanding, no less profound, is that our own well-being is not in someone else's gift, we have to *make it for ourselves*. As Daisaku Ikeda has expressed it for example,

'Happiness is not something that someone else, like a lover can give to us. We have to achieve it for ourselves.'[8]

That is undeniably a hard lesson to learn, because our wants are so many, and because we so commonly believe that our personal happiness *is indeed dependant* upon our partner for example, or our child, or our friends, or our job. Or on earning a million pounds. Whereas Buddhism tells us that we have to go out and make our happiness for ourselves, out of our own determination and action. Just as Stephen Post was asked by his perceptive mother to *take some action*, to go out and help someone else to lift him out of his bad mood. And that phrase 'take some action' is well worth taking to heart because it carries a profound truth of its own. As one utterly practical Buddhist teacher put it to me once, if we think in terms of *pursuing* happiness in some way, then we are very much on the wrong track, because none of us knows how to achieve that. Where do we start? In which direction do we run? We come much closer to it, he argued, if we think of happiness as a sort of *by product*, a quality that comes into our lives when we take action to *create value* in some way, particularly in ways that have beneficial effects in *other people's lives.* It's fascinating to find that view echoed directly, even down to the choice of words, by a modern psychologist, when she writes in a recent book, *The How of Happiness,*

'...even the familiar phrase 'pursuit of happiness' implies that happiness is an object that one has to chase or discover...I prefer to think of the 'creation' or 'construction' of happiness because research shows that it's in our power to fashion it for ourselves.'9

So we are getting a closer fix on what we mean when we use this happiness word aren't we? It's certainly not just forcing ourselves to be cheerful regardless of what is going on. We don't get much joy if we try to chase it. And it doesn't just *happen* to us as a result of good fortune. The kind of durable, deep-seated, and above all resilient *well-being* that we are talking about, can't simply be dependent upon the play of *external* events. This happens and we like it...and are happy. That happens and we don't like it...and we're unhappy. A bit like a cork in a swell. Now up, now down, dependent upon what comes our way. It can only come, we now understand, from one place, it has to come from *within.* We have to make it, through the *values* that we hold and the *choices* that we make, and the kinds of *actions* and *responses* that we fold into our lives.

What about buying it?

We really deal with this complex issue in Chapter 11, but we can't leave this happiness discussion without at least touching upon the immense importance most of us attach to the role of *money* in any picture of happiness we paint for ourselves. It's bound to crop up before long in any modern discussion of what constitutes well-being. And if Buddhism *is* daily life, what does Buddhism have to say about it, to help us deal with it? And what kind of additional insights can the social scientists provide us with?

Edward Diener, for example, from the University of Illinois, psychologist and eminent researcher in this field, is one among many who has written about the materialist dead end, or what he calls *the downside* of today's vastly greater affluence. And there has been a huge amount of research that points to two key ways in which this has a profound effect in diminishing our sense of well-being, both of which I suggest, could sit comfortably in the middle of a Buddhist commentary about the suffering that can come from just wanting things.

One is that there is so much to be hungered after in our modern society, so much more on display in glossy showrooms and shopping malls and supermarkets and so on, that it has become a powerful *external* cause of *inner* discontent. It's a bit like all those sweets and chocolates on display at the checkout queue that can cause children to kick up so much fuss. They *want* them because they can *see* them, and can't understand why they can't *have* them. In very much the same way, people can experience a real sense of loss and deprivation and frustration because they can't *possess*, can't carry away, more of the stuff that is on display. In no way is it difficult to empathise with that situation. It rings absolutely true. Most of us have been there to some degree.

The second is related to the vast wave of media of all sorts that washes over all our lives these days. So we are all constantly being called upon to *measure* ourselves, *who* we are and *what* we have, against an endless procession of supposed role models on film and on television and in countless lifestyle magazines, who are presented as being highly successful, and vastly better off, and therefore by implication *happier.*

The equation seems to go wholly unquestioned, success equals wealth equals happiness. Although of course we all know *intellectually* that that is sheer nonsense, there is no such simple connection, or indeed *any connection* at all. But emotionally it gets to us.

And that of course is precisely the way the modern marketing and advertising machine goes to work, playing with immense skill on our natural human tendency to compare ourselves with others, and therefore focus on what *we haven't got,* as opposed to what we have.

That is to say, it is another immensely powerful *external* cause of *inner* discontent.

Once again, it's clear that Nichiren Daishonin was acutely aware of exactly the same human weakness, in one of his letters written all those years ago, when he highlights the futility, and of course the intense suffering, that can come from that sort of constant comparison itch,

'For example, a poor man cannot earn a penny, just by counting his neighbour's wealth, even if he does so night and day.'[10]

But that having been said, we can't just blank it all out can we? The range of material possessions has never been greater, and with the instant global reach of film and television and the internet, the circle of comparison into which we are drawn is virtually unlimited. The consequent potential for what we might call *induced dissatisfaction* with our own lot is all the greater. And it's important to note that it's not simply a matter of *envy.* Not at all. The psychologists tell us that it is both deeper and more insidious than that. If we can't achieve these sorts of symbols of success we tell ourselves, then what's wrong with us? We persuade ourselves that we are in some measure a *failure,* and since in this equation, *success* is what brings happiness, we just don't have what it takes to be truly happy.

Positive psychology has even coined a phrase to describe this downward spiral into which it is all too easy for us to be drawn. It's called *'reference anxiety,'* the emotional burden if you like, of constantly trying to keep up with the material wealth we perceive so many other people as having...but not ourselves. We have allowed *who* we are if you like, to somehow become synonymous with *what* we have.

What does Buddhism have to say?

So what does Buddhism have to say to help us *re-balance* ourselves in the face of this constant materialist onslaught that can deeply undermine our sense of self-worth? It makes it clear right from the start that it is not about *rejecting* material possessions. It's not about denial, or giving things up, since that doesn't of itself achieve anything. Nichiren Buddhism fully embraces both the material and the spiritual aspects of life, because both are clearly important to us. The absolute key it argues, to establishing a durable sense of well-being is *awareness;* recognising the situation for what it really is, seeing the threat to our stability, and understanding that we need to establish a meaningful balance.

So for example people who take up this practice are positively encouraged to chant for, and of course to take action for, whatever it is they believe they need to achieve full and fulfilling lives. And that might certainly include material things, from a better income and financial security for example, to a better house, and everything in between. They are an integral part of all our lives and can't simply be left out. But undoubtedly, as we continue with the practice it radically changes our perspective. It puts the constant wanting of things into a broader whole-life context.

While acquiring new *things* can undoubtedly be an extremely pleasurable experience…and why shouldn't it be indeed… it cannot be the *basis* for the solid, lasting, resilient sense of well-being that we all seek. The pleasure in new possessions soon wears off, very soon in fact, and the only way to re-ignite that sort of pleasure is to get out there again into a fresh bout of retail therapy. We've all been at least some way down that road. Just look at the level of global credit card debt that was exposed in the crash of 2008. All we need, we repeatedly persuade ourselves, is that *something else* in the shopping mall or the showroom window… and we'll be really truly happy. Promise. And then something else catches our attention…and on and on.

The life state of hunger…and hedonic adaptation

Since it lies at the root of a great deal of self inflicted pain and suffering…and that's a key point to note, it is *self-inflicted*, it is *our choice*…Nichiren Buddhism considers it important enough to flag it up for us, by giving this itch-to-acquire-stuff, a name. It's called the life state of *Hunger*. (see Appendix A) Basically this is a state of more or less constant, restless dissatisfaction with our lives, because we convince ourselves that our happiness lies in *having* something, or *experiencing* something, that is just out of our reach. And in this life state, there's always *something*, just out of our reach. This restless dissatisfaction is not limited of course to material things, it reaches out into all the fields of human activity you can think of, from the desire for particular relationships or partners, to the desire for just a bit more wealth than we happen to have, or status or fame, and on to regaining youth and beauty through plastic surgery. There's always something to want. And it's by no means uncommon for people in this life state to fix their gaze on one thing after another in their environment, in the sure and certain knowledge…*each time*…that this will satisfy their deep hunger, and bring them the happiness that so far has just eluded them.

The extraordinary thing…I use that phrase advisedly because it is I think genuinely surprising…is that modern psychology recognises something very similar indeed to what we have just been talking about. The term it uses to describe it is *'hedonic adaptation.'*[11] *Hedonic* comes from the Greek root that means pleasure. *Adaptation* speaks for itself. So put simply this somewhat esoteric phrase means that we adapt with astonishing speed to new stuff, to any new *material goods* that we acquire. It simply becomes the new norm.

'The things that we get used to most easily and most take for granted are our material possessions- our car, our house. Advertisers understand this and invite us to 'feed our addiction' with more and more spending.'[12]

But the key point is that the acquisition changes *nothing* in terms of how we feel in the depths of our lives. Nothing changes in terms of our fundamental sense of well- being. So, whatever *external* thing we desire in the belief that it will bring us greater happiness, however much we are convinced that we *need* it, however profoundly *life-changing* it might seem when we desire it, and indeed when we initially acquire it, from that shiny new car, to the big house or the huge pay rise, they turn out not to be so life-changing at all. *Indeed not at all.*

There's no question that can be a very difficult lesson for us to take on board. We are so powerfully attached to the idea that these kinds of acquisitions *will make us so much happier*. But the body of research to the contrary is very substantial indeed.[14]

Hedonic adaptation is real

So what does that mean in terms of our ordinary daily life? It's clear that although we may indeed get immense pleasure and satisfaction, and indeed a burst of genuine rapture, at the moment of acquisition, and for a while afterwards, the research shows that the '*while*' is vanishingly brief. This rapid adaptation to the new acquisition, or the new circumstance, is an integral part of the human psyche, and from then on, we're back to where we were. Square one. The new whatever becomes very much a part of the ordinary fabric of our lives.

And I think there's little doubt, if we search even briefly through our own experience, few of us would suggest that our basic sense of well-being or happiness in our lives, was substantially altered by any new *material* acquisition. The new car, the new kitchen, would we really say it has re-shaped our happiness? I think not. I love my new house for example, but has it had a fundamental effect on how I feel about the real substance of my life? The treasures of the heart that we talked about earlier? Definitely not.

So *hedonic adaptation* would seem to be the modern psychological explanation for a factor that Buddhism has been talking about for so long, namely that the *external circumstances* of our lives, or changes in those circumstances, even if on the surface they are quite substantial, have in fact a remarkably small impact on our *enduring* sense of well-being. It is a profoundly unhappy-making *delusion* to believe that enduring, deep-seated happiness can be *acquired* in this way, externally as it were, as a result of some possession, *any* possession.

We only have to give that idea a moment's reflection to see that it amounts to a profoundly behaviour-changing, life-changing lesson.

Who needs problems?

The underlying desire that most of us share for a *problem-free existence* is, I would argue, a special category of that same delusion. It might seem to be something different, but it shares precisely the same characteristics. None of us *wants* problems, not ever. Of course we know in our hearts that problems and difficulties and challenges and crises of one kind or another, are part of the fabric of all our lives, and utterly inescapable. In that sense we are all in the same boat, however different our life circumstances might seem on the outside. But for some reason we cling on to the belief, the deeply-held desire, that the problems, and the pain and suffering they tend to bring with them, are the *exception* rather than the rule.

The research shows that very different people, facing completely different sorts of problems, will use very similar language in explaining it away to themselves. *'This is not really how my life is,'* we say to ourselves. *'I just have to get through this difficult phase I'm going through, and then my life will straighten out and I'll get back to normal'*

We know that once we get over this rough patch we are unlucky enough to be going through at the moment, a tough time at work, or a financial crisis, or an illness, or conflict in a relationship, or whatever, then for sure our life will return to its *normal* state of calm and equanimity. Because that's the life state we desire, *a life state without problems.*

The net result of that understanding of life is utterly inescapable. It is that happiness or well-being, comes to be defined as the *absence of problems.* But of course, there is *no such place.* None of us knows anyone, not a single person, who lives such a life. The reality is that problems and challenges and difficulties just keep coming pretty much all the time, in one area of our life or another. And given this view of life, it is little wonder that we have developed a whole series of ruses or strategies to try to deflect the problems, and the stress and the suffering we associate with them, most of which it has to be said, only make the matters worse.

And that's where we go next, to look at what Buddhism seeks to tell us about living with the problems of life, and how it's possible for all of us to do that, without losing our inner core of hope and optimism and well-being.

CHAPTER FIVE

Buddhism and the
Problem Paradox

Man was born to troubles as the sparks fly upwards, Job tells us eternally in the Old Testament, but few of us if any, are prepared to accept that as an accurate description of the reality of our lives. No way. We're simply not having it. No one wants pains and problems, or the anxiety and the tension and the stress that arise as they threaten to emerge in our lives. So the natural human response is to argue that since we can't stand them, we have to get rid of them! And that in fact is pretty much what we try to do. In our modern societies we spend huge amounts of time and money and energy and ingenuity in trying to create a whole defensive network to keep the challenging and the anxiety-creating side of life at bay. And where we aren't completely successful in the barrier-building business, as we can't be of course, we have evolved a whole series of secondary strategies to fill in the gaps.

So we *ignore* them for example, or run away from them, in the hope that they will just go away or evaporate. The reality is of course that problems ignored have a very nasty habit of becoming problems magnified, so that what was once readily solvable, if only we'd had the courage to face up to it when it first emerged, can become something so big that it can overwhelm us and knock us over.

Or we very commonly *dump* the problem onto someone else. That is to say we mentally shift the blame or the responsibility onto someone or some thing outside ourselves, pointing to anything so long as it's not ourselves, as the source of the current difficulty. If there are problems within a relationship for example, it's not our problem, it's clearly because the *other half* of the relationship has to change something about *themselves* in order to put things right. If there's trouble with the boss or colleagues at work it's bound to be because *they* are being totally obstinate or unreasonable or unfair. Everyone can see that. So we end up in a sort of impasse. Nothing changes, and the frustration or the friction keep on *recurring,* to the extent that it can lead to the break up of an otherwise fine relationship, or people being stuck in a state of tension or dissatisfaction at work.

We have all been there at some stage in our lives, and many times more than once.

A kind of fiction

And if those strategies still don't block up all the crevices in our defences, then we are often complicit in creating a kind of fiction that we are quite happy to share with one another. So although problems and crises, and the anxieties and the suffering they bring, continue to swallow up a considerable portion of our energies, we make it quite clear to ourselves and everyone else, that they are a completely *abnormal exception* to the normal flows and patterns of our life. No matter how frequently they occur, or how disturbing they may be in de-railing our lives, we *persuade ourselves* time and time again, that as soon as this particular setback, hiccup, crisis or disaster has passed us by, our life will revert to its normal, routine, untroubled state. Why? Because that's the life state we've convinced ourselves we need to be happy, the one without any hassle. You could say that is the *idealised, unreal,* life state that we are all pretty much addicted to.

Is there a better way?

Let's be clear, of course several of those strategies have their rightful place in our armoury, we haven't evolved them for nothing. No one for example would question the *prudence* of arranging whatever insulation we can, since we live in troubled times. And although the *fiction strategy* may not keep any actual problems at bay, it probably helps to lessen the anxiety those problems create. But can that possibly be enough? Is that really the best we can do?

The key point is that this is not some remote or theoretical issue is it? It is close up and very personal. We're talking here about real *life-time strategies* that involve all of us throughout *all our lives.* This is how we actually *handle* the daily detail of our lives. And we could certainly argue I think, that learning how to deal with problems effectively, has got to be one of the most important steps along the road to well-being. What can be more important? So we share a deep and common interest, I suggest, in posing this question as to whether or not these strategies are adequate? Are they anywhere close to the *best response* that we can come up with?

So how does Buddhism help us in this sort of situation?

Buddhism is good at dealing with problems, since it was actually born out of the recognition that the nature of human life is always tough and challenging and frequently involves considerable suffering. So that's the starting point if you like that Buddhism asks us to recognise, in setting our levels of expectation. We should *expect* it to be tough and challenging.

So there is absolutely nothing to be gained it argues, from railing at problems as they continue to occur in our lives, which we often do of course…'*Why is this happening to me? What have I done to deserve this?* Or basing our hopes for happiness on some longed-for problem free future. The key Nichiren tells us…in his typically direct style…the key is really just to get on with things.

'Though worldly troubles may arise, never let them disturb you. No one can avoid problems…'[1]

No one. Moreover Buddhism constantly reminds us that in *our* lives, everything begins with *us*. That may not sound on the face of it, to be a particularly ground- breaking idea. But it is remarkable how often this apparently obvious principle is ignored. It is *our* life in every sense. So if there's friction, or frustration or difficulty coming at us from various directions, then Buddhism argues, the place to look for the root cause is…guess where …*within our own life*. That may be difficult for us to accept, very difficult. Indeed we may have to go through a huge internal struggle to accept it, but when you think about it even for a minute or two, that is the real meaning of *taking responsibility* for our life isn't it?

What is it about *our* behaviour, *our* thoughts, *our* words and actions, that is giving rise to *this* difficulty? What subliminal signals are *we* giving off that trigger this response from our environment? How do *we* need to change in order to resolve this difficult issue? That may initially as I've said, be a very hard lesson to swallow. Sometimes we can manage it, sometimes we can't, we're only human after all. But when we *can*, it carries with it an immeasurably huge benefit that arises in no other way; namely if we fully recognise and accept that the *cause* comes from within our own life, then so too does the *remedy*. It lies within our grasp.

So the problem-solving equation becomes, not, '...*if only my partner would change we would be so much happier,...*' which is a very tough call because it is way outside our control; but, '*what action can I take, what things about myself can I change, that will sweep this problem right out of our lives,*' which is so much simpler, because we do have control.

Which means that we can set about sweeping away the impasse, and opening up the possibility of real progress.

Problems are simply facts of life

Buddhism goes on to tell us that we need to use the daily discipline of the practice to train ourselves; we want to learn to see problems and difficulties simply as *facts of life.* Nothing more nor nothing less than that. Once again that is clearly not a particularly earth-shattering idea is it? But again it is remarkable how often we choose to ignore it. For as long as we take everyday problems and difficulties *personally,* Buddhism argues, as a *direct challenge* to our personal equanimity and our happiness, then, absolutely by definition, as the night follows the day, as water always flows downhill, our equanimity and happiness will continue to be challenged! How could it be otherwise?

In a sense by adopting that response, we are *locking ourselves* into a conditioning process from which we can't escape. Round and round we go like a hamster on a wheel. The problems inevitably continue to occur, we *choose* to see them as a disruption to our personal happiness and peace of mind, so inevitably we respond to them with *powerful negativity.* So over the years we carefully forge this more or less unbreakable link in our minds between the occurrence of problems and the negative response, the anxiety and stress with which we have always associated them. It becomes so much the way of the world that we never challenge it. It simply doesn't occur to us that there can be a different response.

You might almost say that Buddhism was created to persuade us that there is.

A change of perception changes everything

Buddhism teaches that the way we look at any situation or environment is of the very greatest importance. That is to say it is not so much the *external* circumstance that governs how it affects us, but how we *choose to see it.* It's not so much the problem that occurs that causes us to suffer, so much as how we *respond* to that problem. That is in itself a huge lesson.

And it takes us directly to a paradox that lies really at the very heart of Shakyamuni's teachings. You could say that it is *the* essential perception we need to grasp to break out of that cycle of self-conditioning. So Buddhism teaches that happiness or well-being, and suffering, are not, as we so often regard them, *entirely different and separate experiences,* that lie at the opposite ends of the wide spectrum of human experience. That is simply the effect of our partial and incomplete view of our reality. On the contrary Buddhism tells us, they are closely and intimately interconnected, almost like the two sides of a sheet of paper.

That's pretty counter-intuitive isn't? What can it possibly mean? We intensely dislike suffering and we run *away* from it whenever we can. And we run *towards* happiness because we love it so much. They must therefore lie in quite different directions. Stop running for a moment Buddhism argues, and look a bit harder at your reality. If we continue to hang on to the view that our happiness in this life is directly dependent on our achieving a smooth, untroubled, sunlit existence, free from anxieties and pains and problems, then it doesn't take all that hard a look to see that it is a strategy doomed to failure, *since there is no such place.*

As I've said, none of us knows anybody who lives such a life. Not a single person.

So all Buddhism is saying essentially is, '*get real!*' Just as today's positive psychologists advise us. If we genuinely seek to establish a strong and resilient sense of well-being at the core of our lives then that can *only* be found, Buddhism argues, in the *very midst of* the problems and suffering that life throws at us, since that is the *only* place there is. *That is the only reality.* They lie therefore, our happiness and our suffering, cheek by jowl, in precisely the same direction.

As one Buddhist teacher puts it so simply,

'Our suffering is us, and we need to treat it with kindness and non-violence. We need to embrace our fear, hatred, anguish and anger.'[2]

Our suffering is us...we can all perceive immediately the deep truth of that statement. Moreover Buddhism goes on, the greater and the more challenging the problems we *embrace* in this way, the greater the potential happiness they can release, since they demand so much more of us. They force us to demonstrate so much more courage and resilience to overcome them. They make us grow you might say, to become our most capable selves. And *personal capability* we learn in the course of our Buddhist practice, is a very important ingredient indeed in the making of the stuff we call well- being. We all dearly want to be, and we want to be seen to be… *capable* human beings.

That chimes with our experience.

And although it may well seem counter-intuitive when we first bump into this idea, if we think about it even briefly, we can see that this kind of perspective on life does indeed chime with our experience. Think back to times when you have succeeded in overcoming a *really difficult* problem in your life, something that you felt had the potential to really knock you off balance, or change your life for the worse, something that even inspired a certain amount of fear or panic. And these events are by no means rare in our lives; loss of a job for example, or break up of a long-term relationship, or cancer, or some other life-threatening illness, or the death of someone you love.

When we overcome these potentially life-diminishing challenges, we may well continue to feel a certain amount of pain, that is not uncommon, but each time the victory gives a powerful boost to our sense of confidence and capability. We feel strengthened, and the bigger the threat to our stability we've overcome, the greater the boost. For some considerable time afterwards we experience a much greater confidence in our ability to deal with things in general, not just in that particular area, but *right across* the spectrum of our lives and activities. And with that increased confidence comes a greater sense of well-being.

Buddhism asks us to hang onto that understanding, that recognition. Since we have some experience of this potential in our lives, it argues, we can learn how to build upon it and extend it. If we can do it once...why not twice...why not many more times? We clearly can't achieve great victories every day of our lives, but then we don't need to! But we can certainly achieve small victories all the time, and the inherent sense of well-being can become a *daily* experience, because we renew the positive energy, and the optimism, and the self confidence, within the structure of the daily practice. That is one of the reasons of course why it is *daily*.

And the key point to hang onto is that it is above all a philosophy built to last, since it is constructed out of the *real circumstances* of our lives, as they really are, tough and challenging, rather than as we frequently wish them to be, soft and easy. Buddhism isn't a soft touch because life isn't a soft touch.

But perhaps most importantly, the sense of well-being that this strategy promises, is constructed and put together, piece by piece, from *within* rather than from without. It comes only from the courage and the resilience and the determination that we steadily learn how to draw out from within, to overcome the problems. So it's not in any way fragile or ephemeral. It's not going to be blown away by something that *happens to us*, because it's not in any way dependant on our ever-shifting, ever-changing *external circumstances*.

Very much in tune with modern psychology

If we look at some of the social and psychological research over the past ten to fifteen years or so, on dealing with stress and hardship and the kinds of problems that confront all of us at some stage in our lives, we find a quite extraordinary similarity of view with some of the things that we have just been discussing. I choose that word 'similarity' with some care, because of course the scientists don't have anything remotely Buddhist *in mind* when they are carrying out their research studies. Of course not. But that having been said, you can find all kinds of familiar and pleasing echoes when you read through their work.

Once you dig beneath the objective and scientific formality of phrases like *'construing benefit in trauma,'* to get down to the actual human detail of the studies, and the under-standing and the advice that emerges from them, we find ourselves in very familiar territory.

So where the problem is of an everyday nature for example, the sort of thing we can all encounter at any time, such as having money problems so you find it difficult to pay the weekly bills, or a troubling and disturbing dispute with a partner, or long running dissatisfaction at work say, the psychologists talk about what they call *problem-focused coping.* Basically that means *facing up to the problem,* embracing it you might say, rather than trying to ignore it and letting it fester on, and then making a *solid deter-mination* to do something about it. Drawing up a plan of action for example, and then putting it into effect. Any practising Buddhist would feel wholly comfortable with that sort of guidance. The only difference is that he or she would also immediately put the problem into their daily chanting to harness their compassion and their courage in tackling it.

Where the problem is clearly not everyday, and not resolvable in that way, because it involves the death of a loved one for example, or the break up of a long-term relationship, or a life threatening illness, where the emotional impact can be utterly overwhelming and uncontrollable, the psychologists talk of *emotion-focused coping*. That is to say, seeking ways to lessen the personal emotional burden by *sharing* it for example. Seeking support from close friends, or by getting involved in activities where you can play a role in helping *others* get through their problems, so you are drawn away from your own grief. Once again that sort of guidance sits right at the very heart of Buddhist compassion, and altruism, seeking to create value in other people's lives, rather than looking inwards and focusing upon our own immediate problems or difficulties.

Moreover the psychologists go on to talk about the immense emotional benefit that can come from encouraging people to try to see beyond their pain and grief, to grasp the *learning,* or the personal *growth,* or the deeper appreciation of the preciousness of each day of life, that can come from going through such a challenging experience, and emerging on the other side as a stronger person. The psychologist Sonja Lyubomirski tells the story for example, of a wife who lost her husband after a long wasting disease, and was able to see beyond her pain to say something quite extraordinary;

'I don't mean to be a Pollyanna, but I had twenty wonderful years with that man. There are people who don't have one day as happy as I had. It took me six months after Charley died to realise that that feeling will never go away. It's like the Grand Canyon. There's this big hole, and it hurts like hell, but it's beautiful.'[3]

I have to say that when I read that I find it not only immensely moving, but deeply hopeful and encouraging. The psychologist concludes,

'Indeed most survivors experience a great deal of distress at the same time as reporting strengthening and progress. So the uphill road that leads to a more fulfilling and more meaningful life may be laid with stones and punctuated by troughs. There's absolutely nothing good about tragedy and loss, but something good can come from the struggle in their aftermath.[4]

Daniel Goleman expresses something very similar when he writes;

'There is much to be said for the constructive contribution of suffering to the creative and spiritual life; suffering can temper the soul.'[5]

So it is clearly possible for us to master this powerful lesson that suffering drives us deeper, that something immensely valuable and life enhancing can come from the struggle against adversity. Daisaku Ikeda, the great modern thinker and writer on Nichiren Buddhism amplifies that idea when he writes,

'Buddhist optimism is not the escapist optimism of those who throw their arms in the air and say, 'Somehow or other things will work out.' Rather it means clearly recognising evil as evil, and suffering as suffering and resolutely fighting to overcome it. It means believing in one's ability and strength to struggle against any evil or obstacle. It is to possess a fighting optimism.'[6]

A personal training programme

So a Buddhist practice isn't in any way about a form of *escapism*, about finding some inner meditative refuge away from the pace and clamour and constant complexity of modern life. Although that of course is one of the most widely held stereotypes of what Buddhism is about, namely getting away from it all, or most of it. Buddhism is above all about that *'fighting optimism.'* About struggle and challenge, about challenging attitudes and behaviours that *don't* create value, or that *don't* lead to positive outcomes. It's far easier of course for us to go on simply complaining about problems that arise, or responding to them instinctively, which often means negatively. As we all know so well, few things in life are more difficult than challenging patterns of thought or behaviour that we have spent years cultivating and nurturing and embedding into our lives. It takes real self-knowledge, and courage and great persistence, simply not being prepared to give up.

Setting out to achieve that change in perspective, that change in attitude, is essentially the role that the daily Buddhist practice plays, the daily Buddhist *personal training programme.* Indeed the true greatness of this practice in my view is precisely that. It enables us to achieve that slight shift in perspective, that slight shift in understanding, and strange as it may seem, that is all that is needed. It may only be a slight change, but time and time again it proves to be enough to enable us to look at the problem with a completely different attitude, that then leads on to tangible, positive, sometimes even remarkable outcomes in people's lives. And every time it does so, it *reinforces* the confidence and the resolve to tackle the next issue that comes along in the same way. And in that way we find ourselves moving steadily from being generally *anxious and negative* about problems to being *focused and confident* about resolving them.

That is the shift in attitude that we are seeking. So the problems remain the same, but our sense of being able to *overcome* them has changed profoundly. And problems that we feel confident we can overcome, actually change in character. They no longer seem so looming or so threatening. In fact we consciously change the way we talk about them and describe them, to ourselves and to others. We start to call them *challenges*, and the change is by no means simply verbal. Problems are negative and threatening. Challenges are stimulating and uplifting. As soon as you say, '*I've got this challenge coming up next month,*' you feel differently about it, don't you? You feel immediately that you are preparing yourself to stand against it…and win.

Given our powerful cultural conditioning it's important to emphasise perhaps, that we are not talking here about something akin to *stoicism,* about merely *putting up* with problems, or being broad shouldered in bearing them as a burden. Not at all. That's a completely different approach. What we are talking about here is *transformation,* about seeing problems differently and turning them into a source of *personal growth,* growing our self-confidence and our sense of our own capability, both immensely important to our overall sense of well-being.

Nichiren Buddhists often describe this approach to problems with the phrase, '*turning poison into medicine.*' That is to say, taking a difficult or seemingly impossible problem and not simply enduring it, but turning it round completely, to create longer term value and self fulfilment out of it.

Concern for others at the heart of Buddhism

And that clearly has wider implications for the people around us in all the various areas of our life. For as long as we are operating under stress in our own lives, then we don't really have much time and space for others. But as we change, and develop this ability to handle our own challenges without being so *taken over* by anxiety and stress, but with courage and confidence and a growing sense of our own capability, so we have more resource *left over* so to speak, to support and encourage those around us. Moreover we find that we have more life-energy to *seek out* more opportunities to help others. From simply sharing our own experiences of coping with troubles, to giving moral and emotional support, to devoting real time and energy to people in the midst of their own crises. Giving and sharing that is, rather than taking and consuming, that's the key change. And Buddhism has always taught that exerting ourselves in this way, focusing outwards rather than inwards, concentrating our energies on the needs and concerns of *others*, rather than on *our own* current little crop of difficulties, which of course we will always continue to have, is what leads to the *most rapid growth* in our own resourcefulness, and capability, and sense of well-being.

Buddhism has been promoting this idea as a value-creating principle of social behaviour for a very long time, but it now finds ample support in modern sociological and psychological research. Richard Layard for example has proposed that it should be built into the school curriculum for all children, so that they come to understand the basic principle of altruism that could be said to lie at the very heart of a healthy and supportive society;

'We should teach the systematic practice of empathy,' he writes, 'and the desire to serve others. This needs a proper curriculum from the beginning of school life to the end, including the detailed study of role models… the basic aim should be the sense of an overall purpose wider than oneself.'[7]

There are many scientists who would agree. As one psychologists expresses it, any act of altruism releases a powerful win-win situation because it triggers…

'…*a cascade of positive effects. It makes you feel generous and capable, gives you a greater sense of connection with others, and wins you smiles, approval and reciprocated kindness.*'[8]

Cooperation with others the key to our humanity

That really brings us to what is perhaps the greatest question of them all, the question that, when it comes down to it, all great philosophies are really about. Where do we turn to acquire our moral or our ethical values, that guide us in the complex maze of relationships and encounters that make up all our lives? How do we understand, deep within ourselves, that behaving like this say is fine and to be commended, and makes us feel good about ourselves, whereas behaving like that isn't really good enough, and leaves us feeling not so good about ourselves, or worse? How do we know that?

It's an important question isn't it? And we learn from the scientists that it sits right at the heart of the human psyche. We find a really fascinating perspective in the work of the evolutionary biologists for example, who suggest that since the very earliest stages of our existence we have always lived as *social* animals, always. Therefore how we relate to others must have been a major factor in our evolution. It is they argue, buried deep within *our heritage*, deep within our DNA. The idea is known technically as *group selection*, but put simply all that means is that our unique ability to *support and cooperate* with one another has been the absolutely *key* factor in the survival and the flourishing of mankind. As the evolutionary biologists point out, we're not a particularly impressive animal physically, we don't have the benefit of natural armour, or strength, or stealth or speed relative to many other species. Essentially therefore it has been our ability to reason, and to plan, and above all to *work together,* that has really set us apart from other animals. Our survival and growth and spreading around the world depended on our *collective abilities,* on our ability to work closely together and band together with others in pursuing a collective goal.

So, the argument goes, in our early history, any groups or tribes who had learned how best to co-operate and support one another and work together, then that *entire group* would inevitably have a much greater chance of success and survival over any other group, whatever they were doing, hunting or seeking shelter or coping with a hard winter. The co-operative group would have by far the greater chance of survival, and so their *entire gene pool* would be passed onto future generations. To us that is, and so become *embedded* as an essential part of our human nature.

In a sense that idea provides a sort of scientific underpinning for many of the fundamental ideas we find in religion and philosophy. Christianity for example tells us to love thy neighbour as thyself. Immanuel Kant, perhaps the greatest moral philosopher of the western world, gave us in the 18th Century, his famous *categorical imperative,* which argues that, in addition to displaying respect for others, if we are searching for a single, overarching guiding principle as the basis for our actions and behaviour towards others, then it ought always to be, how we would wish *others to behave towards us.* Buddhist ethics I would argue embraces both those views, and that in fact is where we go next, to look at the deeply interesting issue of Buddhism and ethics.

Chapter Six

Buddhism and Ethics

What we decide to do, how we choose to behave, unquestionably matters. Moreover, it reveals a great deal about who *we really are*; the principles that we have, the values that we hold and the things that are really important to us. Indeed that is true I would suggest even in what we might consider to be otherwise wholly trivial encounters in our working day. Do I take the trouble to smile at the lady behind the lunch counter and exchange a few pleasant words, or do I choose to keep my head down and ignore her because I happen to have this problem chewing away inside me? Should I respond to that aggressive e-mail equally aggressively? Do I take the trouble to listen to the arguments being put to me, and properly consider their value, or do I just ignore them and cling on to my own views? Do I get up in this heavily overcrowded carriage and offer my seat to that older man who looks a bit weary, or do I just get on with reading my book? It matters.

It matters in the sense that the choices that I make *determine* who I really am. Indeed the psychologists tell us that they determine who I am in two senses.[1] First because my actions and my behaviour are an indication to the people around me what sort of person I am, since it is by my actions rather than by my words that my character can truly be judged. But most importantly they suggest that my character is to an extent *shaped and determined* by my choices and my actions, in the sense that by continually acting in certain ways I develop *habitual* ways of behaving. So in this way my choices yesterday, and today and tomorrow, shape the person I become. Psychologists talk in terms of our developing *habitual dispositions*, or patterns of behaviour. Buddhists might perhaps talk in terms of *life tendencies* or habit energy, but the idea is essentially the same.

Buddhism argues that patterns of choices and patterns of behaviour become so deeply ingrained in our lives that they acquire their own energy, and so become more and more difficult to break out of. And we all instinctively know that to be true don't we? We are very much creatures of habit. We all know that we can all too easily acquire patterns of behaviour that we find difficult to overcome, even when we know full well with our intellect, that these habits really don't help us or create value in our lives, because they are dysfunctional, or unattractive or destructive in some way.

It calls to mind the slightly scary Buddhist mantra that runs...

- *take care of your thoughts because they will become your words...take care of your words because they will become your actions...take care of your actions because they will become your habits...take care of your habits because they will become... your life.*

It's not for nothing that one of the most important things written about the life of Shakyamuni Buddha was that the real significance, the real purpose of his appearance in this world lay in his *behaviour* as an ordinary human being.[2] Not his behaviour as a god notice, or as any sort of special or superhuman being, but just as an *ordinary* human being, one of us.

This discussion lies slap bang in the middle of the slightly fuzzy, often controversial area of thought and debate that is known as ethics or morality, the words are used virtually interchangeably. Morality is essentially about how human beings choose to live their lives *in relation to one another.* It concerns the principles and the values... some religions of course would say the *commandments or the rules...*that we embrace and take on board, to shape and guide the way we think about and deal with, the multitude of relationships and encounters that we have with other people.

And if we think about our lives even momentarily, if we have any concern for the effect our life has on others around us, we clearly need some sort of structure don't we? The plain fact is that all our lives, literally from the moment we are born, until the moment we depart, is made up of *encounters and relationships* of one kind or another; an immeasurably complex network of relationships and encounters of every possible shape and size and frequency and intimacy, from the most fleeting, to the most enduring and long lasting relationships we have within the circle of our family and friends and colleagues.

So if we seek to live any sort of valuable and creative life, let alone the *most* valuable and creative life of which we are capable, we need some structure don't we, some guidelines to point us in the right direction, and keep us on the right track? And that essentially is what this chapter is about. What sort of structure does Buddhism have to offer?

How should I choose to live my life?

As you might expect the discussion as to how we should best handle the relationships that make up the fabric of our lives is as old as civilisation itself. The basic question that we are asking for example, *'What shall I do?'* or to put it in a more comprehensive way, *'How should I choose to live my life?'* didn't just occur out of thin air. It was first put in those very terms by Socrates himself way back in the 4th century BCE. So it is sometimes called *the* Socratic question[3]. And as Socrates taught all those centuries ago, it may sound simple, even banal, but if that is our initial impression then we are deceiving ourselves, because it isn't. Indeed he argued that it is just about the toughest question we can put to ourselves, since it's really about the nature of *our* life. So it's not a question that anyone who cares to think about their lives to any meaningful extent, can avoid or duck under.

It's certainly true that most of us, *most* of the time, live our lives within pretty much well-worn routines, following well-trodden paths and often scarcely thinking about the choices that we make from one moment to the next, one day to the next, in this circumstance or that. Although unquestionably those *accumulated* choices as I've said, come to *shape* us, and our character, even if we're scarcely aware that that is what is going on. We all have huge comfort zones that we take refuge in and hate to depart from. But that fundamental question itself doesn't go away. It sits there you might say, as a sort of constant backdrop to everything we do and say, every single day of our lives.

And then suddenly, as we all know, it can leap out into the very foreground of our consciousness, whenever we encounter something that is not part of the routine. A crisis in our lives that may involve a crucial relationship with a partner or a colleague or a child for example, or the loss of someone we hold very dear, and then…what shall I do we ask ourselves…sometimes in considerable anguish or distress, as we realise that we are being confronted with *who we really are*. We've all been there many times. And it is precisely at times like these that we have the greatest need of that support structure, those *guidelines* of values and principles that we have embedded solidly into our lives, in all those *countless choices* that we have made over the years.

Perhaps the greatest wisdom and the greatest virtue of the Buddhist practice is that it is there *every single day*, renewing its deeply-held positive values and its guidelines. All those days when things are going swimmingly, and routinely, as well as those occasions when the challenge to us is strong and we have to confront who we really are.

Our values are infectious

And this classical age old question has a twin, 'What should *we* do? 'How should *we* live?' Because of course we are all born into families, and families sit within communities, and communities sit within societies.'*No man is an island entire of itself,*' the poet reminds us.[4] The value choices that we make of course have some effect on everyone with whom our lives come in contact. What our friends and work colleagues believe and do affects us, just as what we believe and do affects them. Although it is only very recently that we have become aware of just *how powerful* and how *subliminal* this ripple effect is, as a result of some immensely intriguing research carried out over the past few years, in the US, by sociologist Nicolas Christakis and others at Harvard University.[5]

Very briefly, what their research has revealed is that values and feelings and patterns of behaviour in our life spread, or *percolate* perhaps is a better word, naturally and easily throughout our network of friends and family and colleagues, without any conscious effort or activity on our part, or even without our being in the slightest aware that such a process is going on. That is to say we may not set out in any way with the *intention* of spreading these qualities, which include fundamentally important things about us such as our integrity, and our respect for others, and our habitual life states such as our optimism or our pessimism, but nevertheless, the spreading or the percolation goes on.

Moreover, and this is perhaps the most surprising thing, the research has revealed for the first time the extraordinary *extent* of these emotional networks, if I may call them that. Because they argue, this ripple effect doesn't stop at our own network of friends and colleagues, as we might expect. It goes on to have some effect on *their* network of friends and colleagues as well, and even further beyond that, to *their* friends and colleagues as well. They talk of at least three degrees of influence. It is in my view, a truly surprising result, but it has been established as valid in repeated studies, to become accepted as a wholly new insight. Because these scientists are telling us that *who* we really are, what *values* we really hold, what *behaviour* we demonstrate, has an effect not just on our *close* friends, but on *their* friends as well, and beyond that, to the friends of their friends. People that is to say, whom we personally may actually *encounter* only very rarely, possibly never, or only at second hand through the accounts and stories of friends and work colleagues, and even if we are entirely *unaware* that we are transmitting and receiving those influences in any way.

So clear are the results of their repeated research that he sociologists have actually chosen to borrow a metaphor from medicine to describe them, so they talk about these qualities, these values and states of mind being *infectious,* as if we can actually transmit our basic respect or disrespect for others, our optimism or our pessimism, to other people, across a quite widely spread network.

So this issue that we are talking about, to which we happen to give this slightly forbidding name of ethics or morality, cannot be just a *private and personal issue* as it is so often presented. Of course it starts with individuals, but it's not essentially *about* individuals. It determines the effect that we personally have on those around us, and further out into society, and of course beyond human society, into the environment, since it is becoming increasingly clear that our very survival as a species depends so closely on how we, as individuals and as communities, choose to behave in relation to everything else on the planet.

The modernity of Shakyamuni's teachings

It's important to take note I think of the extraordinary clarity and modernity of Shakyamuni's perception, all those centuries ago, of our fundamental need as human beings, to live in such a way as to create harmonious and balanced relationships within these three dimensions, or these three concentric circles as they are sometimes described, that make up our lives; with *ourselves* first of all at the centre, and then with the extensions of *human society* around us, and then beyond with the wider *environment.*

And it is extraordinary to observe how some of the very latest offerings from today's scientists and philosophers, take up these same themes and express remarkably similar views.

Jeffrey Sachs for example, the noted American economist, when he tries to define what he believes to be the *unique* challenge facing today's society, the society of which we are all a part, clearly embraces all three of those dimensions, ourselves, society, and the environment;

'Ours is not the generation that faced the Cold War. Ours is not the generation to have first grappled with the nuclear demon, although we still grapple with it today. Our challenge, our generation's unique challenge is learning to live peacefully and sustainably in an extraordinarily crowded world…facing the challenge of living side by side as never before, and facing a common ecological challenge that has never been upon us in human history until now…'[6]

Sam Harris, neuroscientist and philosopher, in his stimulating and controversial book, *The Moral Landscape*, in which he puts forward what seems to me the extraordinarily 'Buddhist' argument that the primary basis for making any ethical decisions should be to increase the *well being* of mankind as a whole, writes;

'As we better understand the brain, we will increasingly understand all of the forces -kindness, reciprocity, trust, openness to argument, respect for evidence, intuitions of fairness, impulse control, the mitigation of aggression, etc.- that allow friends and strangers to collaborate on the common projects of civilisation. Understanding ourselves in this way, and using this knowledge to improve human life, will be among the most important challenges to science in the decades to come.'[7]

*'…that allow friends and strangers to collaborate on the common projects of civilisation…'*It's a powerful phrase that projects an immensely bold vision; this inextricable and essential bond

between individual development and social progress. It could be seen I suggest, as very much a scientist's...or perhaps I should say a neuroscientist's... version of the Buddhist vision that we touched upon earlier, presented by the eminent authority on Buddhism, Daisaku Ikeda;

'...only a teaching that gives each individual the power to draw forth his or her Buddha nature can lead all people to happiness and transform the tenor of the times...In other words there can be no lasting solution to the problems facing society that does not involve our individual state of life.[8]

Our individual life state, *our* very own individual values and principles, playing a key role in resolving the profound problems faced by modern society. Buddhism has always taught that although a Buddhist practice is very much an *individual* activity, enabling ordinary people to build a strong and resilient inner self, it only becomes *meaningful* as something that is lived in society. That is to say, the daily determination to *live* as a Buddhist, rather than simply knowing and understanding Buddhist principles, becomes apparent above all in our *behaviour,* and in the way we handle the *relationships* that occur at every level in our lives from the most fleeting, to the most complex.

As you might expect we spend a great deal of time talking about the way in which a Buddhist practice can help us *as individuals* to understand our lives and to develop happy and productive relationships within a relatively close environment, of family and friends and work colleagues. Of course. The fact is that those are the very relationships that have by far the biggest influence on our lives. They make up the very fabric of our lives from day to day and from year to year. And as we all know, maintaining harmonious and creative and fulfilling relationships even within this relatively narrow compass, takes considerable energy and effort and compassion.

But the research of Nicolas Christakis and others now offers us a quite different and, I suggest, an immensely illuminating perspective in looking at what has always been a strong theme in Buddhist teachings. Namely that the way *we* respect and respond to all the people we encounter in the course of the day, from partners and work colleagues to ticket sellers and travelling companions, clearly has effects *well beyond* the people we actually encounter, as they in turn carry those effects on into *their* relationships and *their* social networks.

The power of individual action

And now, as Jeffrey Sachs and Sam Harris and Daisaku Ikeda remind us, almost in unison so close are their views, perhaps the biggest challenge facing us all, as *individuals* in this 21st Century, is how to learn to lift our gaze so to speak. How to extend this courageous and compassionate *value system* that the practice helps us to develop, out beyond the circle of familiar friends and colleagues, out to a wider society, indeed out to a global society, this *global village* that the scientists keep telling us that we now live in. When it is put as boldly as that it sounds like little more than wishful thinking. But Buddhism has always taught that the two are *indivisibly intertwined,* the individual and the social. It argues that a fundamental change in the values and the principles that an individual chooses to adopt, a fundamental shift towards the positive, has this *enduring ripple effect,* spreading out gradually, slowly perhaps but nevertheless continuing to spread, out through family and friends, into the local society and beyond.

Indeed Buddhism teaches that a movement towards a better society, based on the principles of respect for the lives of others, simply cannot be created *as a top down* process. It has to start with a profound change taking place within the lives of countless individuals, gradually changing the way wider communities function.

So Buddhism places the power of *individual action* at the very heart of its ethical teaching. Thus, there is no question for example that most human beings want world peace, although most unquestionably believe that to be an unattainable goal. And in any case, there doesn't seem to be any meaningful path along which it could be achieved. Buddhism however reminds us every single day, of two powerful truths. That however difficult it may be to achieve, it remains a *meaningful and desirable* goal, so giving up is not an option. And however difficult the path, it starts right at our own feet, and we can begin moving along it whenever we choose. It involves each one of us coming to understand *with our whole life,* that we are not powerless and that we can, through the choices that we *personally* make and the *actions* that we personally take, have a profound and beneficial effect upon our society and our environment.

What *we* choose to do, the values and the principles that *we* choose to adopt, unquestionably matter.

So what do we mean by morality?

This is a key question in our understanding of Buddhism. Why? Because we are so completely accustomed, conditioned even, to the idea that religions come *complete* with a clearly defined set of commandments, or dogma, or rules of behaviour that basically tell us the way we should live, the rules we must observe if we are to live what that particular religion defines as the good life, both for ourselves and for the society we inhabit.

In the western world the Ten Commandments might be said to provide the perfect example. So in Judaism and Christianity, they provide what has been described by religious historians as the universal and timeless standard of right and wrong. And so pervasive are they, so embedded are they in the western psyche, that they provide the model, the template so to speak, of what religions do. Even if we are not Jewish or Christian we can make a pretty good shot at listing them…well, most of them! For Jewish believers they cover all the matters of fundamental importance for an individual living in society. The greatest obligation, to worship only God. The greatest injury to another person, murder. The greatest injury to family bonds, adultery. The greatest injury to law or commerce, to bear false witness. The greatest generational obligation, to honour your mother and father. And the greatest obligations to the community in which you live, to be truthful and not to covet or to steal your neighbour's goods.

When Christianity broke away from its Jewish roots it took the Ten Commandments with it. When Protestantism broke away from Catholic theology, it did the same. So little wonder that they provide *the primary model* that most of us brought up in a Judao-Christian culture carry around inside our heads, for what religions have to say when it comes to morality. And of course something very similar occurs in other great religious traditions. They are that is, *highly prescriptive*. Islam sets very precise codes of behaviour that even include details of everyday living such as when you should pray and what you can eat and when. Hinduism, even in the modern world has a strict caste system, laying down the life-paths that people can or cannot follow.

We tend to take it for granted therefore that Buddhism will also come with it's own clearly defined set of dogma or rules of behaviour. *It doesn't.* As we've seen, Edward Conze from Cambridge University takes great care to remind us in his scholarly history of Buddhism, *'The Buddha always stressed that he was a guide, not an authority, and that all religious propositions must be tested, including his own.'[9]*

Buddhism is not prescriptive

The implication of that description is profound, and it could certainly be argued that the great social and ethical power of Buddhism…particularly in the modern world with its powerful drive towards liberalism and individual autonomy…lies in the fact that it is *not prescriptive.* Instead it seeks to make us much more keenly aware of the *effects* of our actions, good, bad and indifferent, for ourselves and for others; always for *ourselves and for others,* the two are inextricably linked. We practice…for ourselves and others. And then it places the responsibility for those actions entirely on ourselves. You could say that *personal responsibility* is the very basis of Buddhist ethics. We and we alone, it teaches, are responsible for the causes that we make, and the effects that those causes plant in our lives.

It could certainly be argued that rarely has there been a greater need for such a principle in western society. There is little doubt that if there were such an understanding, such a movement to cultivate and nurture a profound sense of *personal responsibility* for all one's actions, so that it became widespread in society, taught in schools, promoted in public policies, it could *transform* the quality of our lives, particularly in our ever more crowded towns and cities.

We all seek to live in communities and societies where we *freely experience* fairness and justice and compassion and respect for others as the context of our lives. And creating just such a context is the overwhelming purpose and thrust of the Buddhist approach to morality.

So Buddhism sets out to describe for us in great detail what it sees to be the way that our lives work. What kinds of thoughts and actions are dysfunctional in that they lead to anxiety and suffering, both for us and for those whom our life touches. What kinds of thoughts and behaviour lead to a greater sense of hope and optimism and well-being, again for us and those around us. That is the accumulated body of *understanding and wisdom* about human behaviour that Buddhism presents to us. That basically is what it's all about; a profound understanding of the motives and the impulses that drive human behaviour, and their effect on our sense of well-being. That is one of the reasons for example, why many modern psychologists are so interested in the body of Buddhist understanding.[10]

It's your life, and you are responsible for it

But the key point to take away from this brief exposition is that Buddhism is essentially *observational* rather than *prescriptive*. That is a key differentiator between Buddhism and other great religious traditions. So how does that work? What does it mean in practical terms in our daily life? Essentially it means that in the light of that deep understanding of human nature that it presents to us, Buddhism argues that it's *your* life. No one else can live it for you. No one else can tell you *how* to live it. Only *you* can resolve all the various influences and impulses and opportunities and challenges that come to bear on you as you travel along your *unique* life journey, no one else can do it for you. And so, by the same token *only you can be responsible* for the ways in which you resolve those influences. That is the very heart of the issue.

As Daisaku Ikeda has expressed it;

'*Shakyamuni Buddha explained the fundamental spirit of Buddhism as a sense of individual responsibility,' You are your only master. Who else? Subdue yourself and discover your master.' In other words, we must each take responsibility for our own self-discipline and for cultivating meaningful lives.*'[11]

So Buddhism opens up for us a completely different perspective. Whereas all other major religions are built around what we might call *codes of behaviour*, describing in precise terms, as we have seen with our brief look at the Ten Commandments, what is entailed in the struggle to lead a good and value-creating life. Buddhism is built essentially around this idea of *personal responsibility*. The metaphors that are commonly used vividly reinforce that idea. We alone are the *gardeners* of our own life garden. We alone are the *authors* of our own life story. In every way it is our deal, our choice, our responsibility, and we have to get on with it. It does of course offer intimate and detailed guidance at every step along the way; the owner's handbook if you like, that has been drawn up on the basis of many centuries of experience of human behaviour in a tough world. And the daily Buddhist practice is the essential *support* programme that helps us to develop the *wisdom* and the *compassion* and the *courage,* and the personal *discipline, t*o enable us to handle the responsibility more effectively.

And Buddhism argues, that discipline and that courage are certainly needed.

Life is tough

Indeed Buddhism was *created* out of the recognition that life is tough, and that how we choose to *respond to that toughness* determines the nature of our life. Not just for some of us, but for all of us. Without exception. For those who have a generous supply of the world's goods, as well as for those who don't. It's just that the nature of the toughness is different.

It is something of a digression perhaps, but let me just expand on that thought for a minute or two, because it says something very important about how Buddhist teachings work in the modern world. Whatever we may wish or hope for, or delude ourselves about, there is no perfect *defence* that we can erect to keep at bay the stresses and the strains that come with our humanity. None. Not status, nor wealth, nor success, nor power. Material prosperity may change the superficial circumstances, it may get rid of the hunger and cold, but it doesn't change fundamentally the nature of the human condition. We are all in that sense in the same boat. And I think you could argue that never has that been more evident than in this so-called age of celebrity, when the lives of those who have the slightest claim to fame are laid bare before us every day of the week, in countless magazines devoted entirely to that task, let alone newspapers ferreting around for another scandal to sell a few thousand more copies.

Scratch a princess or a prime minister or a soap star or a football icon, and however glamorous or shining their lives may seem from the outside, the reality is of course that they go through exactly the same pain and suffering as the rest of us, indeed more or more extreme in many cases. Wealth and success bring their own pressures. So what all that is saying is that none of us can *buy* our way, or *insulate* our way, out of life's difficulties. And as we all know, the current crop of difficulties will be replaced by the next crop, and so on. They are as *natural* a part of our life on this planet as gravity. And just as apples always fall downwards, so human life is always filled with complexity and problems.

Problems are the only gym in town

So the plain and demonstrable fact is that Buddhism is not in any way about finding some refuge from the troubling complexity of modern life, in some inner meditative sanctuary. Nor, most emphatically is it about *stoicism*, about bearing the burden, learning how to keep the head down and just tough out the storm. Nor about learning how to remain immensely *calm and patient* when all around you are losing theirs! None of that, or indeed anything like that. If I had to choose a single word to describe a Buddhist practice I think the word would be *challenge.* Because right at the heart of Buddhism is the idea that although of course we cannot change the inherent complexity and problematic nature of human life, it is possible to change fundamentally *our attitude* to those recurrent problems and difficulties. We can that is, *train ourselves* to challenge them, to respond to them positively rather than negatively.

That may not on the face of it, seem to be very challenging. '*Is that all there is to it?*' you might say. But think about it for a moment, because it *is* challenging. Very. Basically Buddhism asks us to come to understand that the problems and the difficulties and the anxiety-making troubles that we all encounter as we go through life, and that we all spend so much time and energy and ingenuity in trying to avoid, are in fact not just an inevitable part of life, they are *valuable* to our well-being. We might even say *essential* to it. How can I say that? Because this constant flow of difficulties and problems provides the only *training ground* there is, the only gym in town you might say, for us to develop our emotional and spiritual muscle. It provides, Buddhism constantly reminds us, the *only* available means for getting the *very most* out of who we are; for becoming the strongest, the most resilient, the most resourceful and the most optimistic individual that we are capable of being. And we all want those qualities don't we? We're just not sure how to get them. Buddhism opens up for us this new perception of how we might do just that.

If that strikes you as an eccentric, not to say a somewhat perverse proposition, I can only say that that is precisely how it struck me when I first encountered it. '*Who needs problems?*' was my initial response? But of course *needing* them isn't the issue, it's *dealing with them* when they inevitably occur that causes us so much pain and suffering. The key to unlocking the situation Buddhism teaches, is to see the situation for what it really is. It's not so much the problem itself that is causing the suffering, as *our response* to it. That may seem an unreal distinction, but in fact it is a fundamentally important one. So fundamental that once we really grasp the truth of it, it can change our whole lives from the inside out.

Indeed, if it is the *only truth* that you take away from this book, the writing of it will have been worthwhile. Buddhism argues that whether a problem, *any* problem, big or small, is a cause of *suffering*, or a source of *personal growth* depends essentially on our attitude towards it. And the difference in attitude, Buddhism argues, the change from a *negative* mind set, to a *positive* one, is crucial to achieving this huge difference in outcome. And let's face it, that's what we all want don't we? Whatever our personal circumstances may be, however good, however bad, we would all wish to dwell in a positive life state, rather than a negative one.

So a Buddhist practice is focused essentially on achieving that crucial attitude change, and it releases a whole new source of energy and determination. We can't simply think our way into it, '*From now on I'm going to live like this.*' Life isn't that simple. We have to *learn* how to make the change. Just as an athlete has to train hard to grow new muscle and to develop new reflexes to get the best out of his or her body, so we have to learn a new set of skills and responses and ways of thinking. It isn't a destination, it's a continuous *journey.*

There is a striking Buddhist text which goes, '*There is no path to happiness… happiness is the path.*' This is that very path. Learning how to achieve this crucial change in attitude towards the tough stuff in our lives.

The connection between cause and effect

Central to a Buddhist practice is this principle that *we alone* are responsible for the actions that we take, or the causes that we make, good bad and indifferent, and in the same way, wholly responsible for the *effects* that those causes plant in our life, like seeds, good bad and indifferent. At some time and in some place Buddhism teaches, those seeds will surely bear fruit. This notion of causes and effects embraces the whole spectrum of behaviour, thoughts and words as well as actual deeds, and it's clearly central to a fuller understanding of Buddhist ethics.

Buddhists often use the phrase '*Buddhism is reason*' to describe their practice. What they are talking about isn't simply that much of it would seem to be sound common sense. They also have in mind that there is a profound sense of balance, a sense of a reasonable, meaningful, *inescapable* relationship, between what we do, the *causes* that we make, and the *effects* that those actions, those thoughts and words and deeds, plant in our life. We inevitably reap if you like, what we sow. Although of course it goes without saying that we may only very rarely, if ever, be able to perceive, or work out, the *connection* between the causes, and the effects they generate.

In fact even to expect that is in a sense to miss the point of the principle. Of course we can all think of some experiences when a connection seems fairly clear; when we made huge efforts say, and achieved what we were after, or when we didn't and saw an opportunity that was within our reach slip away. But those clear connections are very much the rare exception. And since Buddhism is wholly concerned with the down-to-earth reality of everyday, it isn't in any way talking about a direct, *perceptible* connection between causes we make and their effects. That would be simply unreal.

What it is saying however is that once we take on board this central idea, accepting *total responsibility* for the *values* that we embrace, and the *choices* that we make, and the *actions* that we take…and see them as *our causes*…then we are introducing a new and powerful dynamic into our lives. A dynamic that can only have very beneficial and positive results, for us and our families and friends and workmates and communities, all the various societies we inhabit, because it *empowers us*, it puts us in charge of what you might call both halves of the equation.

Doing our human revolution

Of course it's also pretty demanding, particularly when our life is going through a rough patch, and we would much rather point the finger of blame at someone or something else. Just look at what *happened* to me, we say, or look at what *they* made me do. We commonly point at anything else as a cause of our current predicament, rather than at ourselves. We all do it. And of course, accepting complete responsibility in any sphere of life is always challenging. You could argue in fact that Nichiren Buddhism is both immensely *refreshing* in that it doesn't lay down a prescriptive code of behaviour we are expected to follow, and immensely *challenging* in that it asks us *always* to accept total responsibility for the causes that we make.

But as we've already mentioned, with a moments thought we can see that it's an approach to the daily reality of our life that is also full of hope and optimism, since once we accept that the *causes* lie within our own life, then immediately we can understand that so too do the *remedies.* We can see where things are going wrong, and we can set out to put them right. We may not always succeed of course, we're only human, but we can set off down that road.

Nichiren Buddhists often talk about this particular aspect of their practice as '*doing their human revolution*' and the phrase is undoubtedly appropriate, in the sense that simply having the confidence to take hold of part of our life that isn't working, or causing us a fair amount of suffering, and set about changing it, *is indeed* something of a revolution. It's what we all want to be able to do. And if you think about it even briefly, there aren't many teachings or philosophies or life-style techniques around, call them what you will, that help us to *recognise* the source of the problem in this way, and offer a *practical and proven,* down-to-earth method, for putting it right.

Living with respect

Let me round off this discussion by touching briefly upon the subject of *respect,* because it highlights what is an immensely important general point. Undoubtedly one of the most valuable contributions that is made by introducing a consideration of Buddhist values, into any discussion of human behaviour, is that they genuinely *transcend* culture, they don't have any *boundaries,* they are truly *universal.* So if you ask the direct question, what does Buddhism asks us to *demonstrate* in our relationships with other people…all other people without exception…that will enable us to create the greatest value in our own lives and in our wider communities? The answer that comes back as loud and clear as a peal of bells, is this notion of *respect.* It is a central and indeed a dominant pillar of Buddhist thought.

Daisaku Ikeda constantly reminds us of its centrality,

'The misfortune of others is our misfortune. Our happiness is the happiness of others.
To see ourselves in others and feel an inner oneness and sense of unity with them represents a fundamental revolution in the way we view and live our lives. Therefore discriminating against another person is discriminating against oneself. When we hurt another we are hurting ourselves. And when we respect others, we respect and elevate our own lives as well.'[12]

Both Shakyamuni and Nichiren had profoundly revolution-ary views of the way societies should function to create the greatest value for all. Those views were based essentially on everyone learning how to *respect* the dignity and the humanity of every other human being with whom they came in contact, *whatever the circumstances.* It was revolutionary then in the sense of being an ideal to be lived up to. When it is expressed in these direct terms it remains pretty challenging today. But let's be absolutely clear what it is asking of us, because it is a tough call, and it's one that if we take up the practice, we can't fudge or somehow slide around.

Essentially Buddhism argues that if we want to live and bring up our children in a society that is based fundamentally on respect for the lives of other people, as most of us undoubtedly do, then we have to determine to become our own *role model* so to speak. We have to *demonstrate* that respect as a core quality in all our encounters and relationships. Not some but all. We certainly don't have to like everybody, or admire them, still less to love them, or take them into our lives. But we do have to dig deeper than we otherwise might, and recognise their common humanity, whatever the circumstances of our encounter. That's the key point. No more, but importantly, no *less* than that. Like so many other things in Buddhism, we are called upon to make the positive, value-creating choice.

Freedom of choice

And Buddhism is very much based on this central idea of freedom of choice. It is not remember a morality that *tells us* how to behave, we *choose.* And that freedom of choice, coupled of course with the fundamental responsibility we've been talking about, extends right across the spectrum of our lives. One important interpretation of that word responsibility is indeed…*respond-ability*…that is to say, that we always have the choice as to how we respond. Thus the way we experience any *relationship* is also a matter of choice.

Good or bad, negative or positive, constructive or destructive, it's our choice.

It's not something that is done to us if I may express it that way. *No one does it to us.* We do it to ourselves. We can choose of course to respond to the bits we don't happen to like, or what we feel to be the annoyances, or the irrationalities or the inconsistencies in another person's behaviour or manner that happen to *irritate us*, or make the relationship *inconvenient* or awkward for us. That is if you like the *negative* choice. Or we can make the *positive* choice, and dig deeper into our personal resources and determine that we are going to create value out of this encounter whatever our *initial* reaction to it might be. Not always of course. Once again we're only human. But a Buddhist practice is aimed at helping us to be more aware, and thus to recognise what is going on in the encounter or the relationship more rapidly, and so make that positive choice more often.

You'll have noticed that we've been bumping into that word *choice* throughout this whole line of argument, and it's bound to occur again and again on this journey, because it is crucial to an understanding of what Buddhism is about, and indeed to an understanding of what it really means when it talks about happiness or well-being in this life. It has often been said that there can be no happiness without hope or optimism, and no hope or optimism really without freedom of choice…coupled we would hasten to add, to that profound sense of personal responsibility we've been talking about. The two have to be inseparable.

And in a sense that is the bottom line to this entire discussion we've been having about Buddhism and ethics. That *is* the basic Buddhist approach to all relationships of whatever kind, right across the field of human experience. It is based solidly on that central, life-changing perception by Shakyamuni all those years ago, that every human being without exception, has this profound potential of Buddhahood within their lives. And the whole purpose of the *daily practice* is in a sense to sharpen our recognition of that potential in ourselves....and others.

And that's where we go next, to de-mystify that word practice.

CHAPTER SEVEN

Buddhism and Practice

There is a striking phrase that I encountered many years ago that has stuck like a burr in my mind ever since, and every now and again when the circumstances warrant, it resurfaces, and makes its presence felt. The phrase quite simply is,

'We don't see the world as it is. We see it as we are.'

What is remarkable about it I believe, is that it encapsulates in so few words, so profound and bottomless a piece of wisdom, that once heard you might say, it's never forgotten. In this particular form of words it doesn't happen to come from the Buddhist tradition, it comes in fact from the texts that make up the ancient Jewish Talmud.[1] But it expresses an idea that lies right at the heart of Shakyamuni's teaching, that essentially, we carry our *environment* around with us.

It reminds us lest we should forget, that although we might think that what we do each day is to walk through a sort of external reality, to which we respond in various ways, that is very much not the case. It tells us that it is in fact our own *state of mind*, our own attitude, how we are *inside* our heads, that plays so large a part in how we actually *experience* everything we encounter in our world and in our relationships.

We need to perceive our overwhelming responsibility that is, for *shaping and creating* our own reality and our own environment.

With even a few minutes of reflection we grasp the essential truth of that don't we? We all know full well that we can have intensely grey and gloomy days, and we can have brilliantly bright and sunny days, that have absolutely nothing to do with what's going on outside; they are created almost entirely by our own *internal weather*. We have all experienced, particularly in the working environment perhaps, the encouraging and uplifting effect of a colleague who seems always to have a bright and optimistic and resourceful *inner* life, so that a whole team can be energised by such a spirit, however daunting the task in hand. And we've all experienced the reverse, the way in which the spirit of a whole group can be dragged down by a single colleague who tends to turn up full of negativity, and proceeds to tip it out, rather like emptying a suitcase into the office. We have all been there.

But the key thing perhaps that we should take from this piece of ancient wisdom is the hope-filled *life strategy* it proposes. Because it tells us that we do have the ability to *transform* our lives. If we could only find a way of developing and sustaining an internal life state that is *consistently* hopeful and optimistic and resilient, then that will become the dominant perspective from which we will perceive and shape our environment…our reality…our life.

And that essentially is what the Buddhist practice is about.

That may seem a huge and sudden leap to make in the argument, but it's not really. The daily Buddhist practice is precisely about developing a much greater awareness, or mindfulness, of our *internal* weather, of where we are in our heads, and its profound effect upon our own perceptions, and upon all those around us. And then, beyond that, building the determination to do something *positive* about it, to steadily shift our whole lives you might say towards the positive end of the spectrum, nurturing those qualities of hope and optimism and resilience so that they become a consistent part of our daily approach to life.

We want to become that bright and resourceful and optimistic colleague who everybody wants to have around!

A daily training programme

The fact is that Buddhism uses the word practice in very much the same way as we might use it in talking about any other field of human endeavour. It's not a technical term. Why do we practice anything? For one reason only. We don't practice for the sake of the practice do we? We practice to get better at the *skills* we are seeking to acquire. Any sportsman, any musician, any artist knows that unless they practice they cannot possibly hope to achieve their full potential. Moreover having more innate talent doesn't mean less training. The greater the talent, the more, rather than the less sportsmen and musicians have to train because they have a greater potential to fulfil. Few people train as hard as Olympic athletes or as concert musicians for example.

By the same token, however *inherent* the qualities that Buddhism teaches we all have at the core of our lives, learning how to *draw them out,* so that we can understand them more fully, and use them more readily in the stuff of our daily lives, requires a real personal commitment to sustained practice. So from this standpoint the Buddhist practice should be seen not so much as a *religious ritual,* but as a personal daily discipline. Indeed, we might regard it as a sort of daily, life-time, personal *training* programme. Not all that different in a sense from a daily, life-time training programme at the gym for example, aimed at achieving a higher level of physical fitness. Except that with the Buddhist practice we are of course talking about developing *spiritual* muscle, about developing an *inner* toughness and resilience and optimism, that is strong enough not to be dismantled by the problems and the difficulties and yes, the suffering, that we will all inevitably encounter in our lives.

And that word 'training' in this context is very significant, because that in effect is what we are doing with the discipline of the daily practice, we are *training* our minds, we are *shaping* our approach to life. And if we look into the work of the psychologists and other social scientists in this field, their findings directly support the view that a *regular* practice, *sustained* over time...both of those aspects are crucial...is the absolute key to making the most of our qualities in *any* field, including developing these highly desirable life skills that we have been talking about, such as hope and optimism and courage and compassion.

The economist Richard Layard has argued,

'The fact is we can train our feelings. We are not simply victims of our situation, or indeed of our past...we can directly address our bad feelings and replace them by positive feelings, building on the positive force that is in each of us, our better self.'[2]

So he's talking directly about using this regular 'training' to create or to reveal *'our better self.'* And remember that's a social scientist talking, not a Buddhist teacher!

Interestingly like Daniel Goleman, he goes on to use the analogy of professional musicians. You only get to play Mozart on a concert platform so to speak, if you can summon up the inner determination to put in that regular daily practice over long periods of your life. And that sort of regular daily practice, he explains, whether it is to polish our musical ability, or to *train ourselves in the skills of being happy,*[3] will undoubtedly have a profound effect on who we are, and how we behave and respond to the circumstances and the people we encounter.

Professor Ericsson of Florida State University is another great champion of the absolutely primary role played by *effort and practice* in any field of endeavour you care to mention. His research tells us that it is not so much the *innate* skill or talent that we might have been born with, although of course that is important, but the crucial factor in taking any skill or quality that we have to a higher level, is the *effort* we are prepared to put into it. And he equates effort directly with the amount of *time* we are prepared to put into practice, practice, practice.[4]

Professor Martin Seligman from Pennsylvania University from whom we've already quoted on several occasions, not only expresses his wholehearted agreement with that view, he adds the comment that a crucial aspect of this whole process, is that *we* are the ones making the choice to practice; *we* are the ones putting in the effort, its *our* choice, '… *the exercise of conscious choice,'* as he puts it.[5]

No one is forcing us. The life-changing value lies precisely in the fact that we are *wholly responsible* for just how much effort, just how much determination, just how much practice we are prepared to invest into any quality or skill we are seeking to develop. So we are back to that absolutely basic proposition that Buddhism puts to all of us, that if we are prepared to summon up the *determination* to achieve it, and if we are prepared to put in the *effort,* we can *choose* hope and optimism and resilience and well-being, as the way we wish to live our lives.

But how do we achieve it?

But even as I write that I am only too well aware of course that it is far easier to say than to achieve. However attracted we might be by the idea, we can't achieve it without help, without some sort of discipline or structure, some sort of *scaffolding,* around which we can consistently reinforce the determination, and strengthen the will to change. That in essence is what the Buddhist practice offers us. It provides the essential structure, the *method or the discipline,* that enables us to take hold of our lives in a rational and measured way and move them in the direction we wish to move.

Thus despite the many stereotypes and the many misconceptions that are prevalent in the western world, a Buddhist practice is not in any way esoteric or remote and other-worldly. Somewhat different certainly, from our embedded cultural norms, but always immensely practical and down-to-earth. A key thing to hang onto is that it has absolutely nothing to do with the sort of outcome that we normally associate with religious customs, namely some promise of reward in some afterlife. It has wholly to do with establishing a greater sense of well-being amidst the often harsh realities of this one.

What does that mean you might ask, in terms of the ups and downs of ordinary life? It means that instead of finding ourselves responding positively or negatively to those ups and downs, positively to the good things and negatively to the bad, as they occur in our lives. Now up now down, depending on the nature of the circumstances and the events that *we just happen to encounter*, which is how so many of us actually live, if we are honest with ourselves. Instead of that we are seeking, with the help of the practice, to develop a much more stable *inner core* of optimism and resilience and confidence, so that we can *more often* respond positively and optimistically, no matter what circumstances we have to deal with. You will often hear people declare for example that that has been the biggest benefit they have gained from the practice, an altogether greater sense of stability, not being blown around so much by circumstance. Not necessarily more in control of their lives, but unquestionably more in control of their responses.

Does that mean we banish anxiety from our lives? Of course not. We're only human. There is nothing seamless about a Buddhist approach to life. Doubts and anxieties and frustrations all remain part of the daily mix because they are all part of our essential humanity. The key difference in my experience is that they don't take over. You see them earlier, and recognise them for what they are, because the practice is very much about clarifying and strengthening that crucial quality of self awareness, and because we are learning all the time to respond to negative stuff more positively and more creatively.

And we can all see immediately can't we, that an ability to respond strongly and *positively* to negative stuff is an immensely valuable quality to have in life? We could all do with lots of it. Moreover this expressed purpose of the practice turns out to be completely in tune with what modern psychologists tell us about positive and negative responses. They tell us for example that we can't have negative and positive feelings *at the same time.*[6] We can be mixed up and confused of course and often are. We can *alternate* between them, and often do. But we can't *feel* them at the same time. So the objective becomes clear; the more we can learn how to *summon up* our positive responses to tackle the stuff that life presents us with, the *less room* we have to experience the negative ones.

An additional asset

That in itself I suggest, is yet another life-changing lesson, so simple and yet so powerful in its implications. And it is precisely what I have in mind when I talk about the practice being practical and down-to-earth rather than remote and other-worldly. So for example, when Nichiren Buddhists are aware that they are approaching a time of extra stress and difficulty in their lives, such as a change of job for example, or stress in a close relationship, or a major move to a new location, or a challenging illness, or even just a tough set of exams, they step up their *training* you might say. They deliberately step up their practice to give themselves the greater self-confidence and the resilience, and simply the greater life force to be able to push themselves through a difficult and turbulent and stressful time.

It is as deliberate and as conscious, and indeed as *practical* as that. Nichiren Buddhists use the practice as an additional asset available to them. *Buddhism is daily life…* and in many ways that simple sounding phrase is the very heart of the Buddhist message. We are very accustomed in the West…we might almost say trained…by the nature of our educational system and our culture, to live our lives driven by three primary engines; our *intellect and our emotions*, how we think that is, and how we feel, and by our *persona*, how we look or how we present ourselves. We place great emphasis, as indeed we should, on our intellectual ability to *think* our way through life's problems. We all need that basic rationality. We attach great value to emotional expression, to being *in touch* as the modern idiom goes, with our emotions. And we are increasingly concerned, probably to excess, about externals, about physical appearance.

Essentially all Buddhism is saying is, that's fine as far as it goes, but it does only go so far. There's more…there is an inner *spiritual resource* that we can all learn to tap into, and it can lift our life performance to a new level. As the philosopher Robert Solomon reminds us;

'Spirituality …requires action as part of it's very essence. It is a mode of doing as well as of being, thinking and feeling.'[7]

In Nichiren Buddhism the daily practice is the *method* that it offers to enable us to achieve that powerful combination of spirituality in action.

Getting to grips with the practice.
Because it is so important there is an extended and more detailed version of this account in Appendix B. All I want to do here is to give someone who hasn't come across Nichiren Buddhism before, a general understanding of what the practice is about, so that the word doesn't trouble them whenever it pops up, as it has already many times of course. I am keenly aware of that.

So the elements of the practice of Nichiren Buddhism may be expressed in various ways, but if we squeeze it down to its essentials, there are three, namely chanting, study and taking action.

A brief look at chanting

The primary practice is chanting the phrase Nam Myoho Renge Kyo, chanting out loud that is, rather than repeating a mantra silently within one's head as in meditation. The phrase itself is the title in classical Japanese of The Lotus Sutra, and its meaning is explained in greater detail in Appendix B. The first thing you notice is that it is very much a *physical* action rather than a mental one, so it has clear physiological effects. You are for example moving considerable volumes of air in and out of the lungs and that tends to stimulate the circulation, so it feels pleasant, indeed there are many who say it's very good for the complexion because it sets the skin tingling! Certainly people tend to look stimulated, blooming even, after a chanting session. But above all of course it is the *sound* that has the greatest effect. To hear a group of people chanting in unison is altogether an uplifting experience, and that seems to be the case whether or not you happen to be a practising Buddhist. Just to give a very brief example, I was visiting a friend recently who was very sick in hospital, in intensive care in fact, and I sat just chanting very quietly beside his bed for half an hour or so, as he slept. As I was leaving some visitors from a nearby bed came up to me and asked me what that beautiful sound was.

There is no set time, nor any set period for chanting. As with so many other aspects of Buddhist practice, that is entirely up to the individual. It's your life, so you can chant for as long or as little as you can manage before you have to dash out of the door to work. The practice is immensely flexible to fit in with the demands of modern life. But normally we would chant twice a day. In the morning, to launch us into the day with a positive, generous, up-beat life state…we see things as *we are* remember…so we seek that positive life state to shape our perception of our environment. In the evening we are chanting basically in the spirit of gratitude for the day that we've had, whatever it has been like. If it's been good there is plenty to be grateful for. If it's been altogether a bad hair day, then the chanting will help us to lift our life state so that we can get over the frustrations and tackle tomorrow with more confidence.

And I should emphasise that those aren't just casual claims. Not in any way. They are very much an account of my own experience, and that of many others. Many people for example find that they are at their lowest ebb first thing in the morning, not for any particular reason, just because that happens to be their natural state. They find that just 20 or 30 minutes of strong and focused chanting before they go out of the door, can really lift their spirits enough to put a smile on their face and a bounce in their step. But even a few minutes can have a noticeable effect on how you feel.
As Daisaku Ikeda has expressed it,

'The on-going moment –to- moment transformation in our hearts and minds that we achieve through chanting daimoku not only leads to a fundamental inner change, but to a change in the entire way we live our lives.'[8]

And as we can all understand, as with any form of practice in *any* field of endeavour, the key thing is the *regularity*, the daily-ness of the practice. Chanting is no different. Better ten minutes twice a day than an hour every Friday morning. What do we think about while we're chanting? That's a good question, and it raises an important issue. In general I think it's true to say that the western world doesn't place a great deal of value on repetitive chanting, mainly because it's clearly not part of our cultural tradition, but also because it's commonly regarded as a sort of mindless activity, as if we were taking the *intellect* out of gear.

But that of course is precisely the point. It *is* a time to clear the mind and give the intellect, *the fat controller* so to speak, a rest, to allow other immensely valuable bits of the psyche to emerge. So the intention is not to *think,* but to *listen* to the sound, relax into the rhythm, enjoy the chanting for it's own sake. The time for thought is before you start, what do you want to chant about, and after you have finished, when the mind is clear and the spirit is high, and you are deciding on what action you need to take, if any.

Some interesting research

Moreover there has been some very interesting recent research even in this area that is I think worth mentioning. It was carried out by Herbert Benson at the Massachusetts General Hospital, which has a world-class reputation for the range and quality of its medical research. Herbert Benson himself, Professor of Medicine at Harvard University, carried out a long series of studies in the 1990's on the effects on health and general well-being of various forms of religious belief. The results were set out in his detailed account, *Timeless Healing: The Power and Biology of Belief.* His conclusion essentially was that many forms of repetitive prayer, arising from belief, can have powerfully beneficial effects on critical physiological factors such as lower blood pressure, stable heart rates and heightened immune systems. This more recent research however goes even further, it actually looks at the effect of chanting and meditation on the way in which particular genes were switched on or off, so it delves if you like into the very basis of our humanity.

The research group was quite small, only 26 volunteers, none of whom had previous experience of chanting or meditating. Initially Benson and his colleagues carried out an analysis of the complete genomes of all 26, and then they were all taught a brief 20 minute routine of chanting and breathing and *'emptying the mind.'* The volunteers then proceeded to carry out that routine, that practice if you like, every day for 8 weeks. At the end of that time the genomes of all the volunteers were re-analysed. The results were quite startling. As the report in the scientific journal expresses it,

'Clusters of beneficial genes had become more active and harmful ones less so.'[9]

The beneficial effects were related to the energy efficiency of cells, the level of insulin production which improves control of blood sugar, and certain effects of ageing. The clusters of genes that became less active were associated with chronic inflammation, which can lead to high blood pressure and heart disease.[10]

So the process of chanting not only creates *space,* so that if we find ourselves in a troublesome or challenging situation, by chanting about it, it is possible to clear the mind to enable us to *respond* to that situation in a more positive and creative way, rather than, as might otherwise be the case, simply *reacting* to it impulsively. But quite clearly it is a truly re-energising and re-vitalising activity. That has always been part of a practitioner's personal experience. That experience now receives profound support from this extraordinary piece of research.

What do we chant for?

That's an important question isn't it? We are chanting essentially to tap into this potential, this resource within ourselves, that helps us to live with a higher life state *more of the time*. So more optimism, more hope, more courage, more resilience, whatever the turbulence in our lives or whatever circumstances we happen to be living through. That is the dominant underlying thought. But the plain fact is, as we've said so often, *Buddhism is daily life*, so people chant for any goal they wish to achieve in their lives, or in the lives of those around them. People don't often start chanting because they want to 'save the planet' so to speak, or rarely. They are much more likely to start chanting for reasons that are much closer to home, much more personal; for courage in the face of serious illness for example, or for a more satisfying or rewarding job, or to heal a rift in a relationship, or just to have a great day. Many people chant for these and other utterly normal worldly desires every day of the week. They are very much part of our ordinary humanity, and real enough, and therefore part and parcel of our Buddhist practice.

I have no doubt that my Buddhist practice brings immense value into every area of my life on a daily basis. It enriches and strengthens my marriage for example in ways that are too numerous to mention. No marriage is without tension and conflict, and in that sense Buddhism is a great marital aid! Or a great partnership aid perhaps, whichever is appropriate. Why? Because arguments between people who share intimately in each others' lives can be the most destructive, because both parties know so well the other's vulnerabilities. The point is that the daily practice delivers into the hands of both parties, a most powerful mechanism, not simply for slicing through those rows rapidly, but for healing the wounds and for creating genuine value, genuine learning out of the situation. I speak only from experience!

What about material things?

Chanting to achieve things in our life, including material things, runs directly counter of course to a widely held perception of Buddhism, that it is essentially about *renunciation,* about giving up many worldly things, as a necessary step on the road to achieving a higher spiritual state. Nichiren Buddhism however teaches that the mere act of renunciation, *of itself* brings no benefits to our lives. How can it? It argues on the contrary that desire is basic to all human life, and that as long as there is life, there will be the instinctive desire in the hearts of all men and women to make the very most of that life, to live and to grow and to love and to have.

Nichiren saw with great clarity that little was to be gained from people expending huge amounts of thought and time and energy trying to *extinguish* a force that lies right at the core of our lives. On the contrary a great deal more is to be achieved by accepting it as an essential part of everyone's humanity and therefore *harnessing it*, as a powerful engine for individual growth. And indeed there are countless stories to be told of people who have started chanting driven largely by what they saw as their personal needs, who now look back and smile at those somewhat shallow beginnings, in the knowledge of just how profoundly their lives and their concerns have changed towards the *creation of value*, not just in their own lives, but taking in the well-being of family and friends and work colleagues.

But whatever we may be seeking for our own lives at any particular point in time, it is important to hang onto the *vision*, the goal. And the ultimate goal of the Nichiren Buddhist is a world made up of people and communities at every level, that live in peace one with another, and with respect for one another. We chant for it, and we work for it on a daily basis.

What do we mean by study?

Once again Buddhism is essentially like any other subject we might be interested in, in that to gain the greatest value from our practice, then clearly we have to spend a reasonable amount of time studying it, in order to understand more fully its basic principles and beliefs. That is part and parcel of the commitment, part and parcel of the responsibility if you like that we accept in taking up the practice, studying a wide range of things from the letters and other writings of Nichiren himself, which are still extant, to commentaries by Buddhist scholars, and accounts by individual Buddhists of the ways in which their practice has changed their lives. Nichiren makes no bones about its importance. Indeed he goes so far as to say,

'Exert yourself in the two ways of practice and study. Without practice and study there is no Buddhism.'[11]

It could scarcely be expressed more directly, and in a sense study becomes a continuous process. Many practitioners fold it into their daily lives, spending a few minutes each day reading or studying a Buddhist text or a piece of commentary, because it is such a broad ranging philosophy.

But that having been said it is equally important to emphasise that this is not in any way an *intellectual* practice. The practice is not about knowledge so much as about spirit. So the study is not about *acquiring knowledge* in a sort of egocentric way, knowledge as an end in itself. It is wholly about deepening our understanding of the principles that inform the practice and how they play out in everyday life. Because of course, in the final analysis, that is what we are talking about, it's about *our* values and *our* behaviour above all, about how we personally seek to *create value* through the situations and the people we encounter as we go about our daily lives.

Taking the action

This is the essential third pillar of the practice, which anchors the chanting and the study and the basic values of the philosophy into the reality of every day. Taking the action, putting it into practice, the *struggle* some would say, to fold Buddhist principles and values completely into the fabric of our daily life, so that they *are lived*, rather than just perceived or understood. It is simply but memorably illustrated in the example of cooking the rice. If you want to eat rice, the story goes, you can prepare it, put it in the pot and put the pot on the stove. Then you can go off and chant. You can chant until you're blue in the face, but of course not a grain of rice will be cooked…*until you take the action*…until you get up off your knees and light the fire that is. So the chanting is the essential *prelude,* the summoning of the wisdom and the courage and the compassion and the life force, to enable you to take the action to *realise* the change that you seek in your life.

And the reason why we might well use the word *'struggle'* in that list of action words above is because we are so often deeply involved in *change;* we're seeking to change and improve the things that don't work or that we don't like about our lives, and as we all know, few things are more difficult to change than ingrained, often unconscious patterns of thought or behaviour. They might be driven, those patterns, by lack of awareness for example, or by habitual anger, or selfishness, or a basic lack of concern for other people's needs or views. That is part of all our experience. We are all aware of just how loudly our own needs or wishes speak to us, over the concerns of others. What happens is that the Buddhist practice, which has *compassion and altruism* at its very heart, drives the inner transformation towards a fundamental respect for the lives of all others. It's not of course a one-way journey, far from it. One step forwards, two steps back is a common experience, but as we continue with the practice, so we get better at living it out in our lives.

Seeking actual proof

A Buddhist practice is too extensive, too multi-layered to admit of a meaningful summing up. As the late historian and philosopher Arnold Toynbee, who was deeply interested in Buddhist teachings, has expressed it,

'The Buddhist analysis of the dynamics of life is more detailed and subtle than any western analysis I know of.'[12]

But if I had to isolate a single thought that conveys the essence of its meaning and purpose, it would be perhaps, that it enables us to understand altogether more clearly and more vividly, that life doesn't just happen to us, *we make it happen*. This combination of discipline and self-belief that lie at its heart, help us to summon up the determination and the effort and perseverance that can be truly *life-changing*, both for ourselves, and for all those around us.

But it's crucially important to add, that at no stage are we asked to accept the benefits of the practice that we have been talking about, as a matter of *blind faith*. From the outset Nichiren Buddhism asks us to regard actual, demonstrable proof of the benefits or the effects of the practice in our daily lives as the crucial test of its *validity*. Indeed the term *'actual proof'* is used to make this point clear, and if you think about it even for a moment, it is *the* fundamental question isn't it? Does it work? Does it genuinely help us with things like overcoming our problems and facing up to our challenges? Does it enhance our daily lives? Does it help us to live in a more positive, value-creating way despite all the difficulties we are bound to encounter as human beings? Those are the kinds of questions that this practice invites you to ask. As I've said, it requires nothing that might be described as blind faith. It *does* require the commitment and the determination in order to give it a reasonable chance.

And if I look back, that was certainly my own position all those years ago, hanging on to that key question, does it work? And in answering it, I would say that you take note of the doubts and the misgivings about the practice that undoubtedly arise, particularly in the early days, but they can arise at any time, why not? And you ask questions and read more widely in order to seek some resolution of them. But in the final analysis, it will not in my view, be what you read, or what you are told about Buddhism that will convince you of its value, although of course they both have an important part to play, particularly at the outset. In the end it has to be the gradual accumulation of your *own experiences* that prove to you that it makes sense in terms of your own life. Or not indeed. Both options are clearly valid. The practice is too demanding to be continued on the basis of what somebody else tells you about it. The deepening belief and the joy, in the life-changing power of a Buddhist practice *have* to come… can *only* come… from within.

CHAPTER EIGHT

Buddhism and Daily Life

One of the things that struck me most forcibly when I first started to go to Buddhist discussion meetings and seminars, long before I felt ready to take up the practice myself in any steady or meaningful way, was the immensely positive way that people spoke about the influence of the practice in their daily lives. So they would talk for example about having a clearer sense of purpose, and direction, and a value structure that helped them to think constructively about their lives. They would frequently say that they felt more focused somehow, even if they couldn't define precisely why. Or that they no longer felt so blown off course by random events. Or that they could make choices and take decisions more readily, because they had a clearer sense of who they were, and what they wanted in their lives.

In every case there was the sense of ordinary people feeling better about the way they were dealing with the relationships and the events in their lives, and creating more value as a result. Moreover all the qualities they chose to mention, a clearer sense of purpose and direction, more focus, more decisiveness, all appear prominently in the work of the sociologists when they're writing about how we set about establishing a stable and consistent sense of well-being in our own lives, and equally important, how we contribute to the lives of those close around us.

To squeeze it absolutely into a nutshell Buddhism essentially presents the flow life as a constant series of choices that come towards us, all of them lying somewhere on this continuum between the negative and the positive. So that every day, every week, countless times, we are called upon to make this choice between being positive and value creating, or being negative and in some measure…great or small… destructive. And what it seeks to do, as illustrated by those people at those meetings, is to bring to us a greater *awareness*, that in all those countless situations, *we* are the ones making the choice, we have that capability. As we've said earlier, life doesn't *just happen* to us, as we so often see it, *we make it happen.* So instead of just drifting along, or being carried along by our habit energy, we have some clear sense of shaping it and directing its course. Or as the people at the meetings described it, they had a clearer sense of values and purpose and indeed stability, underlying the inevitable daily flux of events.

And all Buddhist practice, at its heart, is about that *heightened awareness*. About helping us grow and nurture, rather as we might grow and nurture a skill at sport or at music or some other skill, as a *conscious act*. That's the key point, as a conscious process of change, in which we invest real time and effort and energy, in order to develop this inner strength. Because it is that inner strength, that emotional muscle you might say, that enables us more often to *recognise and reject* the negative, however persuasive and attractive it might be; and more and more often to make the positive choice. And of course it is only *more often*, rather than always. We all have negativity as a constant presence in our life, and it is pretty skilled at slipping in under our defences.

But it is that steady progression, that growth *towards the positive,* that enables us to become more capable, more effective, more *contributing,* in all the multiple overlapping roles that we all have to fulfil, as parents and partners, as teachers and colleagues at work and as friends at play. And of course as responsible people living in society, which essentially is what we are talking about in this chapter.

And one might add, with a greater sense of *well-being.* That claim is amply borne out in the vast body of social research we now have on what kinds of things contribute to a stable sense of well-being. It's clear that our *awareness* of our own improved self- confidence and our own increased ability to contribute to others, both play a huge role in what constitutes happiness in this life. We all want fundamentally to be *capable people* in all the roles we inhabit.

As we've seen, Buddhism chooses to call that resilient, life-enhancing, inner strength that we learn how to grow, *Buddhahood,* and it chooses to call the confident awareness of it's existence, *enlightenment.* Those are of course unusual and infrequently used words in our western vocabulary, but when it comes down to it, they are just names! We shouldn't allow their unusual-ness and unfamiliarity to deflect us from the central fact that the qualities that they represent are not in any way other-worldly or esoteric; they are demonstrably part of our everyday, down-to-earth reality. But before we dip into some of the important and immensely revealing social research I've mentioned, let's briefly tackle this central concept of Buddhahood.

So what do we mean by Buddhahood?

We are wholly accustomed in the Western world to thinking of 'the Buddha' as being the great historical figure of Shakyamuni. There have of course been many other men who have been given the title Buddha down the intervening centuries, but when we attach that definite article, we are undoubtedly referring to Shakyamuni himself. As we discussed earlier he made no claims to divinity or to divine inspiration during his long lifetime. Indeed he specifically forbade his followers from making any such connection. However, it is unquestionably the case that in western minds he clearly occupies a place alongside the other great founders of religions such as Jesus and Mohammed, who *did* of course claim a divine connection. Indeed that was the very basis of their life on this earth, they claimed to be the only channel through which God's or Allah's purpose was transmitted to mankind.

As a result of this parallel status, if I may put it that way, in the West we are accustomed to attributing to the title Buddha, if not the very special qualities of divinity, something very close to it. For all intents and purposes the Buddha has become god-like. Indeed, across much of South East Asia, Shakyamuni has been virtually deified, with huge gilded statues occupying pride of place in Buddhist temples, and since it was this form of Buddhism that was first encountered and described by western travellers, this sense of *deification* very much colours the western response to the word Buddha.

It is a universal quality

It therefore comes as something of a shock when we first encounter the central teaching of the Lotus Sutra and Nichiren Buddhism, which is that Buddhahood, or the Buddha Nature as it is often called, is not a quality possessed only by one very special man in history, or even by a handful of special men down the centuries. Buddhahood we learn, is a *potential* inherent in everyone, everyone without exception, part of our essential humanity. It argues that whether we accept it or not, whether we believe in it or not, or have the slightest interest in understanding the implications of it, we all have that potential within our lives; everyone you sit alongside in the train, or ride up the escalator with, the man you buy your morning newspaper from, all the colleagues you encounter on a daily basis at work, those you like and those you don't!

The Buddha nature we are told, is a *universal* quality that we can all learn to draw upon or harness in our daily life.

Once again, it is unquestionably a huge, life-changing idea, nothing less than a revolution in the spiritual history of mankind. It was central to Shakyamuni's enlightenment, and was revolutionary when it was first made clear in the Lotus Sutra. It was no less revolutionary when Nichiren spent so much of his life explaining its implications in 13th Century Japan. And I suggest it remains revolutionary today, in the sense of being a very difficult idea to grasp hold of and to act upon, as the *central inspiration* for living through all the mundane muddle of our daily lives.

And as we've seen, that in essence is what the daily practice is about, helping us to move along that path of understanding, and to fold that understanding into the detail of our lives. It's a cooking word of course, *folding,* but it is precisely right it seems to me, for what we are trying to express here. It means taking this bold and utterly uncompromising but somewhat alien teaching, and blending it into the very texture of our lives so that it becomes *indistinguishable* from the rest. From my experience that is by no means an easy thing to do. It takes real commitment and above all constant perseverance. But the rewards in terms of a deep and enduring sense of gratitude and well-being are in my experience, unequalled. Otherwise I wouldn't be writing this!

Human scale qualities

So what do we mean then by Buddha nature? How should we come to terms with it and represent it to ourselves so that it makes everyday sense to us? The somewhat surprising fact is that it is defined quite simply, in terms of ordinary and above all *human scale* qualities or characteristics. There is nothing even vaguely superhuman or other-worldly about them, indeed they are all qualities that we can all make very good use of; a powerful inner resource of courage and resilience no matter what challenges we encounter; a sense of wisdom or judgement that enables us to understand more clearly where and how we can create value; and an overwhelming sense of compassion that enables us always to go towards people warmly and supportively.

Of course we're all ordinary human beings, so achieving these qualities is in no way a static state, a place you arrive at. It is like life itself, dynamic and constantly changing, hence the daily-ness of the practice. But perhaps the key point to hang onto is the essential *down-to-earth humanity* of the idea. Thus all the historically recorded Buddhas were *ordinary* human beings. It's crucially important to remember that, immensely wise and perceptive and deeply compassionate, but still ordinarily human, with their share of the basic human qualities that we would all recognise, as an essential part of their lives, never to be got rid off. Buddhahood that is, has got nothing to do with an aspiration towards perfection, nothing to do with super-human abilities, or transcendental powers.

Just as Buddhism is about daily life, so Buddhahood we learn, can *only* reveal itself in the lives of ordinary people, going about that daily life.

Courage wisdom and compassion

So the *courage* does not mean the soldier's bravery. It's not the *absence* of fear, so much as the courage to *overcome* the fear and the negativity that we all have experience of in our lives, sometimes to the point of paralysis; fear of so many things, fear of failure, of rejection, of isolation, of inadequacy. Winning over our own negative road blocks is often the toughest part of any challenge. We need this *everyday* type of courage to confront problems as they arise rather than denying them until they loom so large they threaten to overwhelm us. As we all know, it takes real courage to face up to our own greatest weaknesses.

The *wisdom* is not about the profound perceptions of the philosopher, but rather a greater awareness of what is really going on in any situation, and an alert and lively common sense as to what action is appropriate. It's also a deeper and closer knowledge of ourselves, our strengths and our weaknesses and the ability to see the repeated patterns in our own behaviour that can cause us so much suffering, so that we can set about changing them.

The *compassion* is not so much concern for those less fortunate than ourselves, but the ability to see and comprehend the true nature of our life and it's relationship to the lives of all those around us. It is much more about profound respect and understanding for ourselves of course as well as others. We can often be all too hard on our own failings, but we find it immensely difficult to see situations from the other person's point of view, whether it's in a disagreement with our closest partner, or a fierce argument with a colleague. It is compassion that breeds the *desire to understand* the other person's point of view, even when it is diametrically opposed to our own. I think we could certainly argue that genuine compassion is always in short supply in today's world. The fact is we can't have enough of it.

But knowing about these qualities isn't the same as *experiencing* them is it? I fully accept that those are just verbal descriptions, just a bunch of words you might say. They mean something on the page of course, but inevitably, they convey little of the challenge of putting them into practice. And still less of the richness of the personal experience as you come to realise that these qualities are informing more and more of your life.

But let me leave it there for the moment and move across the tracks to look at the sort of parallel understanding that is coming out of the world of social research, because it offers us a quite different and illuminating perspective on the same issue, how to go about our daily lives most effectively and most creatively.

A brief sideways look at the research

It is remarkable just how much research there has been over the past decade or so, seeking to define what kinds of things make people feel good about themselves and their lives and their relationships; what kinds of things people have in their minds when they talk about a sense of stability, or a general sense of completeness and well-being when they look across the totality of their lives. And that is of course an important point to emphasise, that we are talking about the *totality* of people's lives, the *average* sense of balance and well-being, rather than the inevitable short-term fluctuations from day to day or week to week.

This sort of research has steadily grown from a trickle a decade or so ago, to a veritable avalanche. And I have to say straightaway, that it's a great pity that most of these findings never, or rarely see the light of day, beyond publication in some...for most of us... remote and inaccessible journal such as the *Journal of Behaviour and Social Psychology*, or the *Journal of Applied Psychology* or the *American Journal of Sociology*, to be read by professionals in the field and quoted in their equally erudite papers, later to be published in the same relatively inaccessible journals! It's a great pity because the plain fact is that this research is opening for us a whole new world of insights into what it is that can really make people's lives sing; make them places of joy and satisfaction and fulfilment. Really important stuff therefore for all of us.

Take for example something as seemingly simple as getting people to keep a *gratitude journal*. That means just taking the time once or twice a week to actually *write down* a handful of things that you feel truly grateful for. Pretty simple yes? But several studies reveal that something that simple and easy to do, can give a genuinely powerful and enduring boost to your sense of well-being, And what's more, this highly desirable result seems to hold true, whatever your actual *life circumstances* happen to be at the time. If you think about it, all these people are doing is actually taking the trouble to *express* their gratitude, even if only to themselves!

Other papers, as we've already discussed in an earlier chapter, confirm just how widely positive changes that we manage to achieve in our own life, begin to filter and ripple out into the social and emotional *networks* of which we are a part, but way beyond anything we might reasonably expect to happen. Another group of findings relates to the fact that quite clearly, positive changes in our own *life state,* as Buddhists might express it, an increase in our general sense of well-being, is not in any way limited to our emotional or our mental activities, inside our heads so to speak. It is undoubtedly a *whole body or a whole life* experience. As one of the most prominent and respected researchers in the field has expressed it recently, when we have a deeper and more stable sense of well-being in our lives,

'…we also improve other aspects of our lives – our energy levels, our immune systems, our engagement with work, and with other people, and our physical and mental health. In becoming happier we also bolster our feelings of self-confidence and self-esteem, we come truly to believe that we are worthy human beings, worthy of respect. A final and perhaps least appreciated plus is that if we become happier we benefit not only ourselves, but also our partners, families, communities and even society at large.'[1]

Those are all life-qualities we would dearly wish to achieve for ourselves and others aren't they? So clearly these findings are not dealing with marginal stuff lying somewhere out on the edges of our experience. They touch upon issues that lie right at the *centre of our lives* from day to day, that's the key thing, our ordinary daily lives. And a couple of things strike me particularly as I read through them, which I think are worth noting.

The Buddhist connection

One is that the issues that the scientists and sociologists are writing about, not the language or the phraseology that is

used of course, but the *basic issues themselves*, would be immediately familiar to anyone who regularly attends Buddhist
discussion meeting or seminars, since these are the very issues
that are discussed at such meetings. These are the very qualities that a Buddhist practice is seeking to initiate and nurture
in our lives. Buddhist teachings that is, and these sociological
studies are walking across the same ground, our daily lives,
and expressing very similar ideas about enhancing them.

The second is in many ways even more significant, since
many of the papers emphasise a point that is so often made
in Buddhist teachings, and that most of us, Buddhists or not,
find very hard to grasp or believe in. Namely that we can
create for, ourselves a profound and stable sense of well-
being in our lives, *almost regardless* of the actual circumstances
and events that we happen to be living through. That is, as
I've said, something that is very hard for most of us to believe
in, and the sociologists clearly understand and accept that
enduring difficulty. But nevertheless, as they make clear,
study after study reinforces the conclusion that the actual
circumstances and events in our lives in fact have only a very
small impact on our overall sense of well-being, either up or
down, negative or positive. It seems clear that it is our basic
attitude, or our *approach* to those circumstances that has the
dominant role to play in our on-going life state. In fact so
sure are they of their ground that the scientists are prepared
to put a figure on it!

And before you exclaim in sheer exasperation, just hear
this passage from the research psychologist we've just
quoted from;

*'As significant as our major life events are to each of us, studies
suggest that they actually determine a tiny percentage of our*

happiness...many past investigations reveal that all life circumstances and events put together account for only about 10 percent of how happy different people are...although you may find it hard to believe.'[2]

I have to say at once that I am not in any way personally attached to that ten percent figure and I'm not asking you to become attached to it either. I quote that passage simply to make the point that there clearly are grounds from both long-established Buddhist teachings, and now from objectively, scientifically managed studies, to *encourage* us to challenge our deeply held assumptions and convictions that our life circumstances play *the* major role in our sense of well-being. They don't. As another sociologist puts it boldly in a single sentence,

'We are not simply victims of our situation, or indeed of our past.'[3]

We have to really work hard to understand that the idea we continue to hang onto, that our *circumstances* are the *dominant* aspect of our lives, is a major delusion or misperception on our part. We are free to rise above our circumstances, as soon as we *choose* to do so. And the sociologists and psychologists believe firmly that they now have a much firmer grasp of the values and behaviours that will most readily enable us to achieve that.

So what do the sociologists have to tell us?

So one of the earliest and most often repeated, and in some ways one of the most surprising results for example was that *wealth*, how much money we earn above a certain basic figure, isn't in any way a big, let alone a dominant factor in our basic sense of well-being. So our grandmothers were quite correct in telling us that money can't buy you happiness! Studies throughout the western-way-of-life parts of the world taking in Europe and Japan as well as the USA, spread over *many decades,* and really digging deeply into this issue, have revealed this somewhat surprising fact. It seems that although we all attach so much importance to money, and spend so much effort and energy in seeking to accumulate wealth, as if our very lives depended on it, let alone our well-being, the fact is that once we've secured a stable financial basis for our needs then *additional wealth* seems to have very little to do with how fundamentally happy we are. There's a huge body of research to substantiate this view however much it challenges so many of our deeply held assumptions, and we will look at it in much greater detail in Chapter 11. But to nail it for us for the moment, let me quote just one of the many experienced economists who argues this case so convincingly,

'This is no old wives tale. It is a fact proven by many pieces of scientific research…all the evidence says that on average people are no happier today than people were fifty years ago. Yet at the same time average incomes have more than doubled. This paradox is equally true for the United States and Britain and Japan.'[4]

But when the psychologists and sociologists move on to describe the kinds of values and behaviour that they've identified as the source of a profound sense of well-being, and confidence, and stability in people, the sorts of qualities that enable people and indeed societies to live and work harmoniously and productively, it immediately becomes apparent just how closely they *echo and mirror* the kinds of values and behaviour that lie at the very heart of Buddhist teachings.

Altruism

Very high on the list for example, they recognise the powerful happiness-effect within our own lives of a compassionate and altruistic approach to life, of developing a fundamentally contributing and giving approach to life rather than a taking and consuming one. So many studies show that even quite small altruistic gestures, simply offering a smile for example, or a helping hand or a word of encouragement on the spur of the moment, they all bring a sense of warmth and connectedness that lasts well beyond the fleeting moment of the event itself. When we give freely of our time and energy in concerning ourselves more deeply with the needs and anxieties of others rather than concentrating, as we so easily tend to do, on our own current problems, it's been shown that this level of altruism can change fundamentally the way we feel about *our own* lives. It delivers a huge boost to our own sense of self-worth and the ultimate value of our lives. Buddhism of course has always taught that exerting ourselves in this way, focusing *outwards* rather than *inwards*, on other people's needs rather than our own, can lead to the most rapid growth in our own inner strength and resourcefulness. Now, as the sociologists describe it, such an outward looking, *giving* approach to life, triggers a cascade of positive effects.

So even though evolutionary biologists have a really hard time of it, trying to put together a meaningful evolutionary explanation for the operation of altruism among human beings, today's psychologists don't have the slightest doubt about the powerfully enriching, harmonising, value-creating contribution it can make to all our lives. And an immensely valuable aspect of altruism of course is giving up our need to *criticise*, criticising people, things, events, anything that we just don't happen to like, or that is in some way *different from* ourselves. Simply giving up the need to criticise has a powerful liberating effect.

Gratitude

Altruism is close to gratitude and there is much discussion in the research findings of the remarkable *transforming* power of a spirit of gratitude,[5] unlocking as it has been described, a whole basketful of positive and beneficial effects for the giver as well as the receiver, and indeed for anyone who happens to be within earshot. It's clear that building a strong dimension of gratitude into our lives is very good news indeed. Just going out of our way for example, to express our gratitude to someone has been shown to have a positive effect on our sense of well-being for days after the event itself. But it's important, the researchers point out, to recognise that gratitude goes well beyond simply saying thank you to someone for help or support. They talk about it as a much broader, *whole-life* attitude to the way we take each day; about having for example a keen and lively sense of *appreciation* for all the ordinary things of life, not taking things for granted, recognising all that *we have* as opposed to focusing on what we don't happen to have. Gratitude if you like as an essential element in the way we experience everything that happens to us.

And it's in this sense I would argue, that it chimes most closely with the Buddhist description of gratitude, as being absolutely fundamental to a positive life state. A sense of gratitude if you like literally *drives out* negative thoughts. You can't be grateful and negative at the same time. Indeed the social scientists make a great deal of this idea in their work, talking of gratitude being 'incompatible with' negative emotions such as anger and resentfulness. One psychologist actually describes it in that way, *'Gratitude helps people cope with stress and trauma'[6]* she writes.

So clearly gratitude is a hugely powerful and valuable quality to nurture in our lives, which once again, is a powerful conjunction of views between the scientist and the Buddhist.

Focusing on strengths rather than weaknesses

The researchers talk of the immense value of coming to know more clearly what our real *strengths* are, and being completely honest to ourselves about our *weaknesses,* which is essential they argue, in developing a far more effective life strategy. Far better they say, to focus our energies and our plans around our strengths, rather than being constantly anxious about our weaknesses, or beating ourselves up over them, or worse, trying to paper over them.

That rings true doesn't it? We know full well that we often devote so much time and energy *worrying about,* and trying somehow to *compensate for* our weaknesses, that it deflects us from what we really want to achieve for ourselves. Whereas we are much better placed in building our lives around what we know we are good at, and where we have a strong base of self-confidence. This immensely practical kind of self-knowledge is one of the things that Buddhism is referring to when it talks about our *innate wisdom,* or being true to ourselves. It's our honesty with ourselves that enables us to respond more capably and more creatively to the events we encounter in all the various sectors of our life. It can certainly have the most powerful underlying effect on our sense of confidence and self-worth, since we all want to be seen and valued as capable and resourceful people.

Professor Ruut Veenhoven for example, from Erasmus University in Rotterdam, one of the most highly respected teachers in this field, talks of the immense value of this kind of utterly practical, down-to-earth self-awareness. He argues that one of the least talked about secrets of a sense of well-being, is learning to be comfortable with who we are, and what our qualities are; as he puts it, *learning to love the life we have.*[7] It's a view that ties in so closely with what we have just been talking about, in relation to gratitude and appreciation for what we *have,* as opposed to spending our energies yearning for what we simply *want.*

Living in the now

Indeed when you think about it, all these qualities that the sociologists describe as being fundamental to a stable sense of well-being, are all closely related; altruism and compassion, being compassionate to ourselves in the sense of focusing on our strengths rather than beating ourselves up over our weaknesses, and this, trying to grasp the value of *the moment.* You might think at first glance that we have Buddhist teachers talking, but they are genuine sociologists, and they talk, at some length and in great detail, about the importance for all of us of learning to live in the now, making the very most of *this* moment, this piece of work, *this* moment of relaxation in a summer garden, *this* conversation…the person who is standing in front of you now is *for this moment,* the most important person in your life. Rather than, as is so often the case, just *passing through* this activity we're involved in, sometimes almost oblivious of it, far too busy or too anxious to grasp it or savour it, because we're on the way to something else. We find ourselves so often wrapped up in anxieties about something that has *happened already,* which we allow to go on spinning around inside our head, or thinking in anticipation of something that will *happen later on,* or tomorrow, or the next day.

When you think about it even momentarily, what you *choose* to notice, what you *choose* to pay attention to, *is* your experience. That is to say, *it is your life.* Or as Eckhart Tolle has expressed it,

'Do I want the present moment to be my friend or my enemy. The present moment is inseparable from life, so you are really deciding what kind of relationship you want to have with life.'[8]

In both cases, it takes us back directly to the lesson that lies at the heart of a Buddhist practice, that we have the *choice.* The *cause* that we make in paying attention to the now of our lives, delivers the *effect* of an altogether richer life experience.

Try it. I'm an extremely active person, indeed overactive, always in too much of a hurry. But I've made real efforts in this past half dozen or so years, to *slow down,* which is the way I express it to myself, in order to experience whatever I'm doing from moment to moment. It's difficult of course. With our hugely active and restless minds it's not a skill that comes easily to us. There is so much stuff coming at us from all directions with our adrenaline-fuelled modern lifestyles. And we can feel considerable guilt if we *don't* go on thinking about that list of uncompleted jobs, or the difficult e-mail we haven't responded to, or the up-coming interview, or that errand we promised to run.

But then, lots of things of value are difficult to fold into our lives. Once we are aware of it, we can undoubtedly learn how to get better at it, and the reward is huge, and growing. It is a genuine life skill. In fact it's interesting that in his recent book, *Flourish*, which is devoted precisely to this issue of how we can enrich and deepen our sense of well-being, Martin Seligman writes on what he calls, '*the virtue of slowness,*'

'*Mental speed comes at a cost. I found myself missing nuances and taking shortcuts when I should have taken the mental equivalent of a deep breath. I found myself skimming and scanning when I should have been reading every word. I found myself listening poorly to others. I would figure out where they were headed after their first few sentences and then interrupt. And I was anxious a lot of the time. – speed and anxiety go together.*'[9]

I think we can all immediately recognise the essential truth of that. We've all taken those shortcuts, and given only half our attention to what's being said. And having been there, I'm just as sure that we can recognise the benefit we would gain from an increased awareness that where we are *right now*, is a pretty good place to be focusing our attention on.

Having meaningful goals

We all need meaningful goals or directions that are bigger and wider than the simple daily progression of our lives. Things that we have to put real effort and energy into trying to achieve, so that we are completely aware that this activity is stretching us, and lifting us up out of our normal comfort zone. Settling down into that comfort zone can become a powerfully restricting habit, to the extent that we develop not just a strong resistance to setting higher goals or targets for ourselves, but even a kind of *fear*, a fear of failure or of rejection, that becomes strong enough to prevent us from attempting anything vaguely testing.

There's plenty of research to show that if we can build this desire, this *willingness to set goals and targets* for ourselves, to the extent that it becomes part and parcel of our lives, with real commitment in making the determination, and real resolution in sticking to it and putting it into effect, then it can spill over into many other areas of our lives, even if they are completely unrelated areas, such as our social and partner relationships and career success and so on. It seems that the sheer *discipline* of setting the goal, and the *perseverance* required into making something of it, act as a sort of catalyst to trigger these beneficial spill-over effects into other areas of our lives.

What has all that to do with Buddhism you might ask? Well a Buddhist practice is precisely about stretching people and lifting them up, about encouraging and challenging ourselves to set goals and determinations for what we really want to achieve out of life. That's an easy thing to say of course, it rolls smoothly enough off the tongue, but it takes real commitment and real application to achieve it. The daily practice is there to help us get better at summoning up that application and that effort. In one sense that is its very point, it is a structured discipline, a structured training programme to help us achieve more.

The connected life

Which brings us to the last and undoubtedly one of the most significant of this little clutch of life-strategies that we have been discussing; we might perhaps call it *the connected life*, because that is the very strong theme that comes out of so much of the research; the importance of a sense of connectedness or engagement as it's often described, a real sense of involvement in the lives of family and friends and colleagues and communities, as a constant reminder of our wider humanity. This turns out to be in many ways *the* fundamental constituent in a well-balanced and happy life. The evolutionary biologists tell us that we are in our deepest nature a *co-operating* animal, that we survive and flourish because of our ability to live and work and co-operate in family and social groups. As Sam Harris puts it in *The Moral Landscape,*

'There may be nothing more important than human cooperation... Cooperation is the stuff of which meaningful human lives and viable societies are made.'[10]

The positive psychologists too tell us something very similar,

'The centrality of social connections to our health and well-being cannot be overstressed.'[11]

What they are telling us is that when we do manage to build or experience these harmonious relationships they don't simply make us feel good about our lives, they seem to buttress and reinforce all our *creative energies* so that we feel released or set free so to speak, and empowered to pursue many other fulfilling activities and objectives in our lives.

And it is even greater than that. The strength of our social connections, the levels of altruism and compassion and willingness to support others, are absolutely decisive factors in how whole communities function. In some of their most recent research for example, sociologists such as Robert Sampson from Harvard have identified a quality that they label the *'enduring neighbourhood effect,'* which determines not simply how communities are able to surmount and recover from major crises such as the Japanese earthquake and tsunami of 2011, and the perfect storm that struck New York in 2012, but how neighbourhoods are able to deal with what he calls, *'everyday challenges'* such as anti-social behaviour.[12]

So our connectedness, our engagement, is clearly a crucial factor in the quality of all our everyday life.

How does all that relate to Buddhism?

That is an all too brief exposition of just some of the important findings that have come from a truly vast amount of social research over the past dozen or so years.[13] It's worth adding perhaps that whenever I raise one or other of these points as a theme say for a group discussion or a seminar, very often the general response is … *'Well it's pretty much plain common sense isn't it? If you have even a few of those qualities in your life, then you're pretty much bound to be happy, they are so positive and reinforcing.'*

What that's doing of course, is simply recognising the validity of the research. But let's be absolutely clear what we do have here. We have modern social scientists, defining in great detail the kinds of *values,* the kinds of *choices,* the kinds of *behaviour* that they now have not the slightest doubt, enhance people's lives. They also make it clear that their work represents a very substantial *addition to our understanding* of what it is that makes people feel good about their own lives, and what kinds of values and modes of behaviour help people and societies work harmoniously and creatively together. And that's what we all want don't we, when it comes down to it? We want to live in peaceful, cooperative and supportive societies, in which people genuinely care about what happens to their neighbour, and fully respect the lives of others.

The key point I would want to make is the sheer *extent of the overlap*, the similarities and the echoes between what Buddhism has been teaching for so long, and the findings of these modern sociologists and psychologists. As I've said before, it's important of course *not* to put it any stronger than that, not to draw too many parallels or inferences. Certainly we shouldn't adopt the research as a sort of *scientific scaffolding* around any particular Buddhist perception, because it patently isn't.

What the research does it seems to me however is to open up a whole series of immensely interesting and illuminating new perspectives, when we are discussing things of the very greatest moment to all of us. What do we really mean when we are talking about happiness in this life, or about creating value in our relationships? Or when we are trying to answer that profound question, how should I live?

It can only be immensely heartening, immensely confirming to any practising Buddhist, to learn that the kinds of answers that modern sociologists are coming up with, are so close to the kinds of values and principles and modes of behaviour that lie at the very heart of a Buddhist approach to life.

But what difference does it make?
In many ways that remarkable conjunction of views reminds us of Einstein's insightful dictum offered so many years ago,

'*Science without religion is lame, religion without science is blind.*'

Even today that statement represents perhaps the most concise and the most powerful expression of the fact that we all need contributions from both.

Science that is, can provide the objective discipline and the method to observe aspects of human behaviour and motivation, right across societies. Religion, Buddhism in this case, with its great body of understanding about the workings of human nature built up over many centuries, can gain not just encouragement and support, but wholly *new perspectives* from the insights that science can now provide. So it is potentially a very rich and fruitful combination of views. And by no means is it just of theoretical or academic significance. Far from it. It has I would argue, huge implications for the future of society. Why do I say that?

We are all deeply concerned, fearful even, about the fact that we live in a time of great turbulence and turmoil, and much of that turmoil is down to violence across religious boundaries. Indeed the violence of inter-religious conflict is without doubt, one of the greatest and most challenging issues of our age. And no one seems to be able to offer any meaningful way forward, let alone anything resembling a resolution. It might seem somewhat fanciful to suggest that Buddhism can offer a strategy for tackling these widespread and seemingly insuperable problems, but that is precisely the *promise* that Buddhism holds out. It represents in a very real sense, the ultimate goal of Buddhist practice. Since Buddhism is not attached to any definition of divinity, it doesn't have *any boundaries*. As we've seen, nothing and no one is excluded. It doesn't have that is, the boundaries across which so much of modern conflict takes place. The only qualification is to be a member of the human race.

The Charter of UNESCO contains a sentiment that echoes to the very heartbeat of the Buddhist vision of a world firmly in the grip of peace. The Charter reads,

'...since wars begin in the minds of men, it is in the minds of men that the defence of peace must be constructed'[13]

Buddhism might well add the words, *individual by* individual, because that, it argues, is how it must begin, in the *minds* of countless individuals. Put simply Buddhism teaches that at any particular time, the environment we find ourselves in is, in large measure, a *reflection* of our subjective life state at that time. If we are in an angry, destructive, aggressive frame of mind, that will be reflected back at us from the reactions of those around us, and from the situations that arise. If on the other hand our life state is high and our approach is consistently optimistic and value-creating, then, Buddhism argues, that will flow out into our environment and have an influence on people we encounter, and the way that situations around us evolve.

I would argue that that claim, huge as it is, fits in completely with our common experience. Even without the recent research we discussed a little earlier, we are aware that both pessimism and optimism are highly infectious. We all prefer to live our lives surrounded by positive, optimistic people. We all find that our energies are sapped and our enthusiasms are extinguished by being amongst those who are persistently pessimistic. And similarly, we are commonly disturbed and can get worked up in all sorts of ways, by being among those who are persistently aggressive or combative.

We can make a difference if we choose to do so

The Buddhist argument is that this understanding that we do, in large measure, *create* our own environment, essentially holds good even when it is scaled up to the level of society, and beyond, to the society of nations. Although at first glance that might seem a somewhat difficult position to accept, we only have to cast around in recent history, in Europe for example, or the Middle East, to find countless examples to suggest that something very similar is taking place; that a nation will find reflected back from its environment, the aggression for example that it projects.

One could certainly argue that the past 100 years has been a clear demonstration of just such a circumstance. It has been described as the bloodiest century in human history, as the cycles of aggression and revenge among nations have been *reflected back* time and time again. Over 70 million people have been killed in wars of one kind or another, estimated by historians as being a greater number than in all previous centuries put together. And yet, despite the world wide suffering and massive destruction, it's quite clear that history, in the sense of human experience, has provided precious few strategies *to break* this cycle. Certainly not diplomacy, and sadly it seems, not the United Nations. At least not yet. There have been over 200 wars since the last great global confla-gration, and today the world bristles with more and vastly more powerful, death-dealing weapons than ever before.

If you take into account also the emergence of the 24 hour news machine that wakes us up and puts us to bed, with stories of violence and disaster from one corner of the globe or another, then you can clearly see the reasons for the sense of *powerlessness and impotence,* that can infect the lives of so many of us. We can grieve in sympathy, or we can give a few pounds to this charity or to that relief organisation, but what else can we do?

Buddhism's immediate response is to say that we can look at the environs *of our own lives,* because that is where change starts, with countless *individuals*. With individuals determining to take responsibility for their own lives, and setting out to develop the courage and the optimism, the compassion and the wisdom, to have a value-creating and positive and peaceful effect upon the lives of those around them.

As Daisaku Ikeda once again reminds us with absolute clarity of vision, *'no one is born…hating others.'*[14]

The great vision

So the Buddhist vision is one of growing numbers of people *seizing* the opportunity…and that word seizing is important, because it does express that element of positively *taking hold* of something that you have come across in your life, rather than simply letting it pass you by… growing numbers of people seizing the opportunity to create this transformation in their own lives, not simply for their own sake, but for the sake of their families and friends and colleagues and all those in the wider circle of their lives. Then indeed we could come to see a *cumulative* change, in the way groups and communities and societies and eventually nations function. It is of course a journey of great vision, and its distant objective is immense…nothing less than peace and harmony in our troubled world.

But the constant Buddhist argument is that it is not a journey that is in any way *remote or inaccessible*. We can all choose to join it, since it starts really at our own feet. Peace, as Buddhism puts it…*begins with me*. And as bold as that sounds, it happens to be a view that has been shared by many great and inspirational leaders down the years, from Ghandi and Martin Luther King to Nelson Mandela and John F. Kennedy. Kennedy chose deliberately, in his Commencement Address at the very beginning of his presidency, to make clear his personal vision of what a bold and positive approach to conflict might deliver. He declared then,

'First examine our attitude towards peace itself. Too many of us think it impossible, too many think it unreal, but that is a dangerous, defeatist belief. It leads to the conclusion that war is inevitable, that mankind is doomed, that we are gripped by forces we cannot control. We need not accept that view. Our problems are man-made, therefore they can be solved by man, and man can be as big as he wants. No problem of human destiny is beyond human beings. Man's reason and spirit have often solved the seemingly impossible, and we believe we can do it again.'[15]

It is a vision and a message that unquestionably continues to resonate in all our lives today. Buddhism too would argue that *'We need not accept that view. Our problems are man made therefore they can be solved by man...'* with each one of us making the determination to create peace in his or her own sphere.

CHAPTER NINE

Buddhism and Negativity

In taking up this practice we are in a sense being invited to take part in what could be described as a huge on-going experiment. We are the focus of the experiment you might say, and our life is the test bed. Practice we are told without being begrudging or half-hearted about it. Give it a sincere and committed trial. And then look for the changes in your life. Put simply the change we are seeking is to shift our whole life towards the positive end of the spectrum. And as we do that, so the promise is, we are also changing our environment. As *we* change, as we move away from a basically self-centred life state say, with it's concentration on our own needs and our own ego, towards a more compassionate and responsive approach to others…which was, I like to think, very much my own progression…so we find those qualities increasingly reflected back at us from our environment. The challenges and the problems are no less frequent or severe. Why should they be, since Buddhism is real life, not magic? It cannot simply sweep life's normal flow of problems away. The fundamental change lies in the *clarity* with which we perceive them, and the strengthened ability to respond to them *positively*.

The clarity is an important factor. Indeed Nichiren describes one of the main benefits of the practice as being the greater clarity of perception it brings; what he describes as a purification of the senses. But what does that mean exactly? The fact is that many utterly feet-on-the- ground people who practice, talk for example of seeing opportunities in their environment that they hadn't previously noticed, or of seeing problems arising at an earlier stage when they can more easily be resolved. They often talk of their life seeming to *run more smoothly* for them, or of being in the right place at the right time. Pure coincidence you might say? Possibly. Of course there's nothing resembling research to *prove* anything either way, and nor would we reasonably expect there to be, but that's not really the point is it? We're talking about how people *feel* about their lives. The fact is that many people express this sense of a greater stability in their lives, no longer so frequently blown of course by tough stuff that comes out of left field, able to make positive choices and decisions more readily, because they had a clearer sense of an objective or direction.

There can be a profound change too in terms of hopes and ambitions and expectations, what we are prepared to *demand* from our lives. It's frequently the case for example that we have allowed ourselves to make huge compromises, to come to terms with a situation or a set of circumstances, despite the fact that deep down we know the situation is unsatisfactory, or even the cause of a great deal of stress or unhappiness in our lives. It might be a job that offers no real opportunity for our talents, or for advancement, a relationship that we have neglected, or a family situation that has become filled with conflict. Through fear or apathy or lack of courage, or simply because we can't think how to initiate change without causing a rupture, we swallow it, we learn to live with these sorts of situations dominating our lives, often for year after year.

As we all know, few things are quite as difficult as bringing about *real, enduring change* in our behaviour or attitudes. It has taken our lifetime to build them up. So it's bound to take real energy and determination and courage to set out to change them. Above all, perhaps, we need *hope,* a real sense that things *can be changed.* And that is precisely the role that the Buddhist practice can play. One of the statements most commonly made about it for example, and one that embedded itself in my mind very early on in my practice, was that when you are faced with a profoundly difficult situation, and have no real idea where to turn, when you start to chant about it, '*as if out of nowhere…comes hope.*'

Of course it isn't out of nowhere, it's from *within.* And it does indeed come when you disengage yourself from the immediate situation or crisis, and just allow yourself the *space* to chant and to rethink. And so often it delivers to us the initial energy and the courage that we need to take decisive action to begin that process of change.

But what about doubts and negativity?

That's all very well, I can hear you say, for those who are fortunate enough to have profound conviction in the practice. But what about those who have doubts? There are many Buddhist commentaries that tell us we should never have doubts. I don't personally see how that is possible since doubts are a normal part of all our lives, just as negativity is inherent in all our lives. Although it is very important to recognise that they are not at all the same thing. We need to examine the cause of the doubt of course, but doubts breed caution, and there is nothing wrong with a bit of caution in a dangerous world. As I've written elsewhere, we might want to call it *prudence,* if that were not such a desperately un-cool word in the 21st Century lexicon!

But negativity is wholly different matter. Negativity can disarm us, or render us completely incapable of action. It can tell us for example that a Buddhist practice may well be able to deal with *other* people's problems, but not *this* one, not the one that happens to have broken its way into *our* life. Because, our negativity tells us, because this one's totally different, or particularly deep-rooted, or because it involves a particularly intractable situation. Our own problems always seem to have a *uniquely* difficult twist to them. There is never any shortage of costumes for us to dress our negativity in.

We all have a negative voice

The psychologists tell us that we all talk to ourselves pretty much all the time. In a sort of on-going dialogue of reasoning with ourselves, and rehearsing and working things over in our mind, we hold this constant inner, ruminating conversation with ourselves. In fact it is so much a part of our life that we tend take this inner whispering voice or voices completely for granted. But one of those voices is a *negative* one, a powerful advocate for *not* doing things, for *not* challenging our situation, for *not* making the effort, because… well, what's the point…we can't win this time.

That modern psychological understanding is very much in keeping with the Buddhist perception of human nature, that we all have a negative side to our personality, to some degree, even those of us who are blessed with the sunniest and most positive of temperaments. Indeed Buddhism teaches that we will *always* have it as a fundamental part of our humanity, however positive the spirit we learn to develop and maintain. And as we know from our personal experience, let alone from Buddhist teachings, it *is* indeed one of our potential life states, lurking there if you like, always ready to take over if we have a low life state. Although we don't tend to describe it openly and directly as our *negativity*. We talk instead about being a bit *low,* or a bit *down*, or feeling less confident and capable at this particular moment, or uncertain or unwilling to challenge this particular situation.

Feeling a bit low seems to be a common experience

Many people talk about their negativity getting up with them in the morning, because that's when it can so often occur. People often say for example that early mornings are a kind of low point for them, when they have to struggle to lift themselves out of a hole. Hence perhaps the global addiction to the regular morning pick-me-up fix of caffeine. But it's not just the mornings is it? There are many times when it can stick around all day. Indeed it seems that to feel generally *'a bit low'* is quite a common experience for many of us these days. Psychologists talk for example about a general, low-level, background anxiety as being one of the features of our time. The psychologist Daniel Goleman for example has dubbed our time, *the age of melancholy*, because there seems to be more depression about than in previous generations.

Even Martin Seligman, the boundlessly optimistic, founding father of the positive psychology movement in the US, comments strongly on this particular aspect of modern society in the West. He writes,

'Why do anxiety, anger and sadness pervade so much of our lives, - concurrent with so much success, wealth and the absence of biological need in the lives of privileged Americans?'

For Americans in that passage, you can of course include all of us who live in the ultra-privileged western-way-of-life parts of the world. He goes on to explain,

'People by and large, are astonishingly attracted to the catastrophic (that is to say the negative) *interpretation of things. Not just neurotics, not just depressives…but most of us, much of the time.'*[1]

Those are indeed broadly inclusive phrases he chooses to use,*'People by and large,'* and,*'most of us, much of the time.'* But if we take them at face value, it would seem that lots of people share in this generalised, low-level anxiety we've been talking about. It is I believe a very significant perception that is being passed on to us, almost you might say, as a wake-up call.

And if we dig a bit deeper, and ask ourselves *why* this might be the case, why are we so inclined to interpret events in a negative way, at least part of the explanation might lie in the fact that this negative voice *knows us* infinitely well. We have no hiding place. It knows all our weaknesses and our vulnerabilities…because of course *it is* us. So it can frame the arguments it whispers into our ear, to match precisely those weaknesses and vulnerabilities. And if we let it, it can go on sniping and whittling away at our self-confidence and our courage for much of the day, constantly taking advantage of those half-formed inner stirrings of doubt and fear and uncertainty, that we scarcely admit to ourselves. So it knows precisely for example *why* we won't succeed in this or that endeavour, *why* we won't get the job, or the praise, or the promotion, or those exam grades we desperately need, or whatever it is that happens to be uppermost in our thoughts.

When we are strong and confident with a *high life state,* or when we've just had a victory, we can often just brush this web of insidious sniping aside, and laugh at it, or ignore it into silence. But when we are down, with a *low life state,* or we've just had a rejection, and particularly when we know full well that what we are reaching for this time is a *real stretch*, then it can often be all that is needed, to tip us into a powerfully negative or defeatist frame of mind.

And as we've seen from the social research we've discussed earlier, that doesn't just affect *us,* it can infect all those around us. And if that pattern is repeated often enough... this time and last time and the time before that...it can stay with us to become what Buddhism describes as a *dominant life tendency*, a habitual mind-set.

And that can be truly life-changing in a negative way. Life can become, *'there's no point in even trying,'* rather than, *'I really think I can make a go of this.'*

Negativity is as real as rocks

The key point towards which this discussion is leading is a greater *clarity.* That's where we started out if you remember, the crucial importance of clarity, or self awareness; a much clearer understanding and awareness of something that may well sit right out on the margins of our consciousness. Because however prevalent it is, we don't spend much time *talking about* the negative side of our make-up do we? But Buddhism argues that in order to recognise it, and combat it effectively, we need to be absolutely *clear-eyed* about just how powerful and damaging an influence in our lives this negativity can be. Indeed it talks about our being involved in combating it on a *daily basis*, hence the daily-ness of the practice.

Negativity that is, *is real*, it's as real as rocks, it's just made of different stuff!

And just to underline how real that point is, in case you find it hard to believe, I came across something in the research recently that really took my breath away. In fact I would have rejected it, were it not for the fact that it occurs in an account with absolutely impeccable academic credentials.[2] That something is called the *Losada Ratio,* named after a psychologist Marcel Losada, who apparently established the underlying facts. Basically it is the *ratio* between the *negative* words or phrases and the *positive* ones, that occur in the regular communications between individuals or groups of people. What took my breath away was that when researchers went into the field and actually looked at *the implications* of this ratio, the results were astounding.

The Losada Ratio

One research group for example was allowed into business meetings across a wide range of sixty or so companies. What they did was, on the face of it, quite simple, quite mechanical even. They transcribed everything that was said at a series of business meetings. Everything. They then worked out the ratio of negative words and phrases to the positive ones. And the implications were startling even to them, because they found that there was a sharp *cut off point.* In those companies where there was a clear majority of positive comments to negative ones between the managers, to get precise about it, about *three positive comments* to every negative one, those companies were flourishing. At anything below that ratio, *less than three positive comments* to every negative one, the companies were ailing in varying degrees. That startling finding is now used at a number of management training courses. If that surprises you as much as it surprised me, it doesn't end there.

John Gottman for example is one of America's leading researchers into marriage, exploring and explaining what it is that makes for a successful marriage or partnership, and what leads to marriages or partnerships breaking up. He can spend whole weekends with couples observing how they talk and relate to each other. He too has applied the same Losada ratio in studying how partners communicate with each other. And…wait for it…he has come up with almost exactly the same observation. He has found that where there are *less than* about three positive communications for every negative one, then the relationship is heading for trouble.[3] In fact he argues that you need at least *five* positive comments to every negative, one to be confident of having a strong and enduring relationship.

I said that you might find this piece of research astounding, and it surely is. But what it illustrates above all I suggest is just how *unaware* we can be of the negative elements in our behaviour and our conversations, and just how powerful the implications of that *mindless* negativity can be for our relationships.

Most of us I'm sure, won't have been aware of anything so specific as the Losada ratio, but if we think about it even briefly, we can all recall some experience of how this kind of *subliminal negativity* can affect us in everyday life. As we've mentioned, we can all recognise at once the huge difference that exists between the positive, optimistic, hope-filled colleague we happen to know at work, who gets things done and inspires others to get things done, even in the most challenging circumstances, and the opposite, the destructive, paralysing effect even a single negatively-inclined colleague can have.

So how does Buddhism help?
So too our own negativity, when it is not *recognised* and resisted and overcome, can have a powerfully destructive

effect, not just on our own lives, but on the lives of all those around us, all those whom our life touches. And as we now know from the social research,[4] the ripples of that effect do spread further afield, to touch the lives of *their* friends and colleagues too. And that word *'recognised'* is obviously crucial, because, as Buddhism argues, it is the recognition above all else, our growing *awareness* if you like, of what is going on, that leads us to take positive action. It is only by being constantly *vigilant* and *mindful* of the reality of our negativity, and its potential influence on our life state, that we are able to go into battle against it, and so begin the process of change, to establish control over the negative functions in our life.

It's not easy of course, nor ever wholly won. As I've mention-ed, Buddhism often presents the battle against negativity as a *daily* encounter, one of the main reasons for the discipline of the daily practice, to help us summon up our optimistic and positive spirit and to drive out the negativity. And it's important to be clear, that being optimistic definitely does not mean, being *unrealistic.* So it does not mean *denying* the existence of the negative, or just pushing away any unfavourable information that comes at us. It doesn't mean constantly trying to control situations that simply cannot be controlled. It does mean applying *effort,* making a conscious effort to make that *difficult* positive choice, rather than that *easier* negative one. Our optimism that is has to be broad enough and deep enough to embrace the *sad and the painful and the suffering,* as well as the joyful.

However hard it may be to achieve, it is undoubtedly a strategy that works. As I write this I am just emerging from a battle with cancer that has gone on over the past three years. I can now hopefully, joyfully, use the past tense, because

I've come through to the other side, I've just been signed off by my consultant! So I can now say it *was* a battle that involved me in a fair bit of physical and mental pain. But the key point I want to make is that as soon as I became aware of the cancer's existence, so too I became aware of my ability to *embrace* it as part of my life. An unwelcome part, but nonetheless *part of me,* and by embracing it I felt enabled to fight it *positively,* rather than be fearful of it. And all the time I was keenly aware that my stable optimism about life, my overall sense of well-being, was not dependent on only good things happening to me.

As Psychology Professor Tal Ben Shahar, has put it in his book *The Pursuit of the Perfect,*[5] being optimistic isn't about being eternally, smilingly cheerful. We need above all to *get real* he argues, and that would be hugely unreal. It's about building our sense of hope and optimism, literally by turning *towards* and *embracing* our pains and our problems, as a normal part of our life, rather than turning away from them.

What is remarkable is just how closely that advice mirrors the sentiment expressed by Nichiren Daishonin in one of his down-to-earth letters to his followers, so long ago;

'Suffer what there is to suffer, enjoy what there is to enjoy. Regard both suffering and joy as facts of life, and continue chanting Nam myoho renge kyo, no matter what happens.'[6]

So we learn, it's only by getting up close to our problems that we can truly understand them. And only by trying to look for the *seeds* of the positive, even in things that go badly wrong, rather than being eaten up by the negative effects, that we can transform them.

As I've mentioned on several occasions because it made such a strong impression on me, one of the things that struck me when I first began to go to Buddhist seminars and meetings, was the powerful sense of optimism, even when people were talking about all kinds of everyday hassles and problems. Life for these people clearly was about *getting real*. About seeing the problems for what they were, and challenging them, rather than being cast down by them. Ordinary people that is, with ordinary everyday problems, learning to see life differently, though the focusing lens of a Buddhist practice. And you can see how that approach makes it possible to establish a sort of *self-reinforcing,* win-win process in our lives; the more we recognise and overcome the negativity, the weaker it becomes, and the stronger becomes our optimism and our hope.

And the greatness of a Buddhist practice, in my experience, is precisely that, its immense *practicality*. It delivers into our hands a method that has enabled all sorts of ordinary people, from every possible personality type, and background and walk of life, to achieve just a slight shift in perspective... from negative to positive. Not a revolution, just that slight shift in perspective, and strange as it may seem, that is all that is needed. It may only be a slight change, but time and time again it proves to be enough to help us to embrace the problem, or handle the anxiety with an optimistic outlook, that then leads on to tangible positive outcomes.

But what does Buddhism have to say about that extreme form of negativity that breaks into all our lives, all too frequently... that we know as anger?

Chapter Ten

Buddhism and Anger

Buddhism has always had a very clear-eyed view of anger. Although it is only too well aware of the powerfully destructive potential of this emotion, that can wreak all kinds of havoc in human affairs, it doesn't simply lament its presence, and condemn its damaging effects. Rather it *accepts* it precisely for what it is, an integral part of what it is to be human, a deeply embedded part of the human psyche that will always be with us. We simply have to *learn* how to live with it and to limit the damage that it can cause in our lives. As one Buddhist mentor put it to me very early on in my practice, '*Anger is very much akin to cow pats...best handled when cold!*'

Homespun wisdom perhaps, but nonetheless very wise, and what is perhaps more surprising, its truth is amply borne out by modern social research!

So Buddhism tells us, we need to recognise that it *will* be there in our lives, and it's only being prudent to learn more about what kind of emotion it is, where it comes from, and how best to set about handling it. And modern psychology takes very much the same long view of anger, namely that it is very much a part of our common humanity.

'Your anger has a long history, one that goes back before your childhood and before your parents' childhoods. It goes back to the life-and-death struggles of your early human ancestors, and further still to our primate ancestors and their forebears…the human capacity for anger is one of the principal reasons why we - and not some other primate line - are the dominant species on earth.'[1]

So there it is, buried deep in our primitive evolutionary roots with a *positive* role to play, and now we have to learn how to handle its destructive potential, in our ever more crowded, fast-moving, shoulder-to-shoulder modern societies. But that particular insight helps us to *embrace* our anger if I may put it that way, because we do need to embrace it as an integral part of our lives, if we are going to understand it more completely, and avoid or overcome the damage it can cause. It also I think, helps us understand what psychologists tell us is one of the most frequent triggers for outbursts of anger; the feeling, rightly or wrongly, that *'I am being trespassed against.'* Trespass in all sorts of ways, being treated unjustly or rudely or being insulted, or very often just a feeling that one's self esteem or dignity is being threatened.

With anger as we know, things can get out of hand so quickly that we may not have any conscious realisation of that thought, but we are told, the thought of trespass is surely lurking there somewhere, and the anger is a sort of counter-attack, to bring the trespass to an end. And simply understanding that point, that this might well be a *perceived* rather than a *real* challenge to our self esteem, can really help us to control our response.[2]

The ten states of mind
Buddhism describes Anger as being one of the ten life states that we all experience on a day-to-day basis. This is not the

place to plunge too deeply into that Buddhist concept, but it is essential to our understanding, so I have added a detailed account of the ten life states, and the important role they occupy in Nichiren Buddhism as an appendix. (Appendix A) But very briefly, the concept of the Ten Worlds as it's often called, or the ten life states, is an analysis of the dynamics of daily human life. It sets out to describe for us in a way that is systematic, and therefore *practical and useful*…that is absolutely the key purpose…something that we all experience, but that we take so much for granted that we rarely give it a moments thought. That something is the extraordinary moment-to-moment *change-ability* in our state of mind as we go about our daily lives. We all know that our life state, or how we feel, changes constantly throughout the day, triggered by the constant flux of thoughts within, and the stream of events we encounter without, so rapid is the mind's response to every stimulus. Every hour can be different, every minute, at times every second, so swift is the ability of the mind to respond to what is going on within our heads, and round about us.

Buddhism argues that the first step in sharpening our *awareness* of what is going on in our lives, and so managing our lives more effectively, is to have a much clearer picture of these shifting mental states. So it offers us a series of what you might call *mini-portraits* of each of them, that we can look at and mull over and take on board.

Why ten? Good question. The short answer is that it passes the all-important test of *practicality*. If there were 50 or 100 life states say, it would become wholly unwieldy and impractical as a way of thinking about our lives. Moreover, it has undoubtedly survived the most challenging test of all, the test of *time*, and remained an immensely useful idea that we can go on using in our daily living today.

The Buddhist view of anger

So Buddhism describes anger as a life state in which our life can be dominated not simply by the external manifestations of anger, all that shouting and threatening and the storms of temper…we've all been there many times…but by the constant over-bearing demands of our own ego. Because at it's heart, anger is about the sense of *superiority* over others, with all the desperate *distortions of perspective* that brings in its wake. I know best. I am right. You are wrong. We're in control. Being right about something puts us in a position of moral superiority over the person or the situation that is being judged. So constantly needing to be right, constantly complaining about situations, are very much an expression of the life state of anger.

So there will be the sudden outbursts of blazing anger that seem to come from nowhere, as we try to impose that superiority, often surprising the owner of the anger as much as the startled victim. But there will also be lots of other immensely *destructive and anti-social* stuff such as rampant intolerance, and cynicism, and sarcasm, lack of gratitude and constant criticism of other people's work. People who frequently inhabit anger state find it just as difficult to live with themselves, as other people find it difficult to be with them, because they seem to have no real control over the source of the anger. The flaring temper, and the corrosive cynicism and backbiting often seem to well up from nowhere; they seem almost to have a life of their own.

It goes without saying that anger of this sort can be immensely destructive of personal relationships, either rupturing them or rendering them intolerable for the suffering partner. But at the wider level of society, anger in this sense of superiority of self, clearly lies at the root of a whole range of widespread and wholly unacceptable injustices, from violent racism and religious intolerance, to the oppression of women and many minority groups.

So anger as a life state is generally bad news, but the Buddhist view is well balanced in that it doesn't exclude the possibility of benefit coming from the *sheer energy* that anger can release, if only it can be properly directed. So it accepts that anger can make a contribution, as a powerful, highly-energised driver towards change, in the fight against apathy for example, or when it stands up against situations that threaten the dignity or the lives of individuals and challenges them.

Buddhism asks us to have the courage to challenge injustice wherever we encounter it.

The psychologists view of anger

It is quite remarkable just how closely that classical Buddhist view of anger and its serious implications for the way we live our lives, is mirrored in some of the latest psychological analyses. They too make the case that anger has a positive role to play when we are fighting for justice for example, or when we are concerned with helping '*to right wrongs and bring about needed change.*'[3]

But they make a very powerful case indeed, both for the immense damage that uncontrolled anger can cause to individual lives and relationships, and the extent to which uncontrolled anger alters and distorts our view of what is going on. Anger we learn '*is a very disorganising emotion,*' our judgement can be completely overwhelmed or switched off. We end up acting in a fog of misperception, so that perfectly harmless and innocent acts by other people in our environment, can, through the *distorting lens of anger*, be seen as highly aggressive and threatening, and therefore trigger a violent and aggressive response that is wholly misplaced or inappropriate.[4]

So Martin Seligman for example talks of anger being the emotion that fuels violence and abuse in society and in personal relationships, to the extent that it can ruin many lives.

'Anger is hot and quick,' he writes, *'Its content, uncensored, is destructive. An angry person never sees things from his target's point of view... Words and brash acts, unlike thoughts, cannot be erased. In a lifetime, most of us wreck dozens, even hundreds, of relationships in the heat of anger.'*[5]

And as if that weren't enough he adds a further point that, if nothing else, should give many of us pause for thought; anger he tells us, is seriously *bad* for our health. Giving in to our desire to explode and vent our anger against some frustrating event or some perceived slight is bad for our blood pressure and bad for our hearts.[6]

That particular view would seem to confirm the profound truth of a Buddhist text on anger that is attributed Shakyamuni himself.

'Holding on to anger,' it argues, *'is like grasping a hot coal to throw at someone else. You are the one getting burned!'*

I could go on, but enough said I think to make the case of just how damaging anger can be to our life. But the key question of course is what can we do about it? Both Buddhism and modern psychology are clear that we can't *eradicate anger* from our lives, however much we might wish that to be the case. As one psychologist puts it,

'Of all the moods that people want to escape, rage seems to be the most intransigent.'[7]

So we have to learn to live with it. It sits there in our psyche, a bit like a slumbering tiger, waiting to leap into action when it's provoked. But can we tame it? Nichiren Buddhism persuades us that we can, provided we make the *determination* that we are going to, and summon up the *perseverance* to achieve that change, despite the setbacks we are bound to encounter.

Taming the tiger

Interestingly both the psychologists and Buddhist commentaries talk in very similar terms, although, as we have already mentioned elsewhere, there is no actual connection between modern research by numerous psychologists and sociologists, and what Buddhism has been talking about for centuries. None. But the fact is that both come to very similar conclusions. The key to overcoming those angry outbursts and those cutting and cynical responses that can have such a destructive effect on our partners and families and friends...is *self awareness*, understanding the life state we are in, so that we can control it.

That is of course the essential purpose of the Buddhist definition of the Ten Worlds, which we've touched upon briefly in this chapter already, and which is set out at greater length in Appendix A. It's only by increasing our awareness that we *are* actually in Anger state, Buddhism argues, that we can learn how to create that *fractional space* between becoming aware of what we see as a 'trespass,' and reacting angrily and violently to it. It may be only a brief gap of time, but that's all we need. It's enough for us to control our tongue, and to defuse that explosive, bite-back expression of anger.

Being advised to count to ten when you're in a potentially angry situation may be a very old saying, but that doesn't stop it from being wise advice. Indeed as one modern psychologist has put it, count to ten, count to twenty, sleep on it if you can![8] You are trying to give yourself the space to cool down and re-evaluate that supposed trespass. Anger remember, like cow pats, is best handled when cold!

And of course, it goes without saying, we can't always manage it. We don't spot it early enough and that old anger flashes out. But the more we practice it, the better we become at spotting it early, and the earlier we spot it, the easier it becomes to grab hold of it and dampen it down, before it has done any damage.

The power of self-awareness in handling our relationships is writ large in these research findings. Psychologist Daniel Goleman for example goes so far as to say,

'*Self-awareness- recognising a feeling as it happens- is the keystone of emotional intelligence.*'[9]

It is, he declares, *the* essential foundation for recognising emotions in *others*, understanding how other people are feeling or responding, or *empathy* as we commonly call it; having the ability to see the situation from the other person's point if view. And empathy of course is the *very basis* of altruism and compassion, and the very *enemy* of anger. We all seek greater empathy. Most of us are pretty fed up with our outbursts of anger.

As we've already seen in our discussion of overcoming negativity, those views are wholly in tune with Buddhist teachings. So the key to overcoming the destructive nature of anger has to come from *within*, from this greater self awareness. It can't just be switched off, or re-directed from *outside*, because we are told, or because we understand *intellectually*, how damaging it can be to our lives. Understanding the theory isn't enough. Each of us has to struggle to tame the tiger by making that crucial determination, and, using the discipline of the daily practice to make sure we persevere at achieving it.

But fundamentally I would argue, this takes us back to a principle that we have already discussed at some length, because it is so central to the Buddhist approach to life, and that is this idea of accepting full responsibility for what goes on in our life.

So who is really responsible?

It's worth revisiting I think, because, on the face of it, it doesn't seem to be a particularly challenging idea does it? I mean something called Personal Responsibility, is scarcely an earth-shattering idea. You wouldn't be overly surprised I suggest, if you were to find it in the small print of some political party manifesto, as being a quality that should be strongly encouraged, or even folded into the secondary school curriculum throughout the land. Indeed that might be a genuinely worthwhile initiative. Properly constituted and put into practice it has the power to offer communities a pathway out of so much of the thoughtless and anti-social behaviour that blights so many of them.

But it's all too easy to point the finger like that isn't it? The real point we need to take on board is that… it's not about *them*. It's about *us*. I'm sure we all like to think that we are wholly responsible for everything that we say and do. No question. Of course we are. We're *very* responsible people. We always have been.

'*Except*' we might add…after a brief thought…. '*except for those instances where clearly someone else was responsible…*' for a bitter and hurtful argument because *they* were so ridiculously unreasonable…or for a nasty squabble in the playground at school…or a punch up in the pub…or a marriage breaking up… or some such thing.
'*We can't be expected to accept responsibility for those kinds of things as well…can we? I mean those things that were…well… clearly someone else's fault?*'

What Buddhism does brilliantly is to lay it clearly on the line for us, so we don't have any doubts about where the responsibility lies. No fudges. No ifs and buts. We *are* responsible it argues, *for what goes on in our lives*. Period. Even if, as so often happens to all of us, we would prefer not to be, and would much prefer to point the finger at someone else, and exclaim, or protest, or shout loudly, about where the responsibility in this or that particular case really lies.

Buddhism says quite clearly, don't look for the causes out there, look for them in here, within one's own life, because that is where they will be. And what's more, we will *benefit* it argues, from taking that view, because it means we can *do something* about them.

Once again, as so often the case with Buddhism, it's a tough principle to take on board, and to live with, among family and friends and work colleagues. Buddhism remember isn't a soft touch, because life isn't a soft touch. And as we all know, it runs so strongly counter to what comes instinctively. It's just so much *easier,* it's also immensely *satisfying,* just to give in to the anger, or the frustration, or the intense sense of self-righteousness, and to shout the blame elsewhere. To offload it onto someone or something else. Anything to get rid of it. We all do it without a second thought.

Basically Buddhism asks us to take that *second* thought. To do what is more difficult and challenging. To calm down. Take a deep breath. Count to ten if you like, or better still twenty. *Remind ourselves that we are Buddhists,* and that we reveal that fact above all in our behaviour, in how we respond to *this particular situation.* Indeed, *every* particular situation. As we've just seen, both Buddhism, and today's psychologists talk about the immense value of *empathy;* of learning how to put ourselves in the other person's shoes, of asking ourselves, what were the causes that *we* made, to arrive at this situation. It has even been suggested that we might wish to create a simple phrase that we can say to ourselves in this kind of confrontational situation that can immediately defuse it for us. Something like this for example:

'I know this seems like a personal insult, but it is not. It is simply a challenge to be overcome that calls on skills I have.'[10]

Skills that I have developed through making that determination that I *will* master my anger, and I will *persevere* in the efforts to achieve that goal.

How it works

There are I think a couple of key points that arise from this all too brief look at negativity in the previous chapter, and at anger in this one, that tell us some fundamental things about the way Buddhism works in daily life, that are worth underlining.

Buddhism asks us, encourages us, helps us, to be clear-eyed and not to fudge the issues; to be clear and confident that is, about *who* we are and *what* our values are. In most situations it is of course far easier to blame other people or other events for things that go wrong in our lives, but we've all tried that many times, and as we know, that approach solves nothing. Nothing gets *improved*. More often than not, it simply serves to *prolong* the conflict, or the pain, or the suffering. And so the relationship breaks up. Or the situation in the office gets fraught.

Even though it is infinitely more difficult and challenging to accept responsibility, and look within ourselves for the causes of whatever it is that hasn't worked out, it is by a long way the most *hope-filled* and the most *productive* choice. We don't lose, we win. We all win, because the anger gets resolved, the situation is improved, and we all move on.

Moreover it doesn't take long to recognise that we are not, with a Buddhist practice, talking about huge, earth-shaking changes in attitude. Indeed as so many people say when they first encounter the practice, so much of Buddhist teaching seems to be plain common sense. It's what works. It's about getting us to look again at some of the ordinary everyday assumptions that we carry around with us, brushing away the *film of familiarity* if you like. Buddhism talks again and again about clarifying our vision, or taking the time to look clearly at our life, so that we get to see just how much letting go the focus on our *own ego* and on our *own needs*, and recognising the needs of *others*, lubricates and creates productive relationships.

So it remains the same old world, it's just that our *perception* of it is slightly shifted, and that's the key. Everything but everything in our lives of course is driven by our *perceptions*, how we *think*, which governs what we *say* and how we *act*. So even a slight shift in our perceptions can change fundamentally the way *we behave*, towards ourselves and towards others. It may only be a slight change, but in my personal experience, time and time again it proves to be enough to enable us to tackle the problem with a different and infinitely more *positive* attitude. And every time it does so it gives us a little lift. A greater sense you might say of our own capability to resolve problems, and we make a mental note to try to deal with the next problem that comes along in the same *personally responsible* way. It means that we open up this possibility of moving on from being generally negative and pessimistic about problems, to being positive and optimistic about them. And that can be life-changing.

Of course it's not all one way. We're only human, so once again it can be one step forward, two steps back. Often. But the point is we're not stuck in a rut. We're growing a *skill* that is not only priceless in the affairs of daily life, but a huge step along the path that we are following, towards building a happier life for ourselves and for those whom our life touches.

CHAPTER ELEVEN

Buddhism and Money

Since Buddhism claims to be about daily life, and since money is an integral part of the complexity of all our lives, we all have bills to pay and ambitions to realise, it's obviously important that we have a clear idea of what it is that Buddhism has to say about our relationship to the stuff. Indeed as it happens money, money that is in a slightly different form, but fulfilling precisely the same functions as we know it today, actually came into the world, and started to have its effects on the way people behaved, at about the same time as Shakyamuni was travelling around and teaching, and in a place not all that far away from where he was in Northern India.

It was actually created by someone whose name is still very familiar to us in relation to money even today, King Croesus, who ruled the ancient Kingdom of Lydia, in Asia Minor, roughly where modern-day Turkey is, during the 6th Century BCE. Up to that time, leaving aside the role of barter, goods were being bought and sold and paid for by bits and pieces of metal, mainly gold and silver of course, that had to be carefully weighed and assessed for purity at every trade. So not only a very laborious and cumbersome process, but one that was clearly open to all sorts of manipulation and corruption and the cause of much conflict and controversy. So, the story goes, it was the smart financial advisers at the court of King Croesus who came up with the simple but brilliantly practical idea of churning out small pieces of gold and silver that were already stamped with marks to validate their weight and purity, and so carrying in a sense the authority and the *guarantee* of the Lydian treasury as to their relative value. It was a whole new paradigm, and it's held by historians to be the birth of *coinage* as we know it.

Sardis, Lydia's capital, rapidly became a mecca for traders from all over the world, because of the surety of its coins, and Croesus gained the reputation for his fabulous wealth that has echoed across the centuries right done to modern times. We still use the phrase *'to be as rich as Croesus,'* to indicate when someone is *very rich indeed*, even today. I notice in fact that in the Wikipedia entry on him Bill Gates is cited as the modern example of the Croesus phenomenon! Although Croesus soon lost his kingdom to the warlike Persians, they too thought that minted money was such a brilliant idea that they just carried on doing what he had started, and you could say with some truth that his coins travelled throughout the world; they've been found for example in Viking hoards buried as far away as York, in Anglo Saxon England.

And basically that same model, that system of minted money, guaranteed by a national treasury, has continued right down to the present day. Economists still generally go on regarding money pretty dispassionately as this sort of *lubricating* device, an impersonal medium of exchange that goes on doing very much what Croesus invented it to do, namely to make the whole business of trade and markets and buying and selling flow more smoothly.

But we all know that it has come to mean much more than that don't we? Much more personal and more intimate, vastly more influential in all sorts of ways. We may not actually think about it too often, or too deeply, we may not ever put it into words, but we all recognise in some subliminal way, that money is right in there close to our sense of self-worth for example. And that personal view is very much confirmed by what the sociologists tell us.

An article in a popular but genuinely scientific journal for example, triggered by the effects on so many people of the on-going economic crisis, carried the sub-heading, *'Why money messes with your mind.'* The article went on to explain in some detail just how far that messing with the mind could go,

'Some studies even suggest that the desire for money somehow gets cross-wired with our appetite for food. And of course because having a pile of money means that you can buy more things, it is virtually synonymous with status...so much so that losing it can lead to depression and even suicide.'[1]

And although that statement might seem at first glance to be way over the top...*'it couldn't possibly affect me in that way,'*... we say to ourselves, if we think about it even briefly the evidence is clearly there. We're all well aware for example of the hundreds of suicides that followed the Great Crash of 1929 in America, people willing to throw away their very lives because their stock values had crashed overnight. Something very similar happened in the UK albeit on a much smaller scale, with the crash in the Lloyds Insurance Market as recently as the 1990's. And as I was actually researching this book, the press and television channels were all covering the truly tragic story of a 50 year old businessman, who was it seems a balanced and loving and thoughtful husband and father, who became so mentally disabled by the thought of an impending bankruptcy, and the fear of losing the wealth and the possessions that he had accumulated over the years, that he simply couldn't face the possibility of *living without them*. So he became virtually a different person, capable of shooting his wife and daughter and then dying himself in the fire he lit to destroy their family home. His money that is, had somehow become more important to him than his life or his loved ones. An immensely tragic messing with the mind indeed!

Not a marginal issue

That is of course an extreme case, and I mention it only with very considerable diffidence because it is so utterly saddening, but the fact that these things can happen at all, underlines the key point we're seeking to establish, namely that whatever we think may be the case, our emotional relationship with money is clearly not a *marginal* issue. In thinking about our relationship to money, to wealth, the accumulation of wealth in all it's forms, we are dealing with something that can undoubtedly have the most profound effects on how we see ourselves, to the point indeed of changing *who* we believe we are. And whether or not we have ever thought about it, or are prepared to acknowledge it, it would be very strange wouldn't it, if *all of us* haven't been shaped and conditioned and affected *in some measure*, by this long-running, supremely-acquisitive, materialist, environment that we all inhabit?

If we ask ourselves the direct question, *how* have we been affected by it, we might find it difficult to give a clear answer, but that that doesn't really undermine the validity of the question does it? Certainly it's a debate that those of us who happen to live in the western-way-of-life parts of the world, can't really duck out of. Nor should we want to I suggest, given that the impact that money has on our general sense of satisfaction and contentedness with life, is such a big deal. On the face of it, it seems to play a very big role indeed in any picture of *happiness* we paint for ourselves. The longing for the kind of life-style that only money can buy seems to be very deeply embedded in the western psyche.

So how might we define the issue itself, because it's clearly a complex one?

What our lives are about?

Put at its simplest, the crux of the argument put forward by the sociologists seems to be that we have allowed the endless cycle of earning and spending, buying and acquiring, to become pretty much what our lives are about. It has been called the *distinctive signature* of our time, although it doesn't sound in the least distinguished does it? Let alone desirable. Is that what we really want this time we live in to be remembered for? The sociologists talk for example about our replacing *meaning* in our lives for the mere *pursuit of money*, and exchanging genuine *quality of life* for mere *standard of living*. As one commentator puts it for example, writing about some of the dysfunctions of the materialist culture,

'*One of those shortcomings may be that we chase money at the expense of meaning. Too many in the Western world have made materialism and the cycle of work and spend as their principal goals. Then they wonder why they don't feel happy.*'[2]

And elsewhere in the same essay,

'Paradoxically, it is the very increase in money – which creates the wealth so visible in today's society – that triggers dissatisfaction. As material expectations keep rising, more money may engender only more desires.'[3]

So in a sense you could say that we're all chasing our tails! Dr. Edward Diener from the University of Illinois, and one of the prime movers in the field of positive psychology has very similar views. He talks of our being so conditioned by the materialist environment we live in that we constantly focus on what we *haven't got,* as opposed to what we have. So he says, as men and women move up the economic ladder, most of them immediately stop thinking about, and feeling in any way *grateful for* their newly improved circumstances. That simply becomes the new status quo, the new base line, and they switch their thoughts instead to what they don't have.[4] And that's by no means the only somewhat scary paradox we encounter when we look into this issue. Our relationship with money is clearly far more involved, far more multi-layered, far more deeply influential than we might be prepared to admit. But let's change direction for a moment and try to determine what Buddhism has to say about this complex issue.

What does Buddhism have to say about all this?

As I mentioned earlier, since Buddhism claims to be about our ordinary daily lives, and since money undoubtedly has a very important part to play in those daily lives, Buddhism somehow has to embrace that fact in its teachings. Man may not be able to live by *bread alone,* as the Christian scriptures tell us, but he certainly has to be able to *buy* bread! The fact is that Buddhism has a lot to say that is refreshingly direct about wealth and how we might best relate to it. Perhaps the crucial point we need to grasp, mainly because it runs directly counter to a widely held stereotype, is that Nichiren Buddhism is not in any way about *not* wanting things, or *not* having things or indeed about *giving things up.* How could it be since it is about the reality of daily life, and part of that reality for all of us, is to have things?

So Nichiren Buddhism is not about diminishing or reducing or setting arbitrary limits on what we might or might not posses. Not at all. It teaches simply that since we clearly have extensive physical as well as spiritual needs, we have to attend to *both* if we are to achieve the most meaningful and the most fulfilling and value-creating lives of which we are capable. That it teaches, is the very purpose of our lives, and the key to achieving success in this, as in so many things Buddhism argues, is establishing a keen sense of *balance.*

Earthly desires

The physical needs are often described as *earthly desires*, not earthly in any pejorative or derogatory way, but simply in the sense that they are needs and wants that relate to the *material* aspects of our life. And Buddhism clearly accepts them as playing an *essential role* in our sense of well-being. That is to say, they are not in any way marginal. Wanting things is part of our basic humanity and has been ever since there have been things to want, from sharp stone hand axes and pretty cowry shells, to a better paid or more satisfying job and a more comfortable home, and a car big enough to carry the whole family and the dog, and a bit of spare cash for an enjoyable holiday. Buddhism *is* ordinary daily life.

So Buddhism makes clear we shouldn't in any way try to reject, or try not to think about these wholly natural wants in our life, or see them as somehow separate from or *in conflict with* our spiritual life. Because there is no conflict, not at *this level* of wanting. It doesn't really matter what it is that launches us down the road of establishing goals for our life, both material and spiritual, and then committing ourselves to a Buddhist practice as a way of strengthening our lives and setting out to achieve them. The understanding that lies at the very heart of Buddhism, and *proven* over countless lifetimes, is that once we set of down this road, it will inevitably draw out the perception that what we are really seeking in life is *meaning and purpose,* and a sense of *self-worth,* and the durable sense of well-being that comes from the exercise of *compassion and altruism,* whether or not we happen to achieve those *material* goals that we set out with.

A sense of balance

So where then do we draw the line between what makes sense for our lives and what doesn't? The key thing Buddhism argues is working hard to maintain that sense of *balance* we mentioned, between the spiritual and the material. The middle way you might say.[5] Not getting swept away by overly strong currents in *either* direction, because both can cause real suffering.

So that means not being overly, even fanatically spiritual for example, just doing too many Buddhist activities and so neglecting the genuine material needs for ourselves and those around us. Just giving *quality time* to a partner and children for example, *is* a crucial material need, among many others.

Conversely real trouble can arise, Buddhism argues, for us and for those around us, when the *hunger* for more money, more stuff, more material goods becomes a dominant or overwhelming life condition.

We may not see it that way of course, because we are *inside* the desire. It is us. Or we may not see it *early* enough, because these things tend to creep up on us. We may regard it as simply ambition, or a desire to get more out of life. But when the drive for yet more wealth, yet more material possessions, becomes the *overriding* motivational force in our lives, the thing we get most pleasure out of, and we find ourselves increasingly drawn in that direction, with decreasing time and space allocated to meaning in our life, or our values, and the lives of those around us, then Buddhism argues, we've lost the plot. We're way out of balance. And the effects of that imbalance can flow into all the other areas of our life, almost without our being aware of it.

In fact Buddhism uses language very similar to that in the scientific article that we touched upon a moment ago. It describes *greed,* because let's face it, that's really what we're talking about here, as a *poison, or addiction* in our system, that can infect *all* the dimensions of our life and be the source of deep, life-changing, pain and suffering.

Witness the story of the bankrupt businessman that I recounted briefly above.

The paradox at the heart of the western way of life

That brings us directly to the vast range of studies that have been carried out over the past 20 years or so by the economists and sociologists and the remarkable paradox that they have brought out into the light. In fact it is so counter-intuitive that I have no doubt that many of us will find it hard to swallow. But it helps if we stick strictly to the science rather than our own instinctive response. The fact is that one of the earliest, and most frequently repeated and unquestionably one of the most surprising findings of all this research is that wealth, how much money we earn, is *not a substantial factor* in our basic sense of well-being. What the studies reveal is that once our basic needs have been met...that is of course an important proviso...then additional wealth seems to have a rapidly diminishing role to play in how we feel about our lives, until eventually it dies out altogether as a contributing factor.

This conclusion has been described by one leading European sociologist as *'the paradox at the heart of western society.'*[6] Why paradox? Because it seems to be so completely out of step with our current immensely aggressive, materialist, consumerist society. Most of us in the western-way-of-life parts of the world, and beyond, are deeply conditioned to believe that much of our happiness and what we describe as *Success*, with a capital S, lies in seeking greater financial wealth.

The plain fact is that we *all* expend very considerable amounts of time and energy throughout our lives in trying to achieve greater wealth. If we were asked the direct question, we all know that we want to be rich or richer don't we? Why? Because we all believe with *absolute conviction,* that although it may not solve every single one of the things that trouble us, it would certainly blow the *vast majority of them* out of sight. So we would be a lot happier... wouldn't we? And if I'm absolutely honest, as I sit here writing these words, having done all the research mind you into this issue, a big part of me wants to shout out the answer..*'Yes.'*

But the accurate answer to that question, and an answer coming from the scientists remember, and from so much research, not from some Buddhist text, comes out as a resounding negative! Listen to this for example from an eminent British economist;

'There is a paradox at the heart of our lives. Most people want more income and strive for it. Yet as Western Societies have got richer, their people have become no happier. This is no old wives' tale. It is a fact proven by many pieces of scientific research. We have good ways to measure how happy people are…and all the evidence suggests that on average people are no happier today than people were fifty years ago. Yet at the same time average incomes have more than doubled. This paradox is equally true for the United States, Britain, and Japan.'[7]

Or this from a leading American sociologist,

'Over the past two decades, in fact, an increasing body of social-science and psychological research has shown that there is no significant relationship between how much money a person earns and whether he or she feels good about life. A Time poll carried out in the US in December found that happiness tended to increase as income rose to $50,000 a year. After that more income didn't have a dramatic effect. Edward Diener, a psychologist at the University of Illinois, interviewed members of the Forbes 400, the richest Americans. He found the Forbes 400 were only a tiny bit happier than the public as a whole.'[8]

'…only a tiny bit happier than the public as a whole!' What an extraordinarily revealing statement that is, because it reveals the sheer scale of the *delusion*…I can't think of a more appropriate word to describe it…that most of us carry around with us. If our sense of well-being were to increase in any way even *slightly in step* with increasing wealth, as we fondly believe, then these Forbes 400 people, the very richest

Americans remember, should be permanently over the moon shouldn't they? Walking on air. Singing in the rain. But the unlikely, the surprising, the oh-so-hard-to-accept truth is… that they *aren't.* They are no happier it seems than the rest of us, sitting as we are on an average income.

More money that is, above a really quite modest level, simply does not seem to turn on our happiness or our well-being switch. Nor it seems does the *stuff* that money can buy.

'If you made a graph of life on both sides of the Atlantic since the end of World War 2, every line concerning money and the things that money can buy would soar upward, a statistical monument to materialism. Inflation-adjusted income per head in Europe and the U.S. has almost doubled in the last 35 years. Owning a small runabout was once a goal; now the average US household boasts nearly three cars, while in the U.K. there are now more mobile phones than people. Designer everything, personal electronics and other items that didn't even exist half a century ago are now affordable. No matter how you chart the trends in earning and spending, everything is up, up, up. But if you made a chart of happiness in the same period, the lines would be as flat as the roof of an S-class Mercedes. Polls in the U.S and Europe show remarkably little change in happiness since Europe began rebuilding itself (after WW2) and America developed into the world's unrivalled economic and military superpower.'[9]

That's another quite remarkable statement isn't it? In fact were it not for the sheer weight of the evidence, the story that it is telling us seems almost inconceivable. But it is given even sharper edge by the figures that are quoted by another researcher. When these surveys are carried out the scientists speak to a sample of people chosen to represent a typical cross section of the entire population, and then those countless personal interviews are reduced to numbers and curves on graphs, so that the sociologists and the economists can make use of them to compare results from one time and place, to other totally different times and places. The American National Opinion Research Centre for example is typical in that it has been carrying out virtually the *same* survey since the 1950's, so that we can compare *directly* how people felt about their lives in the 1950's and the 60's with today.

Back in the 1950's for example, with *infinitely lower* levels of wealth and material comfort, when Americans were asked to rate their *overall satisfaction with life,* they reported an average score of 7.5 out of 10. Despite the simply vast changes in the levels of material wealth and comfort over the past half century, the average score in the same survey today, is just…7.2! So the simply vast increases in material wealth that have taken place over the past 60 years have not been matched in any way by an increase in our overall sense of well-being.[10]

The materialist dead end

Why do we find that so surprising? Because of course in today's western societies the vast mass of the population has *more* of almost everything you care to name; the list is endless, more comfort, more food, more houses, more cars, more health, more leisure, more partners…but not it seems more happiness, or more well-being, or more general satisfaction with life.

So what kind of answers have the sociologists come up with to help us understand this restless modern malaise, because it's only with a better understanding of course that we can do something about it, in order to move on from it. As you would expect, there are no single or simple answers, but there are some truly brilliant insights that help to open our eyes to what is really going on. We can all too easily it seems find ourselves trapped in a sort of materialist dead end.

Professor Layard for example actually talks of the 'hedonic treadmill.'[10] There's that Greek word again meaning pleasure, and the treadmill you might say comes from the hamster's cage, to indicate that we can spend a lot of time going round in circles. It's the phenomenon we touched on a moment ago, the more we have…the more it seems we can want. In an age of immense plenty there is still so much we find to *hunger after*, that it can undermine or diminish, or even cancel out altogether, the pleasure and the joy we might feel in all that we undoubtedly have. We'll come back to that word hunger in a minute because it offers a fascinating link between the social research and what Buddhism has to tell us about this key issue.

The psychologists tell us that *comparison with others* is part of the way we function as human beings, buried deeply in our psyche. We all do it, even if we're not always aware that we are doing it. So it's a constant and immensely influential dimension in our lives, and it has a very real effect on our overall sense of self-worth, and on our general sense of satisfaction or dissatisfaction with our lives. As the psychologist Sonja Lyubomirski has expressed it,

'The more social comparisons you make the more likely you are to encounter unfavourable comparisons; and the more sensitive you are to social comparisons, the more likely you are to suffer their negative consequences…You can't be envious and happy at the same time.'[12]

What a warning line that is…' *you can't be envious and happy at the same time!'*

That in essence is the paradox revealed. It seems that instead of our enjoying a really solid sense of *satisfaction* because of our own considerably improved circumstances, almost the reverse can happen. The vastly greater awareness of *other people's wealth and possessions*, which is so visible in today's western-style societies, seems to have become the source of a much wider and more broadly felt sense of *dissatisfaction*, the *reference anxiety* we mentioned earlier, which chews away at our appreciation of all the good things that we *undoubtedly do have* in our lives.

The life state of Hunger

But the remarkable thing for me I have to say, is just how closely this very modern and scientific analysis, which lays bare for us the powerfully disturbing and unsettling effects of the *constant itch* to acquire more stuff, chimes with the classic Buddhist description of the life state of *Hunger,* which we touched upon briefly earlier. (See Appendix A) It underlines once again just how accurate and therefore how *valuable* to us, is the Buddhist analysis of the dynamics of human motivation and behaviour. Buddhism describes this life state as the root cause of a great deal of *self-inflicted* pain and suffering, with the emphasis very clearly on the fact that it *is* self-inflicted. We *choose* to go there.

Hunger very briefly, is the life state in which we are convinced that our happiness lies in acquiring something that is, for one reason or another, just out of reach. We know for sure that if we can only have this something, we will be *so much happier* than we are now. It will really do the trick. The agony lies in the fact that for people who have this as their

211

dominant life tendency, there is *always something* to want, always something more to reach out for in the saleroom or in the web catalogue…that will really do the trick. And it's not of course limited simply to material stuff, to bigger houses or cars or flat screen TV's, for example. By no means. It reaches out into just about every aspect of people's lives; the desire for more. A modern social network such as Facebook for example even stimulates the desire to acquire and display… more friends. And Twitter…more followers. As if they were commodities.

And that's the key point isn't it? For as long as our lives are largely taken up with stuff, we are essentially treating ourselves as *material* animals. But we know that to be false don't we? We know that we all have a spiritual dimension to our lives, however much we may seek to ignore it, or mask it under a shell of cynicism say. The physical and the material simply aren't enough, and for as long as we try to *live* as if they were, with our lives largely driven by the next acquisition or the next bonus, we know full well that we are in some measure *diminishing* ourselves. Or in Buddhist terms, we are slandering ourselves.

A meaningful spiritual life

As we've seen, Nichiren Daishonin nails this seemingly modern issue so precisely that's it's worth repeating his words; '*more valuable than the treasures in any storehouse…* that is to say more possessions…*are the treasures of the body…*that is to say good health and an active life…*and the treasures of the heart are most valuable of all*…that is to say, a vital and meaningful spiritual life.[13]

And in our deepest selves we know that whenever we manage to pause from the pace and bustle and constant bombarding materialism of modern life, and just take stock of *who* we are, and *where* we are in our lives, and *what* is truly important to us, we recognise that we *earnestly seek* treasures of the heart in our lives. We need a strong sense of the meaning and worth of our lives, totally regardless of wealth or possessions, and warm and generous relationships with all those whose lives touch ours.

It's like a coming home.

And I think it could be argued that that kind of *seeking,* that kind of search for something *more* to life, is at least part of the reason why over the past few decades what might be called this quiet revolution has taken place, quiet because it has never been the stuff of headlines. But in that time frame many tens of thousands of people in the West and elsewhere around the world, ordinary people like us, holding down a job in an office or a factory, falling in love and bringing up families, worrying about the rising tide of bills and caring for aged relatives and so on, have chosen to put that all together under the umbrella of a Buddhist set of principles and values. And for this constantly growing number of people, clearly the choice that Buddhism offers provides a meaningful resolution to the countless challenges that modern life in the West throws at all of us. Meaningful and *happier* indeed, because obviously people in such large numbers are not turning to Buddhism because it makes them less happy, or resolves fewer problems!

It's also possible to argue I think, that this movement of strong Buddhist values and principles westwards is one among several influences that is triggering a profound *re-think* of what we really mean when we talk about the *successful society* in the West, away from the purely material that is, away from traditional measures that have to do largely if not entirely with the *accumulation of wealth* and rising GDP, towards measures that have more to do with quality of life and well-being.

CHAPTER TWELVE

A New Beginning

That brings us just about full circle I think, and time to pull some of many threads of the argument together. This has turned out to be a somewhat more divergent journey than I ever intended when I set out, taking us into many more byways of science for example than I had anticipated, and some that might seem to lie well off the beaten track. Although even if they have started out as seemingly peripheral, in each case they have contributed something special to this central quest; where do we turn in the modern world to tune our moral compass? Where do we go to get a deeper understanding of just how we set about building a life that is genuinely fulfilling and hopeful and optimistic for ourselves, and at the same time, one that creates the greatest value for the communities and the societies in which we live?

As I described right at the outset, I started out on my own long journey into Buddhism with no small measure of reluctance. I cannot say that there was at the start any clear vision or sense of direction. There wasn't an overriding idea or an obvious goal towards which I was heading. I believed I had encountered something that could contribute great value to my life, and to the lives of those around me. But we are all of course to a greater or lesser extent, captives of our time, and the prevailing spirit of *our* time I suggest, is a profound *scepticism* about virtually all institutions, not least institutions that have any sort of religious basis. There is a strong need to *disbelieve* if you like, as part of our modern culture. A need to take things apart and turn them over and question them almost to bits, before considering taking them into our life. That was undoubtedly a strong factor with me when I encountered Buddhism.

And I have to say, I see scepticism as a source of *strength* rather than weakness, a route to a far deeper and a stronger understanding, so long of course as we don't let it degenerate into *mere cynicism,* which must rank as one of the most prevalent and dysfunctional qualities of our time. Cynicism may seem superficially cool, but it has never created anything of value.

But if I try to cast myself back into that situation, there was also I now realise, an inner *resolution.* I was determined that once I had set out down this somewhat surprising road, I would continue on the journey until I was quite sure, one way or the other, about the value of the practice in my daily life. It was easy enough for people to say to me, 'Buddhism *is* daily life.' The question was did it actually work at that level? Could it make a fundamental difference to the way I viewed the mundane stuff of every day?

And if you think about it, that is the acid test isn't it? That's what it boils down to. It's not the theory that is going to change our lives, it's the practice. How do Buddhist values and principles affect the way we *perceive* and the way we *respond* to the constant stream of events and encounters that makes up the daily-ness of all our lives, in all its unexpected, challenging, chaotic, sometimes uplifting, often frustrating detail? The answer can be expressed in many ways of course, but one that makes most sense to me is that Buddhism is both *inspirational and intensely practical.* Inspirational in that it delivers to us a view of ordinary human life that is always hopeful and uplifting and immensely positive and value-creating. It's not for nothing that Buddhist philosophy has been described as the greatest creation of the human mind. At the same time it is intensely practical in that it delivers an utterly down-to-earth, feet-on-the-ground *strategy* for living with the stuff of everyday.

It *does* make a profound difference when you are aware that Buddhism is not about demonstrating allegiance to some external, divinely-inspired set of rules and commandments. It is really about allegiance to one's better self, and one's concern for, and responsibility towards others. That clearly has a powerful impact on how we relate to ourselves, our sense of self-worth if you like, and how we relate to everyone we encounter, not just those who are close, family and friends and colleagues, but those we just happen to bump into on a casual or infrequent basis. Everyone.

It *does* make a profound difference that the Buddhist view of humanity is genuinely all-inclusive. No one is excluded, or sits on the other side of some boundary. It seeks constantly to break down the barriers between self and others. In that sense it embraces all of humanity, and transcends race and ethnic and religious groupings, and nationalities and cultures. One could certainly argue that living as we do on an increasingly crowded a planet, with even its climatic systems and its resources, including the very basics of water and land, under immense pressure, never have we been in *greater need* of such an all-embracing view of mankind.

The celebrated American economist Jeffrey Sachs has put it for us so powerfully,

'...Our challenge, our generation's unique challenge, is learning to live peacefully and sustainably, in an extraordinarily crowded world.'[1]

As to being utterly practical, Buddhism is as we've seen, a man-made religion, so it's not in any way focused on some heavenly *hereafter,* which is consequent in some way on the nature of the daily life we have lived here. Buddhism *is* that daily life. So it's concerned above all with that very here and now. It seeks therefore to engender and nurture wholly practical and down-to-earth qualities that we *need* every day, such as the *courage* to face up to problems rather than sweeping them under the carpet, and *resilience* and *perseverance* in the face of the inevitable setbacks and profound losses we all encounter. And the *compassionate awareness* that enables us to be there for our neighbour whenever he needs help.

And as we've seen, it's about *balance.* We are so accustomed in the West, with our essentially Judaeo-Christian culture, to separate Caesar and God, State and Church, to understand spiritual aspirations as being different from, separate from, and often more *worthy* than material ones. Buddhism argues that both have an essential role to play in the complex spectrum of human well-being. There's nothing about the one that makes it inherently more worthy than the other. It's up to us to establish the *balance* in our lives that enables us to live the most creative and fulfilling lives for ourselves, and the most supportive of others. It's all part of that being wholly responsible for our lives that we have discussed at some length.

Interconnected and interdependent

A crucial part of that down-to-earth practicality is coming to understand with our whole lives the profound *interconnectedness* of all things. We may not be able to see it directly with our eyes of course, or experience it with our senses, but Buddhism, and now of course modern science, ask us to understand that everything but everything in existence, is interconnected and interdependent at the most profound level. Just as, on the surface of things, the island seems to be completely separate from the mainland, but go deeper, to the sea bed, and it is seen to be part of the whole. Or just as each wave on the surface of the sea may seem separate and distinct, but each one is embedded in the great body of the ocean. But those of course are just metaphors to illustrate the idea. The fact is that this deeply rooted Buddhist view, which goes back *directly* to Shakyamuni's great struggle all those years ago, to achieve a deeper understanding of the nature of reality, is now echoed in very precise terms by what modern science has to tell us.

Our DNA for example, the blueprint for making us who we are, we now know connects us to every other living thing. Not just to other humans, but to *every living entity* that has ever existed on the face of the planet. That is an extraordinary mind-blowing idea, most passionately expressed as we saw in an earlier chapter, by one of today's greatest philosopher-scientists, Daniel Dennet. *'You share a common ancestor…*he tells us… *with every chimpanzee, every worm, every blade of grass, every redwood tree.* [2]

And the great Kenyan environmentalist and Nobel Peace Laureate Wangerie Maathai reminds us of something that we could never perceive just with our senses, namely that *all human beings* who walk the planet, are all from the same family stem,

'So far all the information that we have suggests that we come from somewhere within this part of the World, in East Africa, and that of course for many people must be surprising because I think we are so used to being divided along ethnic lines, or along racial lines and so we look all the time for reasons to be different from each other. So it must be surprising for some of us to realise that what differentiates us is usually very superficial, like the colour of our skins, or the colour of our eyes or the texture of our hair. But we are essentially all from the same stem, from the same origin. So I think that as we continue to understand ourselves and appreciate each other, and especially when we get to understand that we all come from the same origin, we will shed a lot of the prejudices that we have harboured in the past.'[3]

So that is the powerful bond that Buddhism, and now modern science, ask us to understand, binds us all so closely to *everything and everyone* that make up our environment on Earth. And remarkably it doesn't stop there. Because the very *materials* of which we are made, connect us intimately to every rock, every planet, every galaxy spinning out there on the edge of darkness. We are that is, made of the very same stuff. It is simply impossible to conceive how a young man living in Northern India all those years ago, and seeking desperately to understand the nature of reality, could possibly have perceived such a level of connectedness, but we are indeed truly connected across the universe, down to the level of the molecule and the atom.

*'...all matter is the same...*the modern particle physicist explains to us... *The matter of which the stars are made is*

known to be the same as the matter on earth...there are the same kinds of atoms there as on earth. The same kinds of atoms appear to be in living creatures as in non-living creatures...'[4]

And let's be clear what we have here. We have a radical modern theoretical physicist coming surprisingly, astoundingly close, to the way in which fully 700 years earlier, the young Buddhist social revolutionary Nichiren Daishonin, sought to transmit to us, Shakyamuni's understanding of the closeness of our connection to everything in our environment.

'Life at each moment, he writes, *encompasses the body and mind and self and environment of all sentient beings in the Ten Worlds as well as all insentient beings...including plants, sky, earth, and even the minutest particles of dust. Life at each moment permeates the entire realm of phenomena and is revealed in all phenomena.'[5]*

Body, mind and self, sentient and insentient beings, and plants and sky and earth and dust. Nothing is excluded. Both Buddhism and Science it would seem, are at one in explaining to us that we live out our lives as part of a totally joined up world. And, I would argue, the more we can grasp and internalise that truth, the more profoundly it is likely to influence our behaviour.

But what difference does it make?

But what difference does it make? Good question. Indeed that might be perhaps the most important question we can ask ourselves. What real difference does all that *theoretical stuff* make to our daily lives? What's wrong you might ask, with seeing ourselves, as we commonly do, stopping at our skin, quite separate and distinct from everything else on the planet? What *practical* difference can it make? Science of course, in presenting us with the clearest possible evidence of our deep interconnectedness doesn't have to take an ethical or a social stance. But Buddhism most certainly does, and the fundamental Buddhist answer to that question would be that everything in our *behaviour,* is driven by our perceptions. Thus a gross *misperception,* that arises directly from the narrowness of our view, strictly limited by what we can perceive with our senses, can lead to grossly *inappropriate* behaviour. As I have expressed it elsewhere;

'Close to it simply means 'me' and 'you.' That's probably easy enough to handle. Further afield it begins to mean 'us' and 'them.' They are different from us, and it begins to get more difficult. You may well be a mild-mannered and altruistic individual who gets on with everybody, but it goes without saying that not everybody is. It doesn't take more than a brief look at human history, old and new, to see that the idea of separation, of them and us, of their lot and our lot, of white skins and brown skins, of Catholics and Protestants, of Christians and Muslims, lies at the root of everything from the brawling between different tribal groups of football fans outside the pub on a Saturday night, to the powerfully disruptive forces of racism and extreme nationalism and religious fundamentalism. And unspeakable events like Rwanda. And Sebrenica. And Auschwitz.'[6]

Those terrible names may come from a different time and a different space, but they are truly part of the *heritage* of every one of us. We can never escape from what they mean.

So the Buddhist answer to that question rings out loud and clear, the difference it makes to all of us is simply immense. Immense, there is no other word for it. As soon as we understand that everything in our behaviour is driven by our perceptions, then keeping those perceptions *sharp and clear,* and keeping our compassion *alert and active* becomes of the utmost importance to the way we encounter everything in our daily life. Are we creating value in this situation, or are we being carelessly destructive? Are we respecting the views and the concerns of others or are we carelessly trampling over them in our pursuit of our own interests?

That clarity is one of the immense benefits that flows from the discipline of the daily practice. That is one of its main functions, to keep that awareness and that compassion fresh and young and active every single day.

Much of the daily-ness of our Buddhist practice is inevitably focused on helping us as *individuals* to understand our own lives and to develop good, strong, productive relationships within a relatively close environment of family and friends and colleagues. Inevitably. Those are the relationships that have by far the biggest influence in our lives. And as we all know, maintaining harmonious and productive relationships even within this relatively narrow environment takes considerable effort and energy.

The greatest challenge

But that having been said, perhaps the greatest challenge facing all of us as individuals, is learning how to extend this understanding, this compassion that the practice helps us to develop and to keep fresh and alive, out beyond the inner circle of friends and colleagues and work mates, out beyond our own community and our own society, to embrace all of humankind. That's a very big ask isn't it? And at first glance it may seem like…well just a bunch of words. They may express what we would like to hear, but are they little more than wishful thinking, little more than a thin pious hope? The history of man's inhumanity to man is so devastating that it can drive out the hope that such a change can ever be achieved.

But Buddhism is by no means alone these days in presenting this challenge to us. There is a growing body of opinion that such a vision is not only immensely, *morally*, desirable, but a profound *necessity*, for the future well being of all of us, more *interdependent* now than ever before in human history. Let's go back to American economist Jeffrey Sachs again, with his passionate argument for global cooperation;

'Most importantly for us on this crowded planet, facing the challenge of living side by side as never before, and facing a common ecological challenge that has never been upon us in human history until now, the way of solving problems requires one fundamental change. A big one. And that is learning that the challenges of our generation are not us versus them...they are us, all of us together on this planet, against a set of shared and increasingly urgent problems.'[7]

*'... all of us together on this planet...*learning to live peacefully and sustainably in an extraordinarily crowded world. It is a powerful vision, and most ordinary human beings would willingly subscribe to it. We desperately want the *resolution* that Jeffrey Sachs describes for us, people of all cultures and of all religions, Jew and Arab and Sunni and Shia and Catholic and Protestant and Buddhist and Hindu, living side by side...not necessarily in *complete harmony*, because history tells us that there are deep rifts in belief that may never be completely healed...but at the very least peacefully and sustainably.

But most ordinary human beings, describing themselves as *realists*, believe that to be an unattainable ideal, and in any case there doesn't seem to be any path along which it can be achieved. One of Buddhism's greatest services to humanity I suggest, is that it simply *refuses* to accept that interpretation of reality. Buddhism reminds us every single day that however difficult the path, it starts right here with each one of us, *at our own feet*, and we can start to move along it whenever we choose. It involves coming to understand that we are not powerless, and that we can start out by seeking to have a beneficial influence upon our own immediate environment, the *sphere* in which *we* live and work. The key thing is making a personal determination that we wish to *make a difference.*

Buddhism asks us to make that determination...every single day.

The wider social impulse

And once again, Buddhism is by no means alone in standing up for that view without compromise. Remember just how boldly John F. Kennedy, galvanised the optimism of an entire nation when he put that same thought into words,

'First examine our attitude towards peace itself. Too many of us think it impossible, too many of us think it is unreal, but that is a dangerous defeatist belief. It leads to the conclusion that war is inevitable, that mankind is doomed, that we are gripped by forces we cannot control. We need not accept that view. Our problems are man made, therefore they can be solved by man, and man can be as big as he wants.'[8]

'And man can be as big as he wants,' or as Buddhism might well put it, as positive and as optimistic and as resilient...as he *determines to be.*

A seismic shift in how we measure progress

And unquestionably, despite the widespread tumult, and the conflict and suffering that we see in the world, the tectonic plates of understanding do seem to be shifting. Buddhism as we've seen, has been teaching this radical idea for many hundreds of years, namely that we create the greatest value in our own lives, when we concern ourselves with the happiness and welfare of others. That is the very basis and foundation of the Buddhist approach to life, respect for and concern for the welfare of everyone with whom we come in contact. We have seen that in the past couple of decades, modern sociological and psychological research has also come to recognise and document something very similar, namely that we do indeed experience great *personal benefit,* a far greater sense of purpose and confidence and pleasure in our lives, when we try to live in this generous and compassionate and altruistic way.

And I have to say, speaking both as a Buddhist and as a responsible citizen, we can only welcome that remarkable *conjunction* of views, since it can only be immensely beneficial to individuals and to the communities and societies we all live in. But the change we are witnessing I suggest, goes even further than that. You might say that we are living through very privileged times in that we are witnessing the slow building of a wave that could bring profound social change.

What do I mean by that? Well over the past ten to fifteen years, perhaps a bit longer, the discussion of what we really mean when we talk about a sense of well-being in our lives, what kinds of values and behaviour make people feel good about their lives and their relationships, has passed out of the hands of philosophers and religious teachers, into mainstream psychological and sociological studies. We have tried in this book to document enough of that movement to illustrate the truth of that. But all the indications are that the circle of this debate is now widening to encompass mainstream, practical, *political and economic* thinking.

The idea that there's much more to life than Gross domestic Product or GDP, is no longer just a passing political joke, it is becoming part of mainstream political discussion. That represents I suggest, a genuinely *seismic* shift, in the way society as a whole thinks about the idea of *progress and success,* away from the strictly limited economic and financial indicators that have been used right across the world up till now, towards a much more meaningful measure that embraces the central idea of *individual well-being.* That would be a revolution. And undoubtedly one that would make social policy infinitely more compatible with a Buddhist approach to life. So it's not a marginal issue is it? It sits slap bang in the centre of all our daily lives, and Buddhism remember, *is* none other than…daily life.

Listen to this for example from a leading American economist John Hall,

'An over reliance on GDP is not just misleading, it's harmful. Focusing on economic growth blinds policymakers to other measures of progress'[9]

So he tells us, it's not just that an over reliance on GDP, as a measure of what our society is like to live in, can lead to *less than the best* choices being made by policy makers, it's *positively harmful* to rely on GDP alone. That is to say, it can blind politicians and lead to choices being made that are *damaging* to our lives. And none of us wants to be governed by blind policy makers do we? We want our policy makers to be clear-eyed and to take fully into account all those things that GDP does not include, since they are the things that directly affect the *daily quality* of our life.

And this from a leading UK economist, adding his very considerable voice to the debate,

'So what is my picture of a better society in which people feel under less threat and pressure and can really exploit the end of scarcity that science makes possible? What should we do if we shifted our goal towards achieving a happier way of life? We should,' he declares radically, *'monitor the development of happiness in our countries as closely as we monitor the development of income.'*[10]

That is a powerful argument for doing something that no one…outside the tiny Buddhist kingdom of Bhutan…has ever tried to do before, although Buddhism, among a small handful of philosophies, has been talking about it for several hundred years. We should be as deeply concerned, it declares, about monitoring the well-being of people in society as we are about the development of income in the economy.

That would undoubtedly represent a major and beneficial revolution

Buddhism is about social change

So, Buddhism argues, we can have the absolute conviction that when we set out on this purely personal journey, towards greater hope and optimism and resilience, even though we may at the outset be focused largely, or even entirely, on our *own* concerns, inevitably, with the *inner* growth that comes from the discipline of the daily practice, it becomes a wider social impulse. Buddhism is crucially about *social* as well as individual change. It determinedly seeks to achieve harmonious societies, and beyond that, global peace. And it determinedly chooses to do so by the only route it can be achieved, individual by individual.

It argues that a movement towards a better society, based on respect for the lives and values of others, and with peace and individual well-being as its objective, cannot be created solely as a top down process. It has to start from the bottom up, with a profound change taking place in the lives of countless individuals, gradually influencing the way the whole of society functions. Daisaku Ikeda reminds us continually that we can all be a part of that crucial process.

'In an age when both society and the religious world are wrought by turmoil and confusion,' as they so painfully are today, *'only a teaching that gives each individual the power to draw forth his or her Buddha nature can lead all people to happiness and transform the tenor of the times. In other words… there can be no lasting solution to the problems facing society that does not involve our individual state of life.'[11]*

It is my strongly held view that Buddhist values and principles, can bring the very greatest value to the daily life of *anyone*, in *any* circumstances, *whether or not* they actually choose to take up the daily practice. But that said, we can come to understand that our daily Buddhist practice is indeed the stone that we personally are dropping into the global pool. And every stone, however small, however personal and intimate and insignificant it might seem, creates ripples, and ripples create change. Initially, as we've discussed, that personal change may only have an effect upon a relatively close-knit group, on family and friends and colleagues at work perhaps. But the effect is *real*. It is crucial that we come to understand that. It's real. And as we carry on, as we *sustain* this movement towards a more positive approach to all the circumstances we encounter, so Buddhism suggests, the ripples extend slowly, gradually perhaps, but nevertheless they continue, out into the local society and beyond.

We can that is, by the way *we personally choose* to live as individuals, by the values and the behaviour *we choose* to adopt, undoubtedly help to transform the tenor of our times.

States of Mind

Buddhism seeks to explain the reality of daily life. It does not present in any way a sort of utopian ideal, or an abstract vision of what might be. It is absolutely real, so real that you can grab hold of it. It is a rich and detailed analysis of the nature of human life, built up on the basis of observations and perceptions, as well as the inspiration, of some quite exceptionally gifted and enlightened people, whom we happen to call Buddhas. It's not scientific, but there are many comparisons to be made with scientific observation. It's no accident that modern psychology for example, is deeply interested in many of the conclusions that Buddhism has arrived at, about the essential nature of human life. As the late philosopher and historian Arnold Toynbee has written, '*The Buddhist analysis of the dynamics of life is more detailed and subtle than any modern Western analysis I know of.*'[1]

The Buddhist concept of the Ten Worlds or the ten states of life is just such an analysis of the dynamics of human life. Its purpose is to describe for us in a way that is systematic, and therefore *practical and useful*, something that we all experience, but which we take so much for granted, as a normal part of our lives that we rarely give it a moments thought. That something is the extraordinary moment-to-moment *changeability* in our state of mind, as we go about our daily lives.

We all know that our life state, or how we *feel* changes constantly throughout the day, triggered by the constant flux of thoughts within, and the stream of events we encounter without. Our mind is so rapid in its response to every stimulus, and everything that we sense or that we experience calls forth a response.

So every hour can be different, every minute, at times every second, so swift is the ability of the mind to respond to what is going on both in and around us.

Since Buddhism is entirely about the ordinary lives of ordinary human beings, it has to cope with this feature of our lives, and the concept of the Ten Worlds is the result. It goes without saying that they are not objective places, these worlds, they are of course purely subjective states, inside our heads, states of mind.

Why Ten?

Although it might seem, when you first encounter the concept, to be somewhat implausible to say the least to reduce the vast range of our constantly shifting responses to just 10 states. But hold your judgement till you have explored the idea a little further. It's worth bearing in mind that this is a structure that has undoubtedly stood the test of time. Moreover it does pass the all-important test of *practicality*.

If there were 50 or 100 life states for example, it would become wholly unwieldy and impractical as a way of thinking about our ordinary daily lives.

That is a crucial point. The Ten Worlds as a fundamental principle of Buddhism, is not intended as a reference book to sit on the bookshelves, or alongside the psychiatrist's couch, it is of value *only* to the extent that it is useful to ordinary people going about their daily lives. It provides us in a sense with a sort of road map, an A-Z of our inner life state. This is where you are, where do you want to be? With this structure we are offered a thoughtful and detailed, and above all an *objective guide*, to help us interpret where we are in our *subjective* or emotional life, so that we can see it more clearly and do something about it.

If we accept, as Buddhism teaches, that both suffering and happiness come not from *external* factors in our lives, but from *deep within*, then knowing more clearly where we are, as opposed to where we would like to be, is a crucial piece of information that we need. Indeed we might ask, where else are we going to get that information?

And this is certainly not superficial stuff. The life states we are in from moment to moment affect *everything* in our life, how we feel, how we think, how we act, even how we *look,* not to mention how our environment responds to us. With a moment's reflection we can all recognise the truth in that. When we are in the state of anger for example, it is instantly signalled by the flushed face, the stiffening in the facial muscles and the raised pitch of the voice. That's an angry man we say! And that set of indicators is likely to trigger an immediate tension in the environment. Everybody responds with their own heightened tension and increased attention to what's going on. Is he going to hit him we might think! Then if somebody happens to prick the tension with a joke or a laugh, in an instant it's all gone. The muscles in the face relax, the voice is lowered again, the eyes lose their glitter, the general tension in the room dissipates. It's all there in those few contrasting moments, how we feel, how we think, and look and act, and how our environment responds.

Not a ladder

Another important point to emphasise is that these ten states are not in any way represented as a sort of subjective or emotional ladder, on which we might move up or down in any progressive way, one rung at a time. Not at all. These ten life states represent rather the entire *universe* of our mind, and we can move from any part of that universe to any other part in a trice, depending on what is taking place within our minds, and what is happening around us, from moment to moment.

There is however a basic problem in putting this idea across. The movement of our mind is so dazzlingly swift, and words by comparison are so slow and cumbersome, that any attempt to describe these kaleidoscopic changes in our subjective or emotional life, *in the slower medium of words*, inevitably appears somewhat laboured and unreal. It feels, and no doubt reads, a bit like walking in wet concrete, everything is slowed down and slightly caricatured. But don't let that put you off, the Ten Worlds are real, and it really helps to know more about them.

OK let's paint brief portraits of all ten life states, so that we can recognise them for what they are.

Hell

Hell is a state of the deepest suffering or depression, often characterised by a feeling of helplessness. We feel we can't escape the pain we're in, we just have to endure it.

That having been said there are many gradations of course, from the somewhat superficial hell of having a really bad day at the office when everything and everyone seems to be against you, and just nothing goes right, to the despair and panic at being made redundant and not knowing where you are going to find another job to pay the bills. The distinctive colour of Hell state is grey; we feel grey within and the world seems grey without.

And then there is the ultimate hell of the deep, deep grief at the loss of a child or a partner, when you cannot believe that the darkness will ever lift, and you don't know how you can carry on.

We all immediately recognise this state as being real. There's nothing in the least *theoretical* about it, it's a real part of all our lives. The examples of course are as many and varied as there are people to experience them. And when we have been cast into hell state the memory of it may remain sharp and clear with us for a very long time, sometimes forever.

Buddhism tells us that all these life states have both a positive and negative dimension, but can there possibly be a positive dimension to Hell? Buddhism argues that there is, that the deep suffering can be the greatest possible stimulus to action. It is so painful that we feel compelled to summon up from somewhere the life force to enable us to climb out of the hole that our life has fallen into. It is also a great *teacher,* in the sense that having been there ourselves, we are immensely more capable of understanding and feeling compassion for, and therefore finding the right way to support, others who are in hell state now.

Hunger

We've already touched on hunger briefly, but just to paint in a little more detail, the world of hunger is essentially a state of constant dissatisfaction with where our life is now because our wants or desires have got out of control, and it's the *out of control* bit that's the problem. Desires are of course fundamental to our human nature, and *essential* to life in many ways. They motivate us for example towards satisfying our basic needs for food and warmth and love and friendship, and move us on to satisfy the need for recognition and reward and pleasure. Once again, as you would expect, there are many gradations of this life state, from a more or less constant low-level itch to have some new thing or experience, all the way up to the stage where the hunger in a sense has become *an end in itself*, so that it can never be satisfied. We end up chasing one desire after another, and yet experiencing no real sense of fulfilment or satisfaction. As soon as the desire has been achieved, the compelling hunger seeks out yet another object to be possessed. A more common term for it I suppose might be good old fashioned *greed*. Since whatever we get is not enough, we end up trapped in a world of frustrated yearning, another kind of hell. We are in the grip of a genuine *addiction*, and like most addictions, it is the source of a great deal of suffering, not just for ourselves, but for all those around us.

What about the positive dimension of Hunger? It lies in the fact that there is often a huge amount of drive and energy locked up in the hunger state. If that energy can be re-directed or re-channelled away from satisfying *our* selfish ends, towards meeting the needs of others who may be severely deprived in various ways, then such hunger can move mountains and achieve great good.

Animality

As the title itself suggests, animality defines a life state in which we are driven pretty much by instinct, with little or no moderation from reason or from moral considerations. So this is a state in which the strong, or those with the special knowledge, take advantage of those who are weak or unaware, in order to satisfy their own ends, regardless of the rights or the morality of the situation.

These days we might think of the widespread occurrence of mindless hooliganism and reckless anti-social behaviour, in which the perpetrators take no account of the suffering or the anxiety inflicted on the people around them. We could argue perhaps that we are being a little hard on the animals when we define this sort of semi-psychopathic behaviour by referring to them. But the point is clear enough, fundamental to this life state is an absence of *humanity and empathy*. It is also characterised by an absence of wisdom or judgement. So that in a state of animality we simply don't care whether our behaviour is *appropriate* or not, we just go ahead and do whatever we want, regardless of other people's feelings or needs. Similarly we pay scant attention to things like rules or regulations that are designed to keep things running smoothly in our crowded urban environments.

These three states, Hell, Hunger and Animality are known in Buddhism as the three evil paths, not so much because they are associated with evil in the conventional sense, but because they are undoubtedly the root cause of a great deal of *suffering.* They can completely tear lives apart, or render them unbearable. People in these life states tend to rotate through them in quick succession, one after the other, driven by their hunger for one thing or another, not really aware of, or caring about, the effects on other people, creating a great deal of pain and suffering and anguish in their own lives and the lives of people close to them.

In that sense they are desperate life states, and one of the great virtues that stems from a knowledge of the Ten Worlds, is that it can act like a clarion call. It can make you starkly aware of the *reality of your situation* and thus act as a powerful stimulus to lift yourself out of it. Who would want to continue to dwell in Hell or Hunger or Animality, once they *realise* where they are?

Anger

Anger is a life state we have already dealt with at some length, but to complete this gallery of mini-portraits, it is a life state we all recognise readily enough, which powerfully underlines the *validity* and indeed the value of this Buddhist analysis. Anger is a state which is dominated not simply by all the external manifestations of anger, the shouting and the threats and the storms of temper, but by the constant over-weaning demands of one's own *ego*. At its heart is the sense of superiority over others, with all the gross distortions of perspective that brings with it. So there will be the sudden outbursts of blazing anger that may seem to come from nowhere, often surprising the owner of the anger as much as the hapless victim. But there will be lots of other destructive behaviour, such as rampant intolerance and cynicism and sarcasm, lack of gratitude, and constant criticism of other people's work.

It goes without saying that anger of this sort can be immensely destructive of personal relationships. At the wider level of society, anger in the sense of superiority of self, clearly lies at the root of a whole range of widespread injustices, from racism and religious intolerance to the oppression of women and minority groups.

But there is positive side to anger because it is also a great achiever. It can be a powerful, highly energised driver towards change, in the fight against apathy for example, or situations that threaten the dignity of the individual.

Once again, the key to overcoming the destructive side of anger has to come from *self-awareness*. It can't just be switched off or re-directed from *outside.* Each individual has to struggle to change his or her life state from within.

Humanity

Humanity once again is a life state we all immediately recognise, it describes those periods, those moments, when we are quiet and calm and at peace with our lot; we like the life we have. So it is fundamentally a *neutral* state. Nothing has excited or upset us, or aroused a passionate or anxious response. It is sometimes called a state of rest because it is at least in part about recharging our batteries. So it is marked by all sorts of positive qualities, such as reasonableness, and sound judgement and consideration for others. When you are in this life state it means that you might be actively seeking to achieve compromise rather than conflict, or you are putting the best gloss on circumstances rather than being critical. You are laid back and relaxed about the situation and quite happy to maintain the status quo.

If there is a negative side to this life state it might be a certain amount of apathy, revealed perhaps in the long-term acceptance of a basically unsatisfactory situation, or an unwillingness to make an effort. We've all been there at one time or another.

Rapture

Rapture represents what is described in Buddhism as *relative* happiness, that is to say, it is very much a transient rather than a deep-seated and long lived state. As its name suggests it is the wonderful up-welling of joy and exhilaration that we all experience when we achieve something that we've really set our heart on. So it brings with it the sense of personal fulfilment and the outburst of energy that comes with passing the difficult set of exams for example, getting that difficult promotion, winning a big prize, or just setting off on a long-awaited holiday perhaps. Or falling in love. Indeed the modern ideal of romantic love is perhaps the most accurate metaphor for what we mean by rapture. Bu however wonderful and exhilarating it may be, however much it enriches our life, the reality is that by its very nature rapture is *short-lived*, a sudden spike of joy in the normal curve of our lives.

Although many people today are inclined to equate this essentially transient state with the highest possible state of life, our maximum happiness as it were, and yearn for some way of making it permanent in their lives, Buddhism, and indeed our own common sense, tells us that the idea of permanent rapture is simply *unreal.* It only takes the passage of time, or a slight change in circumstances, for that peak of exhilaration and joy to pass, to be replaced by another life state. It is by definition, a passing moment. The yearning for it to stay and be there forever, a permanent part of our lives, is a delusion that can only lead to suffering.

The six lower life states

Buddhism tells us that the six life states that we've just outlined briefly describe the reality of life for most of us. These are the worlds we spend a lot of time in, and one of the key insights that Buddhism offers is that we experience them very much as our *response* to what is going on in our external environment. They are very closely interlinked and we can slip very easily from one to another as the day passes. And the argument is that as we fluctuate between these states we are pretty much at the mercy of our environment, now up, now down, now left now right, depending on what is happening. The clear implication is that our life state, and in a sense therefore, our *identity,* from moment to moment, how we think and feel and behave and look even, is to a considerable extent, dependent upon what comes to us from without. Happy when things seem to be going well. Unhappy when they don't. It leaves us pretty much like a rudderless boat, blown this way and that by whatever winds that blow, bounced up and down by whatever waves that strike us. That is obviously a great simplification of the situation. I'm sure we all see our lives as being very much more complicated than that, but the overall message is clear enough, we can all too easily spend a lot of our lives, simply *responding* to what happens to us, rather than *making* and *shaping* our lives.

The remaining four lives are about doing just that. They could be described as representing the great *potential* in human life, not simply responding to changes in our environment in a somewhat reactionary or opportunistic way, but seeking to take greater control of our lives to make the very most of them. So they are all marked, these four life states, by the *effort* that is required to achieve them.

Learning and Realisation
The sixth and seventh life states, Learning and Realisation are often taken together because they are so closely related, they represent in a sense the two sides of the same coin. Both are concerned with the strong desire for self-improvement,

although via different routes. So **Learning** essentially describes the process of study, putting ourselves in a position where we can take on board the knowledge and understanding accumulated in particular fields. In the modern world of course we are likely to spend a considerable portion of our lives in this arena. Acquiring new knowledge and skills, constantly deepening and widening our understanding of how the world works, has become more or less a life-time activity for most of us.

Realisation is slightly different in that it involves the inner process of reflection and consideration that enables us to relate this knowledge and understanding to our own lives and our own circumstances and so make the most creative and productive use of it, to enhance our own lives and the lives of those around us.

Buddhism does make us aware of the potentially negative aspect of learning and realisation that can be manifested in a sense of *superiority* for example, over those who don't aspire to these life states. And we've all encountered unhappy examples of that; doctors for patients for example, professors for students, scientists for the ignorance of the general public. But in general these two life states, Learning and Realisation are seen very practically in Buddhism, as indeed they are presented by modern educationalists, as the veritable springboard to *realising* our individual potential, hence the use of the word, realisation.

Up till now all these life states have been given ordinary names, using words like hell and hunger and learning and realisation that are in common currency. The next two are defined by names that we would never use in any other context apart from a discussion of Buddhism. Bodhisattva and Buddhahood are not just relatively unfamiliar, they are essentially *technical* terms, coming from Buddhist literature. The important thing I would suggest, is not to be put off by them, to get behind the names themselves and to see how they relate to the real substance of our lives. The names might be unfamiliar, the life states are universal.

Bodhisattva

The hallmark of the life state of Bodhisattva is *caring for others*, being concerned about their welfare or their safety or their general well-being. Spending time with an older person living on their own perhaps, supporting a neighbour in a crisis, giving time to a charity, offering a colleague a sympathetic ear, giving oneself in all sorts of ways, big and small, to support other people when they need it. It's not about being a do-gooder. Not at all. It is just being immensely practical and focused in recognising that everybody has need for support at some times in their life. It's also mutually beneficial, although that is not the primary motivation. It is, you will remember, one of the primary qualities that modern psychological research has marked out as being fundamental to our own sense of well-being, being prepared to put ourselves out to help others. Certainly Buddhism argues that one of the most immediate paths out of those tough life states of hell and hunger and animality, is indeed to find some way, however small, to contribute to the lives of others. At its heart is the desire not simply to *help* other people, but whenever possible to *alleviate* the cause of their pain or their suffering and to replace it with a greater sense of well-being.

The prime example of this degree of compassion for others is perhaps the mother, or the parent, whose concern for the child is totally unconditional. Nothing is too much to give. Other obvious examples would be the nurse and the doctor and the social worker. Or the aid workers who are prepared to place themselves in difficult and even dangerous circumstances, in developing countries for example, constantly putting themselves at risk, and challenging their environment, to ease the plight and improve the quality of life of people with whom they may have no connection, except their shared humanity. It's noteworthy that those people in whom the bodhisattva life state is dominant often receive very little public reward or recognition for their work, and they may spend long periods in difficult and stressful environments. Clearly recognition and reward is *not* their motivation. They are driven by a powerful *compassion* to ease the suffering and raise the life state of others. That is the source of their greatest joy and fulfilment. In a sense, in *giving more* of themselves they *become most* themselves. That might well in the end, be the best description of the bodhisattva way.

Buddhism teaches however that the bodhisattva state should not be in any way self-sacrificial, in the sense of neglecting one's own well-being. The care of others is best delivered it suggests, by someone who remains strongly aware of their own basic needs and who takes care of their own welfare. In order to give to others most effectively it argues, we have to develop and make sure we maintain our own strong and resilient life state.

Buddhahood

That brings us to what Buddhism describes as the highest life state of which human beings are capable. It is, as we've already discussed, a name or a title that is overlaid in the West by a huge amount of misconception and misunderstanding, so that it's very difficult for us to believe that it is a life state that can be attained by ordinary people, like us, going about their ordinary daily lives; which might be called perhaps the *What me?* Syndrome. But we shouldn't allow that little local difficulty to put us off. Nichiren Daishonin himself faced very much the same sort of problem. In his day also Buddhahood meant essentially the state of life that had been achieved by Shakyamuni Buddha in the remote past. The word Buddha by the way comes from a Sanskrit verb that means among other things, to awaken, or to see deeply, and is used in Buddhism to describe someone who is awakened to the ultimate truth of life.

It was Nichiren, through his prolonged study of Buddhist writings and commentaries back through the centuries, who brought Buddhism *back down to earth* so to speak. He made it clear that Shakyamuni was at all times an ordinary man, albeit a man of extraordinary wisdom and insight. Indeed the real significance of his life, Nichiren wrote, lay precisely in his *'behaviour as a human being.'* Not as a divine or semi-divine figure, but as an ordinary human being.

Nichiren repeatedly made it clear that Shakyamuni's awakening to the truth of life was not in any way a superhuman state, in some way elevated above ordinary human life. Nor was it a transcendental state; some place of heavenly peace and tranquillity, cut off from the down-to-earth reality of daily life. This is the key understanding that Nichiren went to great lengths to bring to us, throughout his teaching life. Thus Buddhahood, or the Buddha nature, as it is described in Mahayana Buddhism, is not presented as an elevation of some kind, a higher plane or level of life onto which we might step, as if we were leaving behind our ordinary lives. It is rather a deeper and richer understanding *of the mainstream of our life, as it already is,* so that everything we are involved in, the ordinary things, the boring and mundane things, even the suffering and the struggling things, we can experience *as part of* our on-going well-being.

And of course, it's not a destination, somewhere we arrive, as if it were a sort of railway station. It's a path we take up and continue to travel along, trying to understand and experience this deeper sense of the wholeness and richness of our lives. Indeed as one famous Buddhist text puts it, attributed to Shakyamuni,

'There is no path to happiness…happiness is the path.'

Living the ten worlds

So how do the Ten Worlds, or ten life states match up against the reality of our lives?

It doesn't take much self-analysis I suggest, to recall or to recognise in our daily experience, the life states they describe. We've all experienced at some time or another the pain and greyness of Hell state. We've all experienced the frustrations of not getting what we want in Hunger state. Or that spike of intense exhilaration that Buddhism describes as Rapture. And we've all experienced the sense of deep personal fulfilment that comes when we've really been able to help someone else.

There are some key things we should try to remember about them.

Thus there are no barriers *between them* for example. We can move from one to another with great rapidity and with complete freedom depending on what's going on in our heads and in our environment from moment to moment. Nichiren Buddhism chooses to describe this fluency of movement by saying that each life state *contains* the *potential* of all the others. We can immediately see the validity of that idea if we think of incidents in our daily lives. We might for example be in the life state of humanity, completely at peace with our world, but we can move very rapidly to anger say, or to bodhisattva, or indeed to both in quick succession; a certain amount of anger for example that a stream of car drivers won't stop to let an old man who is clearly unsure of himself, across the road, and then stopping and getting out of the car and taking his arm to ensure that he gets across safely.

If you think about that sort of juxtaposition even briefly, if we weren't offered some such concept as the ten worlds, we would have to invent one to explain the immensely changeable…and even contradictory… feelings we demonstrate or experience, every single day of our lives. Of course we're not accustomed to calling these variable and fluctuating states of mind, *life states*, or *worlds,* as Buddhism describes them, indeed we take them so much for granted that we may not dignify them with any name at all. But do we experience them? Yes indeed. And we recognise them rapidly enough when we have them pointed out to us.

The nub of the argument

If we are prepared to accept that argument, and we do need to give it some careful thought, then what follows from it is very important indeed in terms of our understanding of Nichiren Buddhism. Since it brings us to the *central promise* made by Nichiren, namely that it is possible for us to experience the life state of Buddhahood, *in this lifetime,* whatever situation our life happens to be in at any given moment. We have within us that is, the potential to move from the despair of Hell say, to the compassion of Bodhisattva, or the hope and optimism and profound sense of capability and well-being of Buddhahood.

This is the basis for the fundamental argument that has already been touched upon more than once, namely the *normality* of Buddhahood; it's not in any way a *superhuman* life state, but a supremely *human* one. Shakyamuni and Nichiren Daishonin were ordinary men who nevertheless attained the highest life state during their normal life spans on earth. Thus the great promise at the heart of Nichiren Buddhism is that Buddhahood is not some remote and inaccessible goal, it is the immediate, earthly purpose of our daily practice.

Indeed the key implication is unmistakeable. It is that Buddhahood can *only* exist in the presence of the other nine life states, it can *only* find expression that is, in the lives and behaviour of ordinary people. Us. What that means is that all of the lower worlds of Hell, Hunger, Anger and Animality are *permanently* part of our lives. We can't eliminate them or drive them out in some way. They are part of everyone's life. What we need to do if we wish to build a better life for ourselves and those around us, is to face up to our reality, and to set about *transforming* them, through the increased awareness and the determination that the practice builds up, to limit their negative impact on our life. This is undoubtedly one of the most important aspects of Nichiren Buddhism, namely that we can take *any part of our life* about which we have been feeling vaguely uneasy, or downright unhappy, even guilty or ashamed, and set about *transmuting it*, through the practice, into a source of value in our lives. Nothing has to be given up. Nothing has to be abandoned.

Nothing that can exist in the context of our lives is too difficult to challenge.

The overwhelming message

The overwhelming message therefore is one of hope and optimism. This is part and parcel of what we mean when we talk about taking responsibility for our life. As we have seen, one interpretation of that word *responsibility* is precisely *respond-ability*. That is to say, we can learn how to respond to people and situations and events in a more value-creating way. That is why so many people describe the effect of their practice as *enabling*. They come to feel that it helps them to take more control of their lives, instead of feeling at a loss, or even overwhelmed.

In a sense it is a restatement of the analogy of the weightlifter. It is a fact of life that we can't develop stronger muscles by lifting lighter and lighter weights. We all know that to build those muscles we have to go for heavier and heavier weights. From the Buddhist standpoint, it's equally clear that we cannot grow our *inner* strength and resilience, those vital qualities, except by overcoming the biggest obstacles and challenges that life throws at us. The bigger the problem we overcome, the greater the resilience we develop. As Daisaku Ikeda has expressed it so clearly,

'True happiness is not the absence of suffering. You can't have day after day of clear skies... Happiness does not mean having a life free from all difficulties, but that whatever difficulties arise, without being shaken in the least, you can summon up the unflinching courage and conviction to fight and overcome them.[2]

Approaching the Practice

It's important to de-mystify this word practice. The fact is that it is used in very much the same way as one might use it in talking about any other field of human endeavour. The basic objective of any practice is to *get better* at something. Any sportsman, any musician, any artist knows that unless they train, unless they practice, they cannot possibly attain their full potential. Moreover, having more innate talent, doesn't mean less practice. The bigger the talent, the more, rather than the less those sportsmen and those musicians have to practice because they have a greater potential to fulfil. Few people train as hard for example, as top class sports men and women, or concert musicians.

By the same token, however inherent the Buddha nature may be, drawing it out into the light of our daily lives requires a real personal commitment to sustained practice. It is very common to hear Nichiren Buddhists say that the more they practice, the more they feel themselves to be fortunate, in harmony with themselves, and in some way, however difficult it may be to define, in rhythm with the world around them. Unexpected opportunities appear for example, at the most opportune moment, seemingly insoluble problems reach a resolution, relationships improve, anxieties diminish.

That may sound just too good to be true. Maybe. That doesn't alter the fact that the experience is a common one, and that these 'occurrences' continue to occur, as a result of a greater awareness perhaps, or a greater openness to what is going on in the environment, or a sharper sense of the possibilities in any particular situation.

Similarly, when Buddhists are aware that they are approaching a time of extra stress or difficulty in their lives, a set of important exams coming up or stress in a close relationship, or illness or a change of job, they *go into training* you might say. They deliberately step up their practice, to give themselves the greater resilience and self-confidence and judgement, to help to drive them through a challenging time.

It is as deliberate and as practical a process as that.

Thus people use the practice as an additional *asset* available to them. Buddhism *is* daily life, and in many ways that simple sounding phrase is the very heart of the Buddhist message. Trying to learn how to see the problems and the challenges that come ceaselessly from all directions, as *opportunities*, opportunities to grow our lives. And if you think about it for a moment, that necessarily means developing the wisdom to spot them, and the courage to grab onto them, because exploiting opportunities inevitably means change, and change takes courage.

Not going to stop coming

The Buddhist argument essentially is that they are not going to stop coming, those problems. It's a bit like saying something as patently obvious as, water is wet. That's just the way things *are*, the nature of human life. So, Buddhism argues, the *only* part of the equation over which we have control is our approach to those problems. And the key stage in the process of change we go through, is coming to understand that this is not a purely *intellectual* process. The intellect is crucially important of course, but it can only take us so far. Buddhism teaches that we can't simply *think* our way into a radically different approach to life's vicissitudes, we have to work at it, we have to *train* to acquire that persistently more hopeful perspective. That's what the daily practice is about.

Admittedly, that is not an easy truth, either to believe in or to understand. It's not something we are accustomed to doing. If we get a problem the immediate, instinctive, conditioned response is to go to *brain*. That's what we've always done. That we believe, is where the powerhouse is. We are accustomed in the west, trained even, to live our lives driven by three primary engines; our *intellect* and our *emotions*, how we think and how we feel, and by our *persona*, or how we look and present ourselves. We place huge store, as indeed we should, on our intellectual ability to think our way through life's problems. We attach immense value to emotional expression. And perhaps far too much to externals, to physical appearance.

All Buddhism is saying is…'*hang on a bit, there's more…there is a much neglected spiritual resource within you that is capable of lifting your life performance to a new level…your Buddha nature. In learning how you can draw it out into your daily life…it could change your whole life.*'

As the late great philosopher and historian Arnold Toynbee, has commented,

'*Westerners have much to learn in this field from Indian and East Asian experience. In books and articles that I have published,*

I have repeatedly drawn my Western readers' attention to this historical fact, as part of my lifelong attempt to jolt modern Western man out of his ludicrously mistaken belief that modern Western civilisation has made itself superior to all others by outstripping them.'[1]

Three basic elements

There are three basic elements to the practice of Nichiren Daishonin Buddhism. Let's look at each of them briefly.

Chanting

The basic practice is chanting, chanting the phrase or the mantra *Nam myoho renge kyo,* which we'll explain in greater detail in a moment. The chanting is out loud, rather than repeating a mantra within your head as in meditation. The key point is that it is clearly a physical action, and it has clear physiological effects. For one thing it involves moving considerable volumes of air in and out of the lungs for example, and it raises the body temperature.

But above all it is wonderfully uplifting and joyful sound, and it is absolutely central to this practice. It is seen as the essential driving force, the engine that powers the process of change, because it is an essential part of the process of energising and refreshing the spirit. This practice of chanting is known as *daimoku,* and it clearly has a mystical dimension as Daisaku Ikeda explains,

'It would be no exaggeration to say that the practice of chanting daimoku in Nichiren Buddhism is what gave rise to a 'Buddhism of the people.' This practice of chanting daimoku is indeed the supreme Buddhist practice, making it possible for us to fundamentally transform our lives'.[2]

Normally the chanting is carried out twice a day. In the morning to launch you into the day with a wholly positive, up-beat frame of mind. In the evening basically in the spirit of gratitude for the day that we've had, good, bad or indifferent. If it's been good there's lots to be grateful for. If it's been bad then you may need to regain the energy and the determination to tackle the challenges that have arisen. Both morning and evening the chanting is accompanied by the recitation of two brief passages from the Lotus Sutra, that are concerned with the universality of Buddhahood and the eternity of life.

There's no set time to chant, nor any set period of chanting. As with so many other aspects of Buddhist practice, that's entirely up to the individual. It's your life. You can chant for as little time as you can spare before you have to catch the 8.10 commuter train to the office, or for as long as you feel you need. The practice is above all flexible, shaped to fit in with the demands of modern life. As with so many other activities, the key thing is the *regularity*. Better ten minutes twice a day, than an hour every Friday. Just as we need to refuel our bodies with something to eat two or three times a day, so Buddhism argues, we need this regular, daily refreshment of our spiritual resources.

What do we think about?

What do we think about when we chant? Well the short answer is not a lot. The intention if you like, is to become one with the rhythm of the chanting. Listen to the sound, feel the vibration, enjoy the moment for its own sake. It's a kind of relaxation. The time for focused thought is before you start, what is it you want to chant about, and after you have finished, when the mind is very clear, and you are deciding what action you might want to take, if any. What do we chant for? We are chanting essentially to tap into this *potential* within our lives that will enable us to achieve a higher life state. Remember, as both Buddhism and modern psychology teach us, it's our *life state* that governs how we think and how we feel and therefore to a large extent how we act. So that the *higher* our life state, the more fully and creatively we can live the day, and that is the underlying thought.

But the fact is that you can chant for any goal you wish to achieve, either in the short or the long term of your life, and the lives of those around you. In my experience, people don't often start chanting because they want to 'save the planet' so to speak, or rarely. They are much more likely to start chanting for reasons that are much closer and more personal, and for material as well as spiritual concerns. Buddhism is *daily* life remember, and those are elements of all our days. So it might be for a more buoyant spirit for example or more self-confidence in relationships. But it might also be for a better house, or a better job, better health, or just a happy and successful day. Many people chant for these and other utterly normal worldly desires every day of the week. They are very much part of our ordinary humanity and the desire for them is real enough.

But there are two key points to bear in mind. One is that we are of course chanting for the courage and the wisdom and the compassion to emerge in our lives so that *we ourselves* can take the *action* we need, to achieve these goals in our life. And the second is that as we go on chanting on a daily basis, so the practice steadily deepens and broadens our view of what it is we really wish to achieve to enrich our lives and the lives of those around us, and how we might set about achieving these broader goals. So you might say the initial desires serve as the *seed*, or the primary cause, that drives us towards a greater self-knowledge. It is in that sense that earthly desires may be said to lead to self-enlightenment.

Not about renunciation

Chanting to achieve things in one's life, including material things, runs strongly counter to the widely held perception of Buddhism that it is essentially about *renunciation*, about giving up worldly things as a necessary step on the road to achieving a higher spiritual condition. Nichiren Buddhism however teaches that renunciation, giving up things, *of itself,* brings no benefits. It argues rather that desire is basic to all human life, and that as long as there is life, there will be the instinctive desire in the hearts of all men and women to make the most of that life which inevitably means to love and to want and to have.

Nichiren saw with great clarity that little was to be gained from people expending huge amounts of thought and time and energy seeking to *extinguish* a force that lay right at the core of their lives. On the contrary, infinitely more is to be achieved, by accepting it as an essential part of everyone's humanity and *harnessing* it, as a powerful engine for individual change and growth.

But let's be clear, we are not talking about a solely rational or intellectual process. In many ways the effects of chanting on a regular, committed, daily basis, are beyond the reach of the intellect alone. It does change profoundly your view of what is *valuable and meaningful* in life. There are many stories to be told for example, of people who have started chanting in a somewhat inconsequential way, driven largely by personal desires, without any particularly profound knowledge of the practice. They now look back and can laugh openly at those somewhat shallow beginnings, in the knowledge of just how profoundly their lives and their concerns have been changed. They may continue to chant for their personal desires, but now with a far wider horizon, that extends from their own personal on-going human revolution, outwards in ever increasing circles, to take in family and friends and workplace and community, and the global society.

The ultimate goal of the Nichiren Buddhist is a world made up of people and communities that live in peace one with another. We chant for it, and work for it on a daily basis.

Study
The second major element in the practice is study. Studying a wide range of things from the still extant letters and other writings of Nichiren Daishonin himself, to commentaries by Buddhist scholars, and accounts by individual Buddhists on the ways in which their practice has affected their lives. There is a huge and varied abundance of material, because it is such a broad ranging philosophy which touches upon every aspect of our daily lives. Nichiren as we have seen makes no bones about the importance of study. Indeed he goes so far as to say,

'Exert yourself in the two ways of practice and study. Without practice and study there is no Buddhism.'[3]

But that having been said, this is not in any way an intellectual or academic practice. The study is not about acquiring knowledge as an end in itself, it is entirely about deepening our understanding of the principles that underlie the practice, so that we get better at living them, at making them work in our daily lives, at manifesting them in our behaviour.

Action

Taking action is the third pillar of the practice, the effort and the struggle to fold Buddhist principles and values into the warp and weft of our daily lives so that they are lived rather than just perceived or understood. And let's be clear, that is a daily struggle. We have to work at it. Few things are more difficult to change than ingrained patterns of thought and behaviour, of which we have often become almost completely unaware, so much have they become a part of us; driven perhaps by anger, or selfishness, or a basic lack of concern for other people's needs. That is part of all our experience.

The discipline of the Buddhist practice drives what might be called a constant inner *re-appraisal*, an inner transformation of our own life, a real growth in self-knowledge. Out of that grows a fundamental respect for the lives of all others. It's not of course a one-way journey, there can be set backs and regressions as well as advances. It is very much a living, dynamic process. But even so there is no doubt that this change comes to have a profound effect upon the way you handle relationships and encounters with everyone you meet; a greater openness for example, an altogether warmer, wider, welcoming generosity towards other people. I have no doubt that one of the greatest benefits of the Buddhist practice in my personal life for example, has been this transformation in the way I experience relationships at every level.

Not a morality

But we should not forget the point that we have touched upon previously, namely that Buddhism does not depend for its moral force on a *prescribed* set of behaviours. It relies rather on the power of this *inner transformation*, on people learning how to accept responsibility for their own lives and their own actions. This clearly has the potential for far reaching effects, not solely on the person at the centre, but on the community he or she inhabits.

The process begins of course with the individual. It all begins with the personal determination to live one's life, to the very best of one's ability that is, within the orbit of a Buddhist set of values and principles. That's the starting point. But the effect of the changes we make in our thinking and in our behaviour inevitably extends way beyond our own life, in an ever-widening series of ripples

Since the chanting of the phrase, *Nam myoho renge kyo* is central to the practice, and the process of change, where does it come from, and what does it mean?

The meaning of Nam Myoho Renge Kyo

Most of this phrase or mantra comes from the Lotus Sutra itself. *Myoho renge kyo* is the title of the Lotus Sutra as written in classical Japanese. To be precise, it is written in the Chinese pictograms that the Japanese adopted as their own, in order to create their own written language. The five characters used to write this phrase mean literally, 'The Mystic Law of the Lotus Sutra.' The word mystic carries with it the sense of the ultimate or highest teaching, that hasn't previously been revealed.

The key word *Nam* which is placed in front of the title is what you might call the committal word. It comes from the ancient language of Sanskrit and means, among other things, 'to devote one's life to.' So a straightforward literal translation of Nam myoho renge kyo would be, 'I devote my life to the Mystic law of the Lotus Sutra.'

But that is really just the beginning. Many volumes have been written to explain the depths of meaning locked up in this simple sounding mantra. That is partly because in the Buddhist tradition, the title given to each sutra is seen to be immensely important, and is considered to embody the *entire teaching* that it contains. As Nichiren Daishonin explains to us in one of his letters, using the analogy of the name of Japan;

'Included within the two characters representing Japan is all that is within the country's sixty six provinces: the people and the animals, the rice paddies and the other fields, those of high and low status, the nobles and the commoners…similarly included within the title or daimoku, of Nam myoho renge kyo is the entire sutra consisting of all eight volumes, twenty eight chapters, and 69,384 characters without the omission of a single character…'[4]

Moreover, since Chinese is an incomparably concise language, in which each character can be used to express an immense range of different, though related meanings, these 5 basic characters combine to convey a veritable universe of ideas. In very much the same way that in the world of physics for example, the simple seeming equation $e = mc2$, sums up within its five characters the complex relationship between energy and matter across the entire vastness of the universe.

But neither of these partial explanations can begin to explain the depth of meaning that Nichiren himself ascribes to this phrase. He describes it as nothing less than the *Universal Law of Life*, that expresses within its brief compass the relationship between human life and the entire environment within which life is lived. It sums up within itself he says, nothing less than the *'wisdom of all the Buddhas.'*

Shakyamuni himself expresses something very close to that in the Lotus Sutra itself when he writes that this Law,

'can only be understood and shared between Buddhas.'[5]

It's crucially important to make clear that that description is not referring to some sort of exclusivity. Far from it, since the whole purpose of the Lotus Sutra is to convey far and wide to all humanity the breadth and depth of Shakyamuni's hard-won enlightenment, to enable people, all people, to build better lives for themselves. It is simply expressing the crucial point that that the intellect, and words and explanations can only take you *so far* along the path of understanding. You have to practice Buddhism and experience to some extent its *power and potential* to change your life from the inside, before you truly begin to understand. Just as of course, you actually have to bite into the strawberry yourself, before you can begin to understand what it tastes like!

So I don't think we should be surprised or taken aback, if we find some of these issues elusive and difficult to grasp when we first encounter this practice, and indeed throughout our practice. Why shouldn't it be difficult? It is a huge and many-layered explanation of the reality of life. As we have said so often, Buddhism *is* daily life, and since life is infinitely complex, Buddhism will inevitably reflect that complexity.

In my own case I have to say, I certainly did find it difficult. It was one thing coming to understand many of the values that Buddhism proposes, and appreciating just how valuable they could be close to, in terms of human relationships, and further afield perhaps, in terms of how society functions. It was quite another to commit to the practice of chanting a strange mantra, perhaps an hour or more a day. Did I really want to do that?

A mantra moreover that carries with it a whole bundle of meanings and associations and implications that are to a large extent closed off from everyday experience and derived from a quite different cultural tradition. That was quite a struggle.

I started chanting for two principle reasons, and I'm sure my experience is by no means uncommon. The people I met who were practising were to be admired in many ways; positive, compassionate, socially responsible, always constructive in their aims and endeavours. Always supportive of others. But above all it seemed to me that there was only *one* way of coming to understand the true value of Nichiren Buddhism in my daily life, and that was to *allow it* into my life. I have been chanting on a daily basis ever since.

Not a question of blind faith

But a fundamentally important point is that you don't have to understand what this phrase means *theoretically* when you begin to chant. The understanding will grow and deepen as your experience of the practice grows. You certainly don't have to hang onto the many layers of meaning locked up in its characters as you chant. It's not an intellectual process in that way. Not at all. Nor indeed is it a *feeling one,* in the sense that you should expect some sort of emotional response. You chant Nam myoho renge kyo in a steady rhythm, as loudly or as quietly as you choose, or as the environment allows, freeing the mind off from any particular concerns, relaxed, listening to the rhythm in the voice, feeling the slight vibration in the body. The key thing above all is to enjoy the moment for what it is.

If you are thinking about what other more valuable things you could be doing with your time, then it's probably better that you go off and do them.

But that having been said, Buddhism clearly teaches that anything resembling *blind faith* is not an acceptable basis for practice. Does it work? Does it enhance how I feel about myself and my life and my relationships? Nichiren argues constantly that it's up to us to pose these questions to ourselves. Take nothing on trust he tells us, however interesting, however seemingly powerful and profound the teaching. Unless it actually enables us to do something better with our lives...overcome problems better, feel a greater sense of confidence in our own abilities, a greater sense of well-being, become more focused and more capable in achieving what we are seeking for our lives...then what is it for?

As we have seen, in Buddhism the word 'faith' is related not to some external power or force, but to the strength of our belief in *ourselves,* in our own capacities, in our inner resources of courage and compassion and wisdom, and our ability to make use of them in our daily lives. We may indeed take up the practice because we come to value some quality that we see in the practitioners we meet, or because we are attracted by what we are told about the *promise of change* embodied in the practice. But in the long run, we can only continue our practice with *real commitment* when we become aware that it is truly beneficial to our own life.

It is too demanding a practice to continue on the basis of someone else's belief, or someone else's promises. That is certainly true in my own experience. I began slowly, and it was something of a struggle for several months. But as I became aware of this profound sense of well-being that ran right through my life, I started getting up an hour earlier each morning, wherever I was, at home or on location, so that I could fit in at least 45 minutes or so of chanting or daimoku, to launch me positively into the day.

Before we move on let me attempt a fractionally more detailed, and yet wholly practical account of the meanings locked up in these characters, Nam myoho renge kyo. Not one that carries us off into the deeper realms of Buddhist philosophy perhaps, in case we get lost without trace, but one that might serve as a working reference, bearing in mind that if it stimulates you to know more, you can seek out one of the references in the bibliography.

Nam

The word *Nam* comes from the Sanskrit word *namas* and although it is commonly translated as, *to devote oneself to*, it has a multiplicity of meanings. Perhaps the most important among these meanings are, '*to summon up,*' or '*to awaken,*' or '*to draw forth,*' or '*to make great effort.*'

Why is knowing about these different meanings helpful? Because they express subtle differences in our life state or state of mind when we are chanting at different times. When we are faced with something of a crisis for example, we may well be thinking about summoning up, or making great effort to draw out this inner resource, rather than just awakening

Myoho

Myoho is seen to describe the profound relationship between the very essence of life, or the *life force* that is inherent throughout the universe, and the literally millions of *physical forms* in which that life force is manifest or expressed at any given time.

As Nichiren Daishonin defines that idea,

'Myo is the name given to the mystic nature of life, and ho to its manifestations.'[6]

In Buddhism, everything that exists, both sentient, and insentient, is an expression of that life force and is subject to the eternal rhythm of life that we have discussed, formation, continuation, decline and disintegration. Everything but everything is subject to that process of change, or of *impermanence* as it is often called.

So Myoho is made up of two elements; *myo* which refers to the unseen or the spiritual element that is believed to be inherent in all things, and *ho* which refers to the physical manifestation that we can observe with our senses. In Buddhism all things, all phenomena have a *myo* aspect and a *ho* aspect. They are the two different but inseparable aspects of all life, *'two but not two,'* as Buddhism often expresses it, as inextricably interlinked as the two sides of a sheet of paper.

Thus the *ho aspect* of a painting for example, is made up of the canvas and the paint that is spread across it. The *myo aspect* is the feeling or the emotion or the creative energy within the artist as he applied the paint in a particular way, and the emotional impact on us as we view it. Music similarly has a clearly recognisable *ho* aspect in the arrangement of the black and white strokes, or the notes on the page, and the physical vibrations in the air caused by the instruments as they interpret them. The profound *myo* aspect is the effect the music has on our emotions and feelings as we receive the sounds produced by the instruments in that particular sequence. As Shakespeare expressed it so pithily in *Much Ado About Nothing*, it is wholly inexplicable that a sequence of sounds produced on violin strings made out of the guts of a sheep...can move our hearts so readily to tears!

If we think of ourselves, *ho* is used to refer to the all elements in our physical make up, that can be observed with the senses, so that includes our appearance, the way we happen to stand and walk and talk, the way we gesture with our hands, and the various facial expressions we use to communicate. All the elements in fact that enable someone to recognise us as who we are, even from some considerable distance away. But what is quite clear is that so many of those *external* physical attributes, those gestures and movements, the expression in our eyes for example, and the tone and modulation of the voice, the animation in the face and the posture of the body are also an expression of our *inner* life, our myo. These two aspects are so clearly inextricably interwoven.

As we continue with our daily practice, and seek to strengthen the vitality of the *myo* or spiritual aspect of our lives, it can have a very considerable manifest effect upon our physical persona, the general expression on our face for example, the light in our eyes, our tone of voice, our readiness to smile and greet others warmly and generously. The more *active* our inner, spiritual life, the more readily it becomes *apparent* in our external appearance.

What about the inanimate world?

Those are very obvious examples, but rather more difficult to accept, indeed one of the most difficult concepts to understand, particularly if you have a background in science I suspect, is the Buddhist belief that all material existence, everything on Earth and in the Universe both animate and inanimate, has a physical and spiritual aspect. Everything but everything we are told, has both myo and ho, the tree, the rock, the river, the mountain.

That is undoubtedly a difficult idea to take on board, although Buddhism is by no means alone in holding this view. Throughout the length and breadth of human history, artists and poets have been constantly seeking to open our eyes to this view of reality, in all languages and all cultures. Wordsworth for example, the great English romantic poet, when he famously described the *myoho* of a lake and a bunch of daffodils.

'The waves beside them danced; but they outdid the sparkling waves in glee;
A poet could not be but gay,
In such a jocund company,
I gazed…and gazed…but little thought
What wealth the show to me had brought;
For oft when on my couch I lie,
In vacant or in pensive mood,
They flash upon my inner eye,
Which is the bliss of solitude,
And then my heart with pleasure fills,
And dances with the daffodils'

Buddhism stresses this aspect of the continuity and the close association that runs through all things, so it teaches that we are not separate from but closely linked to everything around us. Thus in Buddhist terms, statements such as being in harmony with, or being at odds with, one's environment, are not simply figures of speech. They are held to represent a fundamental truth, a truth that is the basis for the Buddhist principle of oneness of self and environment. Essentially this argues that as we change, as we gradually strengthen and reveal our Buddha nature through our practice, so that change resonates through our environment.

A cart and two horses

One analogy that paints a graphic, if somewhat simplified picture of the relationship between our *myo* and *ho* aspects, is that of the horse and cart, or *horses* and cart to be more accurate. Our life is the cart, pulled along by our *myo* horse, or our deepest spiritual energy, and our *ho* horse, our physical life. In general it's true to say that we are accustomed to spending a great deal of time and effort nurturing the strength and well-being of our *ho* horse, because of course it is so visible and so physically accessible to us. We can look at it in the mirror for example and worry about its shape. We can feed it three times a day, and take it to the gym to work out, and off to play sports to ensure that it's kept fit and healthy and suitably diverted. As a result we tend very much to equate our happiness and our sense of satisfaction with life with how well we are getting on with looking after our *ho* horse.

By contrast we tend to spend relatively little time, if any, nurturing and exercising our *myo* horse, because of course it is wholly unseen and in general has a less powerful presence. The result is a gross *imbalance*. The wagon of our life is at best pulled strongly off in one direction governed by our physical needs. At worst it is pulled round and round in circles, repeating patterns of behaviour, because the spiritual side of our make up simply hasn't been nurtured enough to influence, to *change* that is, our habitual behaviour. We can, as we all know so well, become very much creatures of habit, tending to repeat patterns of behaviour even when they lead to pain and suffering. People very often for example go through a whole series of similar relationships, each one of which might follow a very similar pattern of rise and fall. What we need to do, Buddhism tells us, is to become aware of the danger of this gross *imbalance* between our physical and spiritual lives, and so to allocate more time and energy to keeping both our horses, the *myo* as well as the *ho*, in a fit and active and healthy state. That is very much the role that is played by the daily practice, it is the regular *daily work out* for our *myo* horse.

Renge

Renge means lotus flower. It also means cause and effect. The lotus flower, adopted as the title of Shakyamuni's *ultimate* teaching, is an immensely significant symbol in Buddhism, for many reasons. It is a plant with a particularly beautiful flower and it happens to grow and flourish most strongly in mucky, muddy, swampy environments. In this sense it is seen to symbolise the great *potential* locked up in every human life; the promise that we can build strong and positive and flourishing lives, however difficult the circumstances and the environments we find our lives rooted in. Moreover, the lotus happens to carry both blossoms and seed pods at the same time, simultaneously, and in this sense it is seen to symbolise one of the fundamental and most important principles of Buddhism known as the *simultaneity of cause and effect.*

Once again it is a principle with which Buddhism asks us to challenge the way we are accustomed to thinking about our everyday lives and relationships. Basically it argues that every cause we make, good, bad and indifferent, plants a balancing effect in our lives. That effect, Buddhism argues will, sooner or later, make itself felt, without fail. Thus there is, for all of us, an on-going chain of *causes and effects*. That is, if you like, the *fundamental dynamic* of our lives. It ties together the past, the present, and the future.

Buddhism argues that it is only by coming to understand this constant linkage, that we can grasp fully what it means to take responsibility for our actions, and to seek to change those inherent tendencies in our life that are causing us to suffer. So it's a fundamental teaching that carries within it all sorts of implications, since we are of course, *making causes all the time*, both within our own lives and in relation to those around us, all day every day, in everything we think and say and do. Good causes, good effects. Bad causes, bad effects.

I think it's pretty easy to see how even a superficial understanding of this principle can have a powerful effect on our behaviour, on our *awareness* of the kind of causes that we are making. And since that process of linked causes and effects is going on all the time, you can see that *where* we are now in our lives, *who* we are now in our lives, is the *sum* of all the causes we have made in the past, that have planted effects in our lives.

By the same token, the causes that we are making *now*, Buddhism reminds us, contain the seeds of our future. So you might say, the key factor in shaping our on-going lives is how we *respond* to the situations and events and encounters that face us now, *today and tomorrow and the next day*.

What that is saying so powerfully is that however much we might feel it to be the case, we are *not* simply subject to chance and accident and encounter that come at us out of our environment. The decisive factor is how *we respond* to those situations, the *causes* that we make, and therefore the *effects* that we plant in our lives. The basic message is therefore one of immense hope and optimism; whatever has happened in the past, good *positive causes* made now, will plant good *positive effects* in the future.

Kyo

Just as with *myoho* and *renge, kyo* embodies many meanings. It is literally translated as '*sutra*' or the voice or teaching of the Buddha. But it also means *vibration* or *sound,* so it can be taken to represent the vibrations that spread out from someone in the process of chanting. Indeed there is a well known Buddhist saying that '*the voice does the Buddha's work,*' and there is no question that the sound or the vibration that is created by a group of people chanting, even quite a small group, can be very powerful.

I can still recall with great clarity for example, the very first Buddhist meeting I went to, some time before I actually started practising. It was a dark, cold winter's evening I remember, and we were walking along this street of narrow Victorian houses in West London, with me thinking not particularly positive thought such as, '*Oh well, it can't last much more than an hour this meeting,*' And then as we turned up the short garden path to the house, coming through the closed front door was this wonderful resonant sound. Strong, confident, vibrant. It actually made the hair tingle on the back of my neck I remember. A sound produced by just a dozen or so ordinary people, chanting *Nam myoho renge kyo.*

This has been a necessarily brief account of the many meanings locked up within Nam myoho renge kyo. But having a more comprehensive understanding of those meanings isn't really the key to unlocking the value that it embodies. The fact is that this practice, focused around the chanting of this phrase, is Nichiren's great legacy to all of us. Nichiren was in many ways a great modernist, and he makes it clear in his writings that this practice was fashioned for ordinary people, no matter what place or period they inhabit, 13th Century Japan or 21st Century Europe. People with busy everyday lives and much else to grab their attention, to enable them to get to grips with the values and principles of Buddhism, and so to understand that even in the very midst of life's difficulties and challenges, it is possible to build lives filled with hope and optimism and resilience, and yes…great happiness too.

Understanding the Gohonzon

We can't leave this brief account of the practice without touching upon the meaning and implications of the Gohonzon as a central feature of that practice. The Gohonzon is a simple rice paper scroll, and it marks out Nichiren Buddhism from all other Buddhist schools. It is it's distinguishing characteristic. Hinayana or Theravada Buddhism is very much focused on the person of Shakyamuni Buddha and the worshipping or honouring of him as a unique human being. Mahayana Buddhism, which embraces Nichiren Buddhism, is, by contrast, very much more concerned to bring Buddhist teachings into the daily lives of ordinary people everywhere. That in essence is what Mahayana means, the greater vehicle. And in Nichiren Buddhism, the Gohonzon, allied to the chanting of the title of the Lotus Sutra, Nam myoho renge kyo, make up the primary means of achieving that aim.

The word '*go*' in classical Japanese means '*worthy of honour*,' and the word '*honzon*,' means '*object of fundamental respect*,' so it is clearly an object that is held in the very highest esteem in Nichiren Buddhism. It is also, I have to say, a work of considerable beauty.

The Dai Gohonzon...Dai means *'great'* or *'original'*...was inscribed by Nichiren on 12th October 1279. The original Gohonzon that he inscribed is still preserved in Japan at a place not far from Tokyo, but anyone who is pre-pared to make the personal commitment to practice in accordance with the principles of Nichiren, and to protect and look after their own Gohonzon as an object of fundamental respect, receives a smaller block print version to enshrine in their own house. This is how members of the Soka Gakkai practice. Soka Gakkai means essentially Value Creating Organisation, and it is important to emphasise that it is an entirely *lay* organisation, there are no priests, or temples. Nichiren himself, during his lifetime, established this pattern of committed individuals receiving a personal Gohonzon, to make it easier for them to practice in a place of their own choosing. Not long afterwards he wrote,

'I Nichiren have inscribed my life in sumi ink, so believe in this Gohonzon with your whole heart.'[7]

Sumi is a form of ink used particularly in Japanese calligra-phy, and with that immensely simple phrase Nichiren sums up the scale of the task he had accomplished; he regarded it as nothing less than the fulfilment of his life-long mission as a teacher of men. The characters on the scroll, in Chinese and Sanskrit script, are held to represent the reality of human life. Right down the centre, in bigger and bolder letters than the rest, and as it were *illuminating* all of the human life they represent, are the characters. Nam myoho renge kyo Nichiren. That bold central inscription is the key to understanding the nature and the intent of the Gohonzon. When Nichiren wrote, '*I have inscribed my life in sumi ink,*' he was talking about his life as a Buddha, or in the state of Buddhahood. So we have it there in front of us, a representation of *what it is* that we are seeking to draw out from within our own life, nothing less than our highest life state. It is his great gift if you like to all of humanity, and in that sense it embodies the fundamental principle first declared or revealed in the Lotus Sutra, that all ordinary human beings have the *potential* for Buddhahood, inherent within their lives.

What are we doing when we chant?

It is difficult to think of a meaningful analogy that comes close to expressing what it is that is going on when we chant in front of the Gohonzon. One that might come close is perhaps the musical one. When Beethoven or Mozart for example sat down and wrote out a piece of music, they too were expressing their *life state;* their passion, their spirit, their elation or their melancholy, at that moment in time. A supremely *inner* world, transmuted into bold marks in black ink on white paper. Whatever happens subsequently to that piece of paper, the spirit that flowed through the writer's inner world at that time, has been indelibly inscribed on it, for all of time.

The sheet of paper with the ink marks could rest unnoticed on a dusty library shelf for decades on end. It could be copied out lovingly by a clerk's hand. Or it could be put through a digital copier to churn out a thousand copies. But whatever journey it travels, when the thousandth copy is placed in front of a musician, and played, then the *spirit* embodied in the original ink marks all those years ago is, to a greater or lesser extent, *brought back to life,* to fill the room with its sound and its vibration, and to *recreate* in those who hear it, some measure of the spirit that went into it when it was first written.

The Gohonzon in this analogy, is the musical score that presents to us the *life state* of the writer, when he first wrote it. We occupy the role of the musician, seeking to recreate, *to the very best of our ability*…no more can be asked of us…the spirit or the life state, embodied in the original.

The Gohonzon is said to depict in its complex calligraphy, all the aspects of our ordinary human life, the good, the bad, and the ugly, the positive and the negative, the light and the dark. All those aspects of our everyday lives are there, and Nichiren's too of course, for he was after all an ordinary human being. The ten life states we discussed in an earlier chapter are set out clearly on the Gohonzon, but they are *illuminated* by the principle that can enable us, however strong our anger, or however deep our despair, to move our lives towards the life state of Buddhahood that Nichiren captured in sumi ink. Nothing is excluded. No life state is rejected. We don't have to get rid of anything, or feel guilty about anything. The characters depicted on the Gohonzon are there to make clear that there isn't a life state or a condition that a human being can experience, that would in some way *prohibit* that journey towards our greater self. Everything can be transformed.

That is the huge scale of the promise.

And that really is the Gohonzon's basic purpose, it is something physical to focus on. It is that practical. Something to keep our mind on the task in hand, namely chanting. Nichiren has given us this *picture* of what it is we are seeking to achieve. It is nothing more than that. Nor, it's important to remember, nothing less. It is sometimes described as a mirror, that reflects back to us our true nature. And just as we cannot see our face without a mirrored surface to reflect it back to us, so Nichiren argues, we cannot really perceive our Buddhahood without the 'mirror' of the Gohonzon to reflect its image.

Does it really happen?

Does it really happen? Yes, undoubtedly, and for many thousands, millions indeed, of ordinary people. Can we clearly say why? I do not believe so. There are many explanations offered, but all too often the explanations are couched in terms that are as difficult to grasp as the events in front of the Gohonzon. But are the explanations all that important? There are many things in our universe that lie beyond the scope of our *complete* understanding.

What the practice in front of the Gohonzon *does* require is real application and effort, and the commitment to persevere, to give it our best shot. Of course there are ups and downs. You stride forward one month, and stand still the next. But the stark reality of course, is that people only continue with this practice because of the benefits that appear in their lives. That has to be the acid test, and the implications are profound. We are not talking about a heaven of whatever form in some hereafter, coming for the way one lives this little life. Buddhism as we have said so often, *is* daily life. This life in the here and now.

The benefits have to be felt in the home and in the workplace, and in how one feels about life today, and tomorrow and the day after.

There is no test more exacting, more strenuous, more meaningful…than daily life.

List of References

Acknowledgements.
1. Mr Makiguchi. Quoted in Daibyaku Renge Oct 2010

Chapter One
Setting out on a Journey
1. Gerald Jones, Daniel Cardinal, Jeremy Hayward. Moral Philosophy. p7
2. Daisaku Ikeda. Buddhism Day by Day. p336
3. Daniel Goleman. Emotional Intelligence. p89
4. Daniel Goleman Destructive Emotions p55
5. Richard Layard. Happiness Lessons from a New Science published by Penguin p234
6. C. Nickerson, N. Schwarz, E. Diener, D. Kahneman, Zeroing on the dark side of the American Dream: A closer look at a the negative consequences of the goal for financial success. Psychological Science 14, p531-536

Chapter Two
A Personal Story
1. WH Davies. Leisure. What is this world if full of care 1911
2. Robert C. Solomon. Spirituality for the Skeptic. p6
3. Richard Layard. ibid p230
4. Robert C. Solomon ibid p21
5. Daniel Goleman. Destructive Emotions p 21

6. Nichiren Daishonin. WND Vol 1 p 851
7. Sonja Lyubomirski The How of Happiness published by Piatkus. p1
8. Arnold Toynbee Choose Life
9. Robert C. Solomon ibid p66
10. Tsunesaburo Makiguchi quoted in Daibyaku Renge Oct 2010
11. Daisaku Ikeda The World of the Gosho Vol 1

Chapter Three
Buddhism and Belief

1. Thich Nhat Hanh The Heart of the Buddha's Teaching p3
2. Edward Conze Buddhism a Short History p3
3. Lotus Sutra. Chapter 16. line 232 'At all times I think to myself / How can I cause living beings / to gain entry into the unsurpassed way / and quickly acquire the body of a Buddha.'
4. Daisaku Ikeda. Lectures on On Attaining Buddhahood in this Lifetime pp6-11
5. Nichiren Daishonin WND Vol 1. p1137
6. Nur Yalman. Prof of Anthropology Harvard. Quoted in Sekiyo Shimbun 26.11.93
7. Bruce Springsteen Lyrics of Saving Up
8. Nichiren Daishonin WND Vol 1. p848
9. Richard Feynman The Character of Physical Law p149
10. Daniel Dennet Kinds of Minds
11. Daisaku Ikeda. The Wisdom of the Lotus Sutra Vol 1. p14
12. Daisaku Ikeda ibid p7
13. Mark Williams, John Teasdale, Zindel Segal, Jon Kabat-Zinn. The Mindful Way Through Depression, Freeing Yourself from Chronic Unhappiness
14. Nichiren Daishonin WND Vol 1. p3

15. Daisaku Ikeda Lectures on On Attaining Buddhahood in this Lifetime p 70
16. Sonja Lyubomirski The How of Happiness p5
17. Nichiren Daishonin WND Vol 1. p 386

Chapter Four
Buddhism and Happiness
1. Martin Seligman What You Can Change…and What You Can't. p5
2. Daniel Goleman Emotional Intelligence p89
3. Sonja Lyubomirski The How of Happiness p14
4. Martin Seligman Flourish p9
5. Daniel Goleman Working with Emotional Intelligence p228
6. Tal Ben-Shahar Pursuit of the Perfect
7. Martin Seligman ibid p20
8. Diasaku Ikeda Faith Into Action
9. Sonja Lyubomirski ibid p15
10. Nichiren Daishonin WND Vol 1. p601
11. S. Frederick and G Loewenstein Well Being: The foundation of Hedonic psychology p302-29
12. Richard Layard ibid p49
13. Sonja Lyubomirski ibid p20

Chapter Five
Buddhism and the Problem Paradox
1. Nichiren Daishonin WND Vol 1. p302
2. Thich Nhat Hanh Heart of the Buddha's Teaching p29
3. S. Lyubomirski The How of Happiness p 157
4. ibid p163/4
5. Daniel Goleman Emotional Intelligence p57
6. Daisaku Ikeda Buddhism Day by Day p249
7. R. Layard Happiness p234
8. Feature Article Time Mag. Feb 7th 2005

Chapter Six
Buddhism and Ethics

1. Gerald Jones, Daniel Cardinal, Jeremy Hayward. Moral Philosophy, A Guide to Ethical Theory. p5
2. Nichiren Daishonin WND Vol 1. p851
3. Gerald Jones, Daniel Cardinal, Jeremy Hayward ibid p2
4. John Donne Devotions XV11. 1624
5. Nicholas Christakis. Prof. of Medical Sociology, Harvard. Article New Scientist. 03.01.09
6. Jeffrey Sachs, economist. BBC Reith Lectures. 2007
7. Sam Harris The Moral Landscape p55
8. Daisaku Ikeda World of the Gosho Vol 1
9. Edward Conze Buddhism a Short History p3
10. Mark William, John Teasdale, Zindel Segal, Jon Kabat-Zinn The Mindful Way Through Depression, Freeing Yourself from Chronic Unhappiness
11. Daisaku Ikeda Buddhism Day by Day. p338
12. Daisaku Ikeda. Wisdom of the Lotus Sutra Vol.1 p149

Chapter Seven
Buddhism and Practice

1. Talmud. The Talmud is the first written compendium of Judaism's oral law and the central text of Rabbinic Judaism. It is written in Hebrew and Aramaic and contains the views and opinions of thousands of rabbi's on a huge range of subjects, including law, ethics, philosophy, customs, history and theology.
2. Richard Layard Happiness Lessons from a New Science 183
3. Ibid p189
4. Martin Seligman Flourish p115
5. Ibid p125
6. Richard Layard ibid p189

7. Robert C. Solomon Spirituality for the Skeptic p15
8. Daisaku Ikeda Lectures on On Attaining Buddhahood in this Lifetime p68
9. Andy Coughlan. Article New Scientist. 11th May 2013. p12
10. ibid
11. Nichiren Daishonin WND Vol 1 p386
12. Arnold Toynbee Review of Life an Enigma, a Precious Jewel by Daisaku Ikeda.
13. Nicholas Christakis Prof. of Medical Sociology Harvard. Article New Scientist 03.01.09

Chapter Eight
Buddhism and Daily Life

1. Sonja Lyubomirski The How of Happiness p26
2. Ibid p 41
3. Richard Layard Happiness Lessons from a New Science p188
4. Ibid p3
5. R. Emmons and C. Shelton, Handbook of Positive Psychology, Oxford. pp 459-471
6. S. Lyubomirski The How of Happiness p92
7. Ruut Veenhoven Professor of Happiness Studies, Erasmus University Rotterdam. Article Time Mag. Feb 7th 2005
8. Eckhart Tolle A New Earth: Create a Better Life
9. Martin Seligman Flourish p110/111
10. Sam Harris The Moral Landscape p55
11. S. Lyubomirski The How of Happiness p125
12. Robert J. Sampson. Feature Article New Scientist. 11 May 2013 p 28
13. S. Lyubomirski ibid p 1
14. Robert Solomon Spirituality for the Skeptic p66
15. Charter of UNESCO

16. Daisaku Ikeda. Notes accompanying Painting a World of Friendship Exhibition
17. John F Kennedy. Commencement Address June 1963

Chapter Nine
Buddhism and Negativity

1. Martin Seligman What You Can Change... and What You Can't p 49/50
2. Martin Seligman Flourish p66
3. Ibid p67
4. Nicholas Christakis Prof. of Medical Sociology Harvard. Article New Scientist. 03.01.09
5. Tal Ben- Shahar The Pursuit of the Perfect
6. Nichiren Daishonin WND Vol 1.p681

Chapter Ten
Buddhism and Anger

1. Martin Seligman What You can Change...and What you Can't p121
2. Ibid p120
3. Ibid p126
4. Ibid p127
5. Ibid p129/30
6. Daniel Goleman Emotional Intelligence p59
7. Martin Seligman ibid p139
8. Daniel Goleman ibid p43
9. Martin Seligman ibid p132

Chapter Eleven
Buddhism and Money

1. Mark Buchanan Article New Scientist 21.03. 09
2. Gregg Easterbrook Article Time Mag. Feb 7th 2005
3. Ibid
4. Edward Diener Article Time Mag. Feb 7th 2005

5. Dictionary of Buddhist Terms and Concepts. p263
6. Dylan Evans Emotion; The Science of Sentiment
7. Richard Layard Happiness p3
8. Gregg Easterbrook ibid
9. Ibid
10. R Lane The Loss of Happiness in Modern Democracies Yale Univ Press 2000 p5
11. Richard Layard Happiness p48
12. Sonja Lyubomirski The How of Happiness p116
13. Nichiren Daishonin WND Vol 1. p 3
14. Nichiren Daishonin WND Vol 1. p 851

Chapter Twelve
A New Beginning

1. Jeffrey Sachs, economist. BBC Reith Lectures 2007
2. Daniel Dennet. Kinds of Minds
3. Wangerie Maathai BBC Radio 4 documentary May 2010.
4. Richard Feynman The Character of Physical Law p149
5. Nichiren Daishonin WND Vol 1. p3
6. William Woollard. The Reluctant Buddhist p27
7. Jeffrey Sachs. BBC Reith Lectures 2007
8. John F Kennedy. Commencement address June 1963
9. John Hall Economist. Article Time Mag. 01.11.09
10. Richard Layard Happiness p232
11. Daisaku Ikeda World of the Gosho Vol 1

Appendix A

1. Arnold Toynbee with Daisaku Ikeda Choose Life
2. Diasaku Ikeda Faith Into Action

Appendix B

1. Arnold Toynbee with Daisaku Ikeda Choose Life p27
2. Daisaku Ikeda Lectures on Attaining Buddhahood in this Lifetime p24
3. Nichiren Daishonin WND Vol 1. p922
4. Nichiren Daishonin WND Vol 1. p4
5. Lotus Sutra
6. Nichiren Daishonin ibid p412

Bibliography

Lectures on On Attaining Buddhahood in this Lifetime. Daisaku Ikeda. Soka Gakkai Malaysia 2007

Lectures on the Expedient Means and Life Span Chapters of the Lotus Sutra. Daisaku Ikeda. World Tribune Press. 1996.

What You Can Change...and What You Can't. The Complete Guide to Successful Self Improvement. Martin P. Seligman. Nicholas Brealey Publishing. 2007

The Moral Landscape. How Science Can Determine Human Values. Sam Harris. Bantam Press 2010

The How of Happiness. A Practical Guide to Getting the Life You Want. Sonja Lyubomirski. Piatkus. 2010

Flourish. Martin P. Seligman. Nicholas Brealey Publishing. 2011

Destructive Emotions. A Dialogue with the Dalai Lama narrated by Daniel Goleman. Bloomsbury Publishing Plc. 2003

Emotional Intelligence. Why it can matter more than IQ. Daniel Goleman. Bloomsbury Publishing Plc.1995

The Mindful Way through Depression. Freeing Yourself from Chronic Unhappiness. Mark William, John Teasdale, Zindel Segal, and Jon Kabat-Zinn. The Guilford Press. 2007

Moral Philosophy. A guide to ethical theory. Gerald Jones. Daniel Cardinal, Jeremy Hayward. Hodder Education 2006.

Advice on Dying and Living a Better Life. His Holiness the Dalai Lama. Rider 2002

Kinds Of Minds. Daniel C. Dennett. The Phoenix Press. 2007

The Character of Physical Law. Richard P. Feynman. Penguin Books 1992

Buddhism a Short History. Edward Conze. Oneworld Publications. 2000

Choose Life. A Dialogue. Arnold Toynbee and Daisaku Ikeda. Oxford University Press. 1989

The Fabric of the Cosmos. Brian Green. Allen Lane 2004

The Buddha in Daily Life. Richard Causton. Ebury Press 1995

The Living Buddha. Daisaku Ikeda. Weatherhill Inc. 1976

Mind Body Medicine. Daniel Goleman and Joel Gurin. New York Yonkers. 1993

Emotion. The Science of Sentiment. Dylan Evans. Oxford Paperbacks 2002

Authentic Happiness. Martin P. Seligman. Free Press 2003

The Wisdom of the Lotus Sutra. Daisaku Ikeda. World Tribune Press 2000

The World Of Nichiren Daishonin's Writings:Vol 1. Daisaku Ikeda. Soka Gakkai Malaysia 2003

Lectures on the Expedient Means and Life Span Chapters of the Lotus Sutra. Daisaku Ikeda. World Tribune Press. 1996

Conversations and Lectures on the Lotus Sutra: Vol 1. Daisaku Ikeda. SGI-UK 1995

Conversations and Lectures on the Lotus Sutra: Vol 2. Daisaku Ikeda. SGI-UK 1996

Happiness Lessons from a New Science Richard Layard. Penguin Press. 2005

The Reluctant Buddhist. William Woollard. Grosvenor House Publishing. 2007

A New Earth: Create a Better Life. Eckhart Tolle

Varieties of Moral Personality. Owen Flanagan 1991

The Pursuit of the Perfect. Tal Ben Shahar 2009

Spirituality for the Skeptic. Robert C. Solomon Oxford University Press 2002

The Power and Biology of Belief. Herbert Benson. Scribner 1996

The Living Buddha Daisaku Ikeda Bungei Shunju Tokyo 1973

Printed in April 2021
by Rotomail Italia S.p.A., Vignate (MI) - Italy